Michael Neubert
Editor

Virtual Slavica:
Digital Libraries,
Digital Archives

Virtual Slavica: Digital Libraries, Digital Archives has been co-published simultaneously as *Slavic & East European Information Resources*, Volume 6, Numbers 2/3 2005.

Pre-publication
REVIEWS, COMMENTARIES, EVALUATIONS . . .

"REMARKABLE. . . . To my mind what makes this work most valuable is its relevance to anyone involved in humanities digital projects or in scholarly research methodology. Librarians, IT specialists, teaching faculty, and library students planning to become subject specialists will all find something of value in this collection. The chapters are of consistently high quality and address a wide variety of practical issues. The authors are all well-known in the field: Janice Pilch, for example, is the leading authority on Eastern European and Slavic copyright law in the U.S. today and Miranda Remnek, as Head of the Slavic and East European Library at the University of Illinois at Urbana-Champaign, is responsible for the many innovative services that distinguish that library."

Marta Mestrovic Deyrup,
MPhil, MLS
Associate Professor and Librarian II
Seton Hall University Libraries

More pre-publication
REVIEWS, COMMENTARIES, EVALUATIONS . . .

"This collection is CERTAIN TO INSPIRE THOSE WORKING IN THE FIELD OF SLAVIC LIBRARIAN-SHIP to launch new projects . . . and to help ensure that 'best practices' and lessons gained from these pioneering projects are widely shared in the U.S. and the broader international library and archives community. Especially interesting are the CLEARLY WRITTEN AND INFORMATIVE analyses of a number of ambitious digital library and archive projects that have been undertaken, in most cases on a cooperative basis, by institutions in the U.S., Western Europe, and Russia. These include the Comintern archives project, the Library of Congress' *Meeting of Frontiers* project, the Central Eurasian Interactive Atlas Project at the University of Washington, and several others."

John Van Oudenaren, PhD
Chief, European Division
The Library of Congress;
Project Director
Meeting of Frontiers

"BROAD IN SCOPE BUT PACKED WITH USEFUL DETAIL, this collection provides an overview of the current state of Slavic librarianship as it crosses over into the digital frontier. It describes in considerable detail the planning, development, and application of several ambitious Slavic digital projects, including the Comintern Archives Database and its online offspring; the Central Eurasian Interactive Atlas Project; the highly useful *Fundamental Digital Library of Russian Literature and Folklore*; and the cross-cultural *Meeting of Frontiers* project hosted by the Library of Congress. *Virtual Slavica* is one book that every Slavic librarian will want to read cover to cover. It is AN ESSENTIAL ACQUISITION FOR EVERY COLLEGE LIBRARY facing issues of making Slavic digital resources readily available. There is a useful index as well as reference notes."

Jon Giullian, MA, MLS
Slavic Librarian
University of Kansas

The Haworth Information Press®
An Imprint of The Haworth Press, Inc.

Virtual Slavica: Digital Libraries, Digital Archives

Virtual Slavica: Digital Libraries, Digital Archives has been co-published simultaneously as *Slavic & East European Information Resources*, Volume 6, Numbers 2/3 2005.

Monographic Separates from *Slavic & East European Information Resources*™

For additional information on these and other Haworth Press titles, including descriptions, tables of contents, reviews, and prices, use the QuickSearch catalog at http://www.HaworthPress.com.

Virtual Slavica: Digital Libraries, Digital Archives, edited by Michael Neubert, MLS. MAIS (Vol. 6, No. 2/3, 2005). *An examination of the most significant aspects of presenting Slavic studies materials via the Internet in libraries and archives, including copyright issues, digital references, and text encoding.*

A Guide to Slavic Collections in the United States and Canada, edited by Allan Urbanic, PhD, and Beth Feinberg, MS (Vol. 5, No. 3/4, 2004). *A directory of libraries with collections of Slavic materials; provides general information about each library, specifics about its collections and electronic resources, and contact information.*

Russian and East European Books and Manuscripts in the United States: Proceedings of a Conference in Honor of the Fiftieth Anniversary of the Bakhmeteff Archive of Russian and East European History and Culture, edited by Tanya Chebotarev and Jared S. Ingersoll (Vol. 4, No. 4, 2003). *This book documents the concerted effort to preserve Russian and East European written culture outside the bounds of Communist power.*

Judaica in the Slavic Realm, Slavica in the Judaic Realm: Repositories, Collections, Projects, Publications, edited by Zachary M. Baker, MA (Vol. 4, No. 2/3, 2003). *A collection of essays, bibliographies, and research studies illustrating the state of Jewish-related publishing ventures in Eastern Europe and the former Soviet Union, and documenting efforts by Judaic scholars, librarians, and genealogists to provide access to archival collections in those countries.*

Libraries in Open Societies: Proceedings of the Fifth International Slavic Librarians' Conference, edited by Harold M. Leich, MLS (Vol. 3, No. 2/3, 2002). *"The papers collected in this book are not only the product of this international conference, but also are concrete evidence of how far Slavic librarianship has progressed over the past 30 years. Valuable–not only to those with an interest in the Slavic field but to any librarian with an interest in area studies librarianship, international networking, and collection development." (Robert H. Burger, PhD, MLS, former Head of the Slavic and East European Library, University of Illinois at Urbana-Champaign)*

Publishing in Yugoslavia's Successor States, edited by Michael Biggins, PhD, MS, and Janet Crayne, MLIS, MA (Vol. 1, No. 2/3, 2000). *"A valuable tool, one which has been sorely lacking. All regions of the area are covered. The list of vendors, most with contact information that includes Web sites, will certainly be of service to those charged with acquiring these publications. An indispensible resource for anyone needing access to the publications of this region." (Allan Urbanic, PhD, MLIS, Librarian for Slavic Collections, University of California, Berkeley)*

Virtual Slavica:
Digital Libraries,
Digital Archives

Michael Neubert
Editor

Virtual Slavica: Digital Libraries, Digital Archives has been
co-published simultaneously as *Slavic & East European Information
Resources*, Volume 6, Numbers 2/3 2005.

The Haworth Information Press®
An Imprint of The Haworth Press, Inc.

New York • London • Victoria (AU)
www.HaworthPress.com

Published by

The Haworth Information Press®,10 Alice Street, Binghamton, NY 13904-1580 USA

The Haworth Information Press® is an imprint of The Haworth Press, Inc., 10 Alice Street, Binghamtom, NY 13904-1580 USA.

Virtual Slavica: Digital Libraries, Digital Archives has been co-published simultaneously as *Slavic & East European Information Resources*™, Volume 6, Numbers 2/3 2005.

The development, preparation, and publication of this work has been undertaken with great care. However, the publisher, employees, editors, and agents of The Haworth Press and all imprints of The Haworth Press, Inc., including The Haworth Medical Press® and Pharmaceutical Products Press®, are not responsible for any errors contained herein or for consequences that may ensue from use of materials or information contained in this work. Opinions expressed by the author(s) are not necessarily those of The Haworth Press, Inc. With regard to case studies, identities and circumstances of individuals discussed herein have been changed to protect confidentiality. Any resemblance to actual persons, living or dead, is entirely coincidental.

Cover design by Marylouise E. Doyle.

Library of Congress Cataloging-in-Publication Data

Virtual Slavica : digital libraries, digital archives / Michael Neubert, editor.
     p. cm.
    "Co-published simultaneously as Slavic & East European information resources, volume 6, numbers 2/3 2005."
    Includes bibliographical references and index.
    ISBN-13: 978-0-7890-2685-9 (alk. paper)
    ISBN-10: 0-7890-2685-6 (alk. paper)
    ISBN-13: 978-0-7890-2686-6 (pbk. : alk. paper)
    ISBN-10: 0-7890-2686-4 (pbk. : alk. paper)
    1. Europe, Eastern–Digital libraries. 2. Slavic countries–Digital libraries. I. Neubert, Michael E. (Michael Edward), 1957- II. Slavic & East European information resources.
  DJK7.75 V57 2005
  025.06'947–dc22
                                           2005007857

Indexing, Abstracting & Website/Internet Coverage

This section provides you with a list of major indexing & abstracting services and other tools for bibliographic access. That is to say, each service began covering this periodical during the year noted in the right column. Most Websites which are listed below have indicated that they will either post, disseminate, compile, archive, cite or alert their own Website users with research-based content from this work. (This list is as current as the copyright date of this publication.)

(continued)

Special Bibliographic Notes related to special journal issues (separates) and indexing/abstracting:

- indexing/abstracting services in this list will also cover material in any "separate" that is co-published simultaneously with Haworth's special thematic journal issue or DocuSerial. Indexing/abstracting usually covers material at the article/chapter level.
- monographic co-editions are intended for either non-subscribers or libraries which intend to purchase a second copy for their circulating collections.
- monographic co-editions are reported to all jobbers/wholesalers/approval plans. The source journal is listed as the "series" to assist the prevention of duplicate purchasing in the same manner utilized for books-in-series.
- to facilitate user/access services all indexing/abstracting services are encouraged to utilize the co-indexing entry note indicated at the bottom of the first page of each article/chapter/contribution.
- this is intended to assist a library user of any reference tool (whether print, electronic, online, or CD-ROM) to locate the monographic version if the library has purchased this version but not a subscription to the source journal.
- individual articles/chapters in any Haworth publication are also available through the Haworth Document Delivery Service (HDDS).

Virtual Slavica:
Digital Libraries,
Digital Archives

CONTENTS

ABOUT THE EDITOR

Michael Neubert, MLS, MAIS, is Digital Projects Coordinator at the Library of Congress, and Team Leader for the Digital Conversion Team whose staff produce American Memory, Global Gateway, and other digital conversion projects. He has been active in negotiating and implementing Global Gateway collaborative projects with Russia, Brazil, France, and other countries' national libraries. Previously Mr. Neubert was a librarian at the Library of Congress specializing in Russia. He was a United States Information Agency/American Library Association Library Fellow in Yekaterinburg, Russia in 1997-1998. In 2004, he was selected as a "library world mover & shaker" by *Library Journal*.

Introduction

In October of 2004, as I am completing editing the articles for this volume, Brewster Kahle of the Internet Archive announced at the Web 2.0 conference that he believes that the twenty-six million volumes in the Library of Congress can be scanned for 260 million dollars and fit into a terabyte of space. As a digital projects coordinator at the Library of Congress, I frankly find this prospect both exciting and frightening (even as I find his math somewhat doubtful).

Of course, digital conversion is just one part of the virtual, or digital, information world that continues to develop around us. Area studies, or at any rate Slavic studies, has tended to follow behind the progress of developments in the digital realm in other disciplines. This gives us in Area studies the advantage of seeing what our future may bring so that we can try to shape that future, but it also means that we must deal with users who come to us with expectations that they may have from their interactions with tools available for other disciplines.

This volume provides a snapshot of different aspects of what can be called Slavic digital librarianship. Interestingly, much of what is presented here is not closely focused on bits and bytes, but on such topics as wrangling with copyright issues (in Janice Pilch's article) or wrestling with the requirements of a TICFIA grant (Bradley Schaffner's article).

The greatest focus is on some interesting and, it is hoped, representative digital projects: *The Fundamental Digital Library of Russian Literature and Folklore* (Joseph Peschio et al.), the Comintern archives, both as a standalone product (Ronald Bachman) and online (Tatyana Doorn-Moiseenko), and a spatial database for large Russian cities (Alexander Perepechko et al.).

[Haworth co-indexing entry note]: "Introduction." Neubert, Michael. Co-published simultaneously in *Slavic & East European Information Resources* (The Haworth Information Press, an imprint of The Haworth Press, Inc.) Vol. 6, No. 2/3, 2005, pp. 1-2; and: *Virtual Slavica: Digital Libraries, Digital Archives* (ed: Michael Neubert) The Haworth Information Press, an imprint of The Haworth Press, Inc., 2005, pp. 1-2.

Available online at http://www.haworthpress.com/web/SEEIR
doi:10.1300/J167v06n02_01

Bits and bytes are not completely ignored: the FAQ (frequently asked questions–and answers) for Cyrillic multilingual computing (Kevin Hawkins) provides considerable technical detail, as does the article on implementing a Cyrillic OPAC at Queens Public Library (by Jane Jacobs and Malabika Das). Technical aspects of Slavic text encoding (TEI) are covered in an overview article (by Miranda Remnek).

Users are not ignored. An article (by Sandra Bostian) describes how focus group information is being used to influence design of the *Meeting of Frontiers* website. And finally, there is an extensive review of the state of Slavic digital reference, covering both digital information resources and virtual means of communication, including QuestionPoint and online chat (by Angela Cannon).

I want to thank the authors who contributed to this volume. I learned a lot myself as I read through their articles and I think the readers will find much of interest as well.

Michael Neubert
Library of Congress
Washington, DC

Frequently Asked Questions
and Selected Resources
on Cyrillic Multilingual Computing

Kevin S. Hawkins

SUMMARY. The persistence of multiple standards, both *de jure* and *de facto*, for handling text on the computer is perhaps the most perplexing problem facing those who wish to use a computer in more than one language, or even to provide access to data across more than one operating system and application platform. Using Cyrillic as an example, this article attempts to answer questions commonly asked by non-expert computer users who wish to work in more than one language. *[Article copies available for a fee from The Haworth Document Delivery Service: 1-800-HAWORTH. E-mail address: <docdelivery@haworthpress.com> Website: <http://www.HaworthPress.com> © 2005 by The Haworth Press, Inc. All rights reserved.]*

Kevin S. Hawkins, MS, is Electronic Publishing Librarian, Scholarly Publishing Office, University Library, University of Michigan.

Address correspondence to: Kevin S. Hawkins, 300 Hatcher Graduate Library North, 920 North University Avenue, Ann Arbor, MI 48109-1205 USA (E-mail: kshawkin@ umich.edu).

The author wishes to thank David Dubin and the other members of the GSLIS Research Writing Group at the University of Illinois at Urbana-Champaign for their comprehensive advice, and Troy Williams, Benjamin Rifkin, Michael Brewer, David Dubin, Tatiana Poliakevitch, Irina Roskin, Peter Houtzagers, and Uladzimir Katkouski for their specific corrections and suggestions.

[Haworth co-indexing entry note]: "Frequently Asked Questions and Selected Resources on Cyrillic Multilingual Computing." Hawkins, Kevin S. Co-published simultaneously in *Slavic & East European Information Resources* (The Haworth Information Press, an imprint of The Haworth Press, Inc.) Vol. 6, No. 2/3, 2005, pp. 3-21; and: *Virtual Slavica: Digital Libraries, Digital Archives* (ed: Michael Neubert) The Haworth Information Press, an imprint of The Haworth Press, Inc., 2005, pp. 3-21. Single or multiple copies of this article are available for a fee from The Haworth Document Delivery Service [1-800-HAWORTH, 9:00 a.m. - 5:00 p.m. (EST). E-mail address: docdelivery@haworthpress.com].

doi:10.1300/J167v06n02_02

KEYWORDS. Character encoding, character sets, keyboard layouts, multilingual computing, fonts, computers, Cyrillic

INTRODUCTION

Nearly everyone who has used a computer has experienced what are often called "font problems" or "encoding problems": letters or punctuation marks outside of the very basic ones used in English, which show up on screen or in print as something other than what was originally intended. While in some cases, such as jumbled punctuation marks, the reader can "read around" these characters, when using non-Latin writing systems it becomes impossible to use a document without decoding it.

While a scrambled document can sometimes be decoded simply by using a different *character encoding scheme* (*character encoding* or *character set*) or a different font, the solution is often not so simple. The problem might involve settings in software used to create, copy, view, or deliver the file, or a combination of these. Information providers, including librarians, have the responsibility to use settings in their own software properly and make choices that will guarantee wider access to their materials. Furthermore, while settings in the user's software are out of the control of information providers, steps can be taken to minimize the likelihood that these settings will interfere with properly reading the document.

We have so many different standards, both *de jure* (official) and *de facto* (unofficial), because multilingual computing, like most technologies, caught on faster than a standard could be agreed upon, especially since dominant commercial and political interests tend to oppose standardization initially in order to preserve market share, sphere of influence, or ideology. The proliferation of conflicting, inferior standards is the result of a history we have not yet succeeded in fully escaping, but all stakeholders, even dominant ones, now agree that it is in everyone's interest to escape this history.

It is so complicated to store and enter characters used in the writing systems of natural languages because there are many software layers and levels of abstraction involved, all of which are easily confused with one another. Terminology is inconsistent, with some terms having common usage but a different technical meaning.

I will address common points of confusion in multilingual computing, using Cyrillic as an example. However, everything that I say applies to those using non-U.S. computers, those writing in languages in the Latin alphabet other than English, and those using other *scripts* (*writing systems*)[1] on the computer besides Cyrillic. I gloss over distinctions when I believe that they are insignificant to users of contemporary operating systems and software: my loose use of terminology, guaranteed to offend experts in text processing, is designed to make this very complex topic accessible to the lay audience. I hope that my conversational style and use of the frequently-asked-questions (FAQ) format, while unorthodox for a scholarly journal, will make this very difficult topic easier to understand. Following the FAQ is a short bibliography of resources on multilingual computing.

IMPORTANT POINTS OF CLARIFICATION

There is one terminological and ontological distinction that must be explained up front: the difference between a *character* and a *glyph*. Characters are basic, abstract units in a writing system and are not to be confused with their particular appearance in any font (called a glyph).[2] The Latin character *B* is not the same as the Cyrillic character *V*, despite appearances, and the Latin character *M* is not the same as the Cyrillic character *M* even though the latter pair are used for essentially the same sound. A character is still the same character no matter what glyph you use: whether you write it in a serif font or a sans serif font, or whether you write it in italics or boldface or large or small. Storing text as characters rather than glyphs enables searching within and across files, where the particulars of appearance are rarely significant.[3] Characters can be correlated when helpful in searching–for example, capital and lowercase letters are correlated at the operating system level (and in many programs), whereas it is not helpful to correlate Latin *M* and Cyrillic *M*. Which languages are considered for the purposes of character sets to use the same writing system has the potential to be a contentious issue, but such decisions are increasingly made by experts who strive to balance linguistic and pragmatic needs. French *B* and English *B* are considered the same character, as are Russian *G* and Ukrainian *H*. That is, the notion of character is writing-system dependent, not language-dependent.

Another common point of confusion among computer users is over whether it is possible in creating a digital document of any sort to guarantee that the reader will see it exactly as the creator does. While the exact appearance of a document can be preserved in PDF format,[4] it is impossible to preserve it in HTML and even word processing formats since many of these details change as you view the file. There are non-standard and deprecated practices in HTML for specifying and even embedding fonts, but there is no way to be sure that the document will show up exactly as you see it when viewed by another person, who may have a different operating system, collection of fonts, web browser, and browser settings. The appearance of word processor documents is subject to the user's settings in the word processor, the fonts available, and the printer driver. So you should never create a document whose proper appearance depends on text appearing at a certain location on the page or appearing in a certain font or size.

FREQUENTLY ASKED QUESTIONS

1. I want to read text written in Cyrillic. Do I need to download a special font? What if I know I can view text in Cyrillic already but the website claims I need a special font? Do I really?

Until the mid-1990s special fonts were needed to work in "exotic" languages on major operating systems distributed in the U.S. Since then all major operating systems come with some built-in or freely available capacity for displaying documents in Cyrillic. At first this involved adding optional components–especially fonts and keyboard layouts–to work in exotic languages. These fonts often had "Cyrillic" or "Cyr" appended to the name but otherwise matched pre-installed fonts in name and appearance. Since then, due to standardization on Unicode,[5] any given font usually has Cyrillic "built in" to it, so separate fonts for different scripts are no longer needed and one web page can now contain characters from more than one non-Latin script. In today's operating systems the fonts and keyboard layouts are installed by default for many languages and need only be activated, or at least they are included on the installation disks.

However, sometimes websites providing textual resources in Cyrillic will claim that a certain font is necessary to view the text properly. While this is never strictly true, there are three reasons why it can be practically true. First, if the resource was created using a custom font with a non-standard *font encoding*,[6] such as those that allow you to type in Cyrillic by changing fonts but not changing keyboard layouts, you will need to use some font with the same font encoding, and chances are this font is the only one out there. (See question #6 for reasons to avoid such custom fonts.) Second, it is possible that the resource uses a standard encoding but includes at least one character whose glyph is simply missing from common pre-installed fonts; in this case, you will need to download this font or use another one that includes all the glyphs required. Third, the author might have attempted to guarantee the *exact* appearance of the document. While using the specified font can help, there is no guarantee that this will give the exact desired appearance, as explained above.

Therefore, to read documents including Cyrillic text, no special fonts should be needed if the document was created using a standard font (with a standard font encoding). Word processing documents with a standard font generally open without problem, whereas the proper viewing of HTML files is subject to browser and server settings, either of which can cause the wrong character encoding scheme to be chosen. If this is the case, see question #2.

2. I have trouble viewing certain websites. Why?

As explained in question #1, you generally do not need any special fonts to view text in Cyrillic; therefore, problems with garbled Cyrillic text are most likely caused by improper settings on the server where the file is located or on your browser, and possibly both. The following explains how to decipher pages you come across; see questions #9, #10, and #11 for information on how to minimize problems for viewers of your own websites.

Regardless of what is causing the garbled text, web pages are best deciphered by enabling the character encoding "auto-detect" feature of your browser since this feature usually selects the character encoding you need. In some browsers, there are different auto-detect features for different languages. If the feature ever selects the wrong encoding when viewing a web page, you can override it by selecting an encoding from the list, usually without disabling the auto-detect feature. Auto-detect is usually not enabled by default in browsers for some strange reason, and it can easily be disabled by accident. There is no particular disadvantage to leaving this feature on unless you are testing your own web pages for encoding compatibility. Note that auto-detect features poorly judge web pages with HTML frames, so you will most likely need to manually choose an encoding when viewing such pages.

3. I want to type in Cyrillic. Do I need to download a special keyboard layout (driver)? Is there any way to type without adding a keyboard layout?

First we need some background on keyboards. When you buy a computer, it almost always comes with a keyboard made for users in the country in which it was purchased, with keys labeled for the most commonly used characters. Some characters do not have their own keys but instead are sent to the computer by typing a combination of keys simultaneously, for example, by holding down Ctrl, Shift, Alt, or AltGr (the right Shift key on American keyboards). While American keyboards only use the Shift key to enter alternative characters, in other keyboard layouts it is common to have access to more than one script through the keyboard by using key combinations. A similar functionality might be provided by your operating system, word processor, or both, but these are in fact layered on top of what is provided by the physical keyboard.

Thankfully for users, keyboard layouts are quite standard in all countries: the QWERTY layout, with slight national variants, is nearly universal for languages using the Latin script, and languages using Cyrillic have just a few basic layouts.

Your operating system can be set to work with any keyboard layout you specify, and today's operating systems come with all the major international layouts by default, just as they contain all fonts for non-Latin scripts. Choosing a keyboard layout is one of the first steps in an installation process. Since keyboards all over the world have almost the same number and arrangement of keys, just with different arrangements of characters, it is generally possible to use any physical keyboard with any keyboard layout. Furthermore, operating systems allow you to change the default keyboard layout or to install more than one keyboard layout with one or more convenient ways to switch between them (such as by clicking in a special toolbar for language settings) or by using a key sequence like Alt + Shift.

The problem, then, after changing your keyboard layout or adding an additional one, is knowing where to find the characters you need if your physical keyboard is labeled with the characters of the country where you purchased it. Keyboards almost all use the same type of cable to connect to a computer,[7] so one often overlooked solution is to buy a keyboard in another country while traveling there. Keyboards sold in their target market, even in the West, are quite inexpensive. Foreign keyboards can be purchased online from domestic websites but cost much more this way. You can also buy clear stickers online for your domestic keyboard, thereby allowing you to fake a keyboard that you might buy in another country. A cheaper solution is to make your own stickers. Transparent (scotch) tape works well but is difficult to remove after being constantly pressed by warm fingers. Masking tape is more easily removed but tends to slide under the heat of your fingers and is annoying to the touch for some users. If you type in another language frequently enough, you might instead print a picture of the keyboard layout you are using and learn to touch-type by looking at it. Learning the layout doesn't take as much effort as you might think.

I highly recommend one of the above methods of learning a standard keyboard layout so that when traveling to Slavic, East European, and Eurasian countries you will be able to adapt to the commonly used keyboard layout immediately. Some Western users, however, prefer a *homophonic* ("transliterated" or "phonetic") keyboard layout, in which characters are arranged similar to those in one's native layout. This layout is easier to learn for the non-native user and does not require stickers or a new keyboard. Numerous web pages explain how to download and install such keyboard layouts (there are various versions but no one accepted standard) on your computer (see Further Reading section).

Some text editors have a built-in "de-transliteration" function, by which you type in transliteration and the editor converts to Cyrillic characters. Some also have built-in phonetic keyboard layouts, allowing you to use a phonetic keyboard just in that program without changing your operating system keyboard layout.

For especially small input needs, there are three options, none of which requires changing the operating system keyboard layout. Websites such as *Translit.ru* allow you to type in transliteration and the site will convert your text to Cyrillic on the fly. Some text editors and websites have virtual keyboards in small windows that allow you to choose Cyrillic characters. These applications can be used to copy and paste text into other programs or websites. Another option is to copy and paste letters from other programs. This usually works smoothly, especially with Unicode-conformant software. A third option is to use a *character palette* (or map) to insert characters. A palette may be found within a word processor or as a standalone program in the operating system. If using this, it is best to select from the default font; otherwise, you risk selecting characters from a font with a non-standard font encoding (see questions #1 and #6).

4. When I copy and paste between programs, my characters get jumbled. How do I fix this?

More often than not, this is a sign that one of the programs you are using is not fully Unicode-conformant.[8] Try using other combinations of programs.

5. Say I need to type just one Russian word in the middle of a document in English and it uses letters also found in the Latin alphabet. Can I just type these letters using my default American keyboard layout?

Please do not. The three characters in the Russian word *mat* are not the same as the three characters in the English word *mat*. Storing them as different characters prevents the Latin lowercase *T* from ever being displayed like the Cyrillic lowercase *T* (which in most typefaces are not identical), and it prevents a search for the English word from finding the Russian word or vice versa.

6. What font should I use to type in Cyrillic?

When using a contemporary word processor to compose a document involving characters from more than one script, choose characters from a Unicode-conformant font (one that uses Unicode font encoding)[9] rather than a font like Symbol, Zapf Dingbats, or one of the pre-Unicode custom fonts for typing in a non-Latin script. These fonts use only the first 255 *code points*,[10] replacing the Latin glyphs and basic punctuation that should be in these code points with Greek glyphs, printer's dingbats, or glyphs from another non-Latin script (respectively). While these fonts can be used with old programs that recognize only fonts with 255 code points and were especially useful before special keyboard layouts became common, the documents created with them are entirely dependent on the arrangement of glyphs in this font–an arrangement that does not conform to any particular standard and therefore will likely require conversion in case the font is no longer available.[11] For example, while the Symbol font might continue to be shipped with operating systems for the foreseeable future, Greek texts using it are not interoperable with Greek texts in Unicode, so cross-searching is not possible unless the document in Symbol is converted. In such a case you will need to find a utility that will do this conversion, and unless you write one yourself, the chance that you find one is related to the size and technical expertise of the user community for that font with a non-standard encoding.

Using Unicode rather than an older standard allows you to capture almost every character likely to be encountered in a printed text[12] and store the electronic text in a standard broadly accepted by industry and the international standards community. If you have scholarly or practical problems whereby the 96,447[13] characters of Unicode version 4.0.1 are inadequate for the kind of transcription you would like to do, you can use Unicode's Private Use Areas, which contains unassigned code points.

In short, I recommend that you never switch fonts in a word processor just to type in another language. Stick to one font, using a second keyboard layout or other input method as described in question #3 to insert glyphs for the character you need.

7. I want to be able to use diacritical marks with certain characters in Cyrillic, but I don't see the glyphs I need in Unicode. Can I still use Unicode? Do I need a special font?

Unicode aims to include all characters in all scripts, so one font could have all the glyphs for every character needed in any document. However, the designers of Unicode realized that many diacritical marks can be used on nearly any character, and therefore it makes sense to define *base characters* and *combining characters* separately.[14] Since Unicode includes all the diacritical marks you'll ever need, I recommend against using another font just because it has particular *precomposed characters* that you need. A document relying on such a font would suffer the same compatibility problems as affect other pre-Unicode fonts (see question #6). Instead, I recommend using Unicode base characters and combining characters.

However, many programs that can read, write, or print files using a Unicode character encoding scheme have trouble displaying *base characters* and *combining characters* together properly, especially if there is more than one combining character applied to the base character. This can even be true when going from the same program running on different operating systems. If you are unhappy with the way your program renders *composite characters* (decomposable characters, including base characters with combining characters applied to them), you might try using other Unicode-conformant fonts. If you cannot find a font that works acceptably with the editor or word processor you are using, it is best to find another program that works better: the strong disadvantages of using a font with a non-standard encoding, as explained in question #6, outweigh the convenience of using a program you are most familiar with. Support for Unicode character sequences involving combining characters can only improve in the future.

8. I see that Unicode contains a number of precomposed characters to guarantee round-trip compatibility with earlier standards, but "the same" character can be encoded by finding the appropriate base character and combining character and using them together. Which should I use?

The World Wide Web Consortium,[15] stewards of HTML and other web standards, recommends using precomposed characters (using Unicode's Normalization Form C) for web documents.[16] Even if your documents are not intended for the web, you will find it easier to work with precomposed characters since many programs handle composite characters poorly, as explained in question #7. There are utilities for automatically converting between normalization forms in Unicode (between using precomposed and composite characters), so you can always decompose later. Note that the Unicode Consortium refuses to admit any new precomposed characters to the standard, and a major design goal of Unicode is to decompose all characters as far as possible (to the atomic level).

9. What character encoding (character set) should I use for saving my web pages or other documents?

Word processors often do not present the user with a choice of character set when saving in their native formats; instead, they translate to a standard character set when saving in a text format or in HTML.

For text and HTML including any number of languages but no more than small amounts of CJK (Chinese, Japanese, or Korean) text, I personally recommend using UTF-8, one of the seven Unicode character encoding schemes.[17] UTF-8 has the advantage over the other Unicode encodings of working fairly well with most pre-Unicode software for the first 128 characters (basic Latin characters and punctuation marks). Since Unicode encodings allow you to encode practically any known character, it is superior to earlier script-specific encodings, such as ISO 8859 encodings, Windows codepages, and national standards such as the KOI encodings. Support for Unicode is now well-established in Internet standards, major operating systems, and office software, and the proportion of computer users using pre-Unicode software will continue to shrink as software and hardware are upgraded.

While scholars and librarians are right to be concerned about accessibility overseas, where older hardware and software are the norm, the value of international standards and the need for long-term accessibility must be borne in mind as well. There are many utilities for converting files between character sets, as well as web forms that let you cut and paste chunks of text for conversion or transliteration, so documents in a non-Unicode character encoding scheme can be automatically converted to UTF-8 or another Unicode character encoding scheme. When creating new files, it is best to start in UTF-8 rather than convert to it later because you will never be limited by the set of characters found in any particular pre-Unicode character set; however, converting to UTF-8 at a later stage is effortless. Note that this conversion is not the same as converting from a font with a non-standard encoding (as explained in question #6), for which there are few utilities available.

I also recommend using UTF-8 with documents entirely in English to be consistent and to encourage the adoption of this superior standard.

For character set recommendations for e-mail, see question #13.

10. How do I specify the character encoding (character set) for my web pages?

There are a few levels at which encoding can be specified for an HTML web page:

a. If composing HTML in a text editor, you need to choose an encoding in which to save the file. An option may be presented to you when saving, or it might be set by default.
b. The HTML file itself can contain a declaration of the encoding being used (explained below). In HTML editors this is tied to (a).
c. The server on which the file is stored can be configured to declare an encoding when serving files to users, directing their browsers to use this encoding when displaying the file.

Step (a) must happen, even if you're not aware of it because your program for generating HTML (an HTML editor or word processor) takes care of this for you. Neither (b) nor (c) is required, but if neither is used, you rely on the user's auto-detect feature being enabled and your text being sufficiently predictable to have its encoding guessed. There is no need to risk this when the encoding can be specified otherwise.

Popular web page editors and text editors do not default to UTF-8 for (a) and (b) because most users do not require multilingual capabilities and want their web pages to be accessible to as many users as possible, even those using outdated web browsers and operating systems. However, current editors can be customized to work entirely in UTF-8, and contemporary browsers have no problem reading files in UTF-8 encoding.

Even if you save your web documents (HTML or otherwise) in UTF-8, there are other settings which could interfere with their proper delivery online. There are four different sources of information a web browser uses to determine which character set to use to view a page, given here in order of precedence (the browser stops as soon as it finds a suitable setting):[18]

1. The value of the *Content-Type* field in the HTTP header sent by the server
2. The XML declaration (applies only to XHTML and other XML documents): <?xml version="1.0" encoding="utf-8"?>
3. This line (or an equivalent for using another character encoding) in the HTML or XHTML head element: <meta http-equiv="Content-Type" CONTENT="text/html;charset=utf-8" /> (*Exact syntax varies depending on the version of HTML or XHTML. This is an alternative to reconfiguring the HTTP header but is considered an unofficial fix.*)
4. The most recent setting in the user's browser for which character set to use (if auto-detect is not used), or the auto-detect feature of the user's browser

While the last is completely out of your control as the creator of a web page, the first can be properly configured with the help of your server administrator, and the second and third can be included in your HTML code.

11. Should I offer more than one encoding of all my documents?

Some websites offer more than one encoding of their pages because there was a time when browsers could only view certain encodings and because you can automatically generate files converted into another encoding–or even transliterated–quite easily. Today, however, in my opinion there is little reason to provide your documents in more than one encoding. For multilingual documents, the only real choice right now is between UTF-8 and any of the earlier script-specific or national character encoding schemes.

12. How can I be sure others will be able to view my web page or other documents properly?

PDF is the only major format preserving the exact appearance of a document. It's a good option for providing documents meant to be printed, for guaranteeing exact appearance, and for archival preservation, but it is a bad choice for building a website.

If not using PDF, you cannot guarantee that a document provided in another format will appear for the user exactly as you intended: there are simply too many factors outside your control. However, by following the directions in questions #9, #10, and #11, you will minimize the chance that a user will not be able to view your pages. It would not hurt to try viewing your pages on a variety of operating systems using a variety of browsers to make sure there are not any problems. Doing so will help you spot not only character encoding problems but also design problems caused by browsers–even major ones–that are not fully standards-compliant.

13. What character encoding (character set) should I use in e-mail messages?

Character encoding in e-mail is even more complicated than in HTML and word-processing documents. Unicode support in e-mail software lags behind operating systems, word processors, and web browsers, so a Unicode encoding should be used only if you know all recipients of your message can view it. It is better to use a pre-Unicode encoding standard (as long as you can limit your conversation to Latin plus one additional script) or transliterate[19] everything if you must.[20]

Note that some e-mail clients and servers that can handle "exotic" character sets in the body are not able to display or even process these character sets when found in the header of the message, which includes the *to*, *from*, and *subject* fields, among others. So you may find it best to use only basic Latin characters in your subject lines and even your name as it displays in the *from* field.

14. My colleague can't read my e-mail message written in Cyrillic. Have I done something wrong, or has my colleague?

There are three types of *e-mail clients* you can use to read e-mail: a program that runs on your e-mail server (such as Pine), a *stand-alone* program that runs on your computer (such as Microsoft Outlook, PC Pine, Netscape Messenger, or Eudora), or a web interface hosted by whatever service you use for e-mail (such as Hotmail, Gmail, or a university's "webmail" service). Most, though not all, e-mail clients allow you to set the character encoding of an outgoing message. Either this setting is program-wide for all messages, or it is a default setting that can be overridden for an individual message. In the former case, if you find yourself needing to compose in a different encoding than usual, you should change the setting before you begin composing a message. Clients of all types work similarly to browsers when deciphering a received message: most have auto-detect features and allow you to override the current setting.

When using a program on an e-mail server, both sender and receiver need to have a client capable of understanding the character encoding used in the message, and their software for connecting to the server (such as SSH or Telnet) must be able to understand and display the character encoding using a font on the user's computer.

When using a standalone client, both sender and receive need to make sure their clients can understand and display the character encoding used in the message using a font on their computer.

When using a web interface, both sender and receiver need to make sure their clients can understand the character encoding and that their browsers are configured to display this encoding, as explained in question #2.

15. I can read messages from individual colleagues without any problems, but messages I receive from e-mail lists consistently give me problems. How can I fix this?

Electronic distribution lists (*electronic mailing lists* or simply *e-mail lists*) present additional problems beyond the pragmatic solutions to today's e-mail situation explained in #13. As with web pages, you can never really guarantee how your message will appear to recipients, and this is especially true for messages sent to mailing lists because the software running them intervenes while relaying your message. Users who subscribe to a list in a non-MIME digest mode receive messages forced into one character encoding, and some list software (such as ListProcessor, which runs SLAVLIBS[21]) strips the encoding declaration out of all messages. In order to guarantee that you will reach the maximum number of people, you will need to stick to Latin characters (and avoid sending HTML or "rich text" mail). Using the lowest common denominator of e-mail standards is also important for e-mail distribution lists since many are archived, and archive interfaces are not always friendly to multiple character sets.

16. Do search engines reach all documents no matter what their character encoding (character set), or do they only pick up certain encodings?

Any major search engine is bound to understand more than one encoding and allow searching across documents.

17. Now that I can type in Cyrillic on my computer, can I search online library catalogs (OPACs) in Cyrillic?

This depends on the capabilities of the software behind the OPAC, as well as on whether the records have Cyrillic text in the 880 field (in addition to the usual transliterated fields). Generally speaking, records must have Cyrillic text and the OPAC software must be Unicode-conformant. Because of the way shared cataloging works in Western libraries, it might be the case that some records have Cyrillic text while others have only transliterated text. In this case a search in Cyrillic would yield only records with Cyrillic text while a search using proper transliteration will yield all records. Therefore, users should continue searching in transliteration for the near future for languages written in Cyrillic, for which use of the 880 field among catalogers has been sporadic.

NOTES

1. I give alternative terms in parentheses following the form I prefer, which is either more closely aligned with computer, as opposed to linguistic, terminology or more precise than another computer term.

2. There are many attempts to elucidate the character-glyph distinction, as well as some to discredit it. For an analysis of medieval Slavic arguing that a language-independent distinction is ultimately unsustainable, see David J. Birnbaum, "Standardizing

Characters, Glyphs, and SGML Entities for Encoding Early Cyrillic Writing," *Computer Standards and Interfaces* 18 (1996): 201.

3. For times when appearance is significant and could be helpful in searching, texts should be encoded using *descriptive markup*, such as that prescribed by the Text Encoding Initiative <http://www.tei-c.org/>, to enable such searching.

4. Software and printer drivers for generating PDFs try to replicate the exact appearance of a printed document; however, such software is not without flaws. *Combining characters* (defined in question #6) in Unicode are known not to work in some PDF-generating software and printer drivers. Furthermore, the PDF standard allows for only the most common fonts to be used without embedding them in the PDF file, so if a PDF file uses a rare font that is not embedded, it will display as intended. See Adobe Systems, *PDF Reference, Fifth Edition: Adobe® Portable Document Format Version 1.6* (San Jose, CA: Adobe Systems, 2004), <http://partners.adobe.com/public/developer/en/pdf/PDFReference16.pdf> (accessed December 22, 2004), 15-16.

5. See the website of Unicode, Inc., <http://www.unicode.org/>. Unicode is actually the common name for two separate standards synchronized since 1991: the Universal Multiple-Octet Coded Character Set (UCS), defined by ISO/IEC 10646 (JTC 1/SC 2/WG 2), and the Unicode Standard, defined by the Unicode Consortium, an industry group that allows for limited outside participation.

6. Think of the difference between *font encoding* and *character set encoding* like this: *font encoding* concerns the arrangements of glyphs within the font itself, reflected, for example, in how the characters are arranged in a character map program, whereas *character set encoding* concerns how the data (numbers) that make up the file are matched to characters.

7. Macintoshes here are the most significant exception: recent models would mostly but not entirely work with PC keyboards, but the latest models do not work with PC keyboards or even earlier Macintosh keyboards. See MacWindows Solutions, "Sharing Keyboards and Monitors Between Macs and PCs: Cross-Platform KVM Solutions," <http://www.macwindows.com/keyboard.html> (accessed September 12, 2004).

8. It is possible for both programs not to be Unicode-conformant but both to use the same character encoding in communicating with the clipboard, but this is decreasingly likely when using recent software.

9. At least one Unicode-conformant font comes with all major operating systems today. See question #1.

10. A *code point* is the unique number assigned to each character for data storage.

11. One such conversion effort, involving various Cyrillic fonts from the 1980s and early 1990s, is the Cyrillic Font Project: <http://www.stg.brown.edu/projects/indexcard/displaycard.php3?card=9> (accessed September 12, 2004). Similar work has been done by the staff of the Slavic and East European Language Resource Center <http://www.seelrc.org/>.

12. For the Slavicist, note that Unicode includes Glagolitic and all the Cyrillic characters needed for any modern language written in Cyrillic, but some historical Cyrillic characters are still missing, according to Deborah W. Anderson's presentation "Unicode in Multilingual Text Projects: A Status Report from the Script Encoding Initiative, UC Berkeley" delivered at the Joint International Conference of the Association for Literary and Linguistic Computing and the Association for Computers and the Humanities, Göteborg, Sweden, June 11–16, 2004.

13. Unicode Consortium, "*The Unicode® Standard*: A Technical Introduction"; "Unicode 4.0.0," <http://www.unicode.org/versions/Unicode4.0.0/> (accessed August

21, 2004). This number was calculated by summing figures given in these two documents.

14. This is the same principle used in MARC (where it originated), though Unicode combining characters follow base characters rather than precede them in the file's sequence of characters, as was originally the case in MARC.

15. See <http://www.w3.org/>.

16. Patrick Rourke, "Unicode Normalization Forms," *Unicode Polytonic Greek for the World Wide Web (version 0.9.7)*, <http://www.stoa.org/unicode/normalization. html> (accessed September 23, 2004).

17. *Wikipedia: The Free Encyclopedia*, s.v. "UTF-8," <http://en.wikipedia.org/ wiki/UTF-8> (accessed September 23, 2004). CJK ideographs are more efficiently stored in UTF-16.

18. Web Standards Project, "Specifying Character Encoding," <http://www.webstandards. org/learn/askw3c/dec2002.html> (accessed September 13, 2004); Alan J. Flavell, "Notes on Internationalization," <http://ppewww.ph.gla.ac.uk/%7eflavell/charset/internat. html> (accessed September 15, 2004); Richard Ishida, "Tutorial: Character Sets & Encodings in XHTML, HTML, and CSS (DRAFT)," <http://www.w3.org/International/ tutorials/tutorial-char-enc/> (accessed September 15, 2004).

19. What transliteration scheme you use is up to you. Ideally you will use a *reversible* transliteration scheme–one that can be de-transliterated automatically. Library of Congress (LC) Romanization schemes are reversible if combining characters are used (difficult to represent outside of MARC software), as are proposed standards like Russkaja Latinica <http://www.kulichki.com/centrolit/rl/latinic1.html>. Note that multiple systems of transliteration, like multiple character encodings, are a barrier to cross-searching and future reuse of material. (See question #6.)

20. Use of Unicode in e-mail is less important than in other electronic documents for which long-term accessibility and preservation are of greater concern. While social historians may one day be interested in your correspondence and having some trouble deciphering electronic records of it, they will have to decipher everyone else's as well and will be quite good at it.

21. For more information on SLAVLIBS, see "Internet Links 'As Seen on SLAVLIBS,'" <http://www.columbia.edu/~jsi19/slavlink.html>.

SELECTED BIBLIOGRAPHY

Czyborra, Roman. *Czyborra.com.* <http://czyborra.com/> (accessed September 12, 2004).

This personal web page contains links to many comprehensible sub-pages on multilingual computing. While some are aimed at computer experts and focus on Linux and the pages are generally a bit outdated, the historical information is quite well-digested. Unfortunately, the site is frequently unavailable.

Drozd, Andrew M. "Slavic Fonts and Keyboard Drivers." *American Council of Teachers of Slavic and Eastern European Languages.* <http://www.aatseel.org/keyboards. html> (accessed September 24, 2004).

This section of the AATSEEL website contains links for fonts and keyboards (including homophonic keyboards), but as explained, there is very little you need to download if you are using recent software.

Gorodyansky, Paul. *Cyrillic (Russian): Instructions for Windows and Internet*. <http://www.ruswin.net/> (accessed September 24, 2004).

This fully bilingual (English and Russian) site contains exhaustive, accessible information about "russifying" many versions of Windows, including installing a homophonic keyboard created by the author.

Il'in, Igor'. *Translit.ru*. <http://www.translit.ru/> (accessed September 24, 2004).

This online tool allows you to type in Latin characters and have them converted to Cyrillic based on the transliteration scheme built in. You can copy and paste in text for transliteration or de-transliteration.

Korpela, Jukka "Yucca." "Characters and Encodings." *IT and Communication*. <http://www.cs.tut.fi/~jkorpela/chars/index.html> (accessed September 24, 2004).

The subpages from this site contain a huge amount of highly accessible information, including historical perspective. Especially useful is "A Tutorial on Character Code Issues."

Main, Linda. *Building Websites for a Multinational Audience* (Lanham, Md.: Scarecrow Press, 2002).

This book explains basic terminology in depth and explains how to use current and emerging web standards. Particularly useful to librarians is Appendix A: Library Automation Vendors and Unicode Compliance.

Mashkevich, Stefan. *Automatic Cyrillic Converter*. <http://www.mashke.org/Conv/> (accessed September 24, 2004).

This online tool allows you to type or paste characters in any Cyrillic encoding or in one transliteration scheme and convert them to another encoding (or to transliteration). You can also upload whole files for conversion, or convert the page at a given URL.

Microsoft Keyboard Layout Creator (MSKLC) Version 1.3.4073. <http://www.microsoft.com/downloads/details.aspx?FamilyID=fb7b3dcd-d4c1-4943-9c74-d8df57ef19d7&displaylang=en> (accessed September 24, 2004).

This program, available from Microsoft for Windows 2000, Windows XP, and Windows Server 2003, allows you to make your own keyboard layouts.

Palchuk, Matvey B. *Russification of Macintosh*, <http://www.friends-partners.org/partners/rusmac/> (accessed October 15, 2004).

This site in English gives full russification instructions for many versions of Mac OS and common software. As with Windows, many of these steps are no longer required when using recent operating systems and programs.

Rourke, Patrick. "Unicode Polytonic Greek for the World Wide Web: Version 0.97: Draft." *Stoa Consortium*. <http://www.stoa.org/unicode/index.html> (accessed September 24, 2004).

Though this resource has not been updated since 2002, its clear description of Unicode for the non-specialist is still highly useful. It is useful to those using Unicode for languages other than Ancient Greek.

Sidorenkov, Igor. *Otpad 2.3–Russian Text Editor.* <http://www.ingenit.com/home/programs/otpad/index> (accessed September 24, 2004).

This free Windows text editor that has built-in transliteration and encoding conversion capabilities.

Wood, Alan. "Unicode and Multilingual Support in HTML, Fonts, Web Browsers and Other Applications." *Alan Wood's Unicode Resources.* <http://www.alanwood.net/unicode/> (accessed September 24, 2004).

This site is updated regularly and very easy to use. There are many pages to test encodings, as well as the best listing of freely available Unicode fonts on the web. (If using recent software, you do not need to download a special font. See question #1.)

The Comintern Archives Database: Bringing the Archives to Scholars

Ronald D. Bachman

SUMMARY. As one of nine institutions participating in the International Committee for the Computerization of the Comintern (INCOMKA), the Library of Congress (LC) played a primary role in making the archives of the Communist International available to researchers around the world. LC assumed responsibility for converting some 175,000 personal names from Russian Cyrillic to their standard spelling in American English usage and translating nearly 20,000 keywords from Russian to English. As a result, researchers who do not know the Russian language have access to the vast Comintern database, including more than a million pages of digitized manuscripts.

KEYWORDS. ArchiDOC, browsing, Comintern, Communist International, CPSU, Communist Party of the Soviet Union, descriptors, digitization, ECCI, El Corte Inglés, INCOMKA, Library of Congress, name vetting, personal files, RGASPI, Romanization of Cyrillic, Rosarkhiv, text searching, transliteration

Ronald D. Bachman, PhD, is Polish Area Specialist, European Division, Library of Congress, Washington, DC 20540-4830 USA (E-mail: rbac@loc.gov).

Opinions stated in this article are those of the author and not of the Library of Congress.

[Haworth co-indexing entry note]: "The Comintern Archives Database: Bringing the Archives to Scholars." Bachman, Ronald D. Co-published simultaneously in *Slavic & East European Information Resources* (The Haworth Information Press, an imprint of The Haworth Press, Inc.) Vol. 6, No. 2/3, 2005, pp. 23-36; and: *Virtual Slavica: Digital Libraries, Digital Archives* (ed: Michael Neubert) The Haworth Information Press, an imprint of The Haworth Press, Inc., 2005, pp. 23-36.

Available online at http://www.haworthpress.com/web/SEEIR
doi:10.1300/J167v06n02_03

BACKGROUND

The Communist International (Comintern) was established in March 1919 to foment world revolution. Within a few years, communist parties existed in nearly all the countries of Europe and by 1930 in most countries of the world. These generally small, often illegal parties looked to Comintern headquarters in Moscow for support and guidance. After the dissolution of the Comintern in 1943, the Communist Party of the Soviet Union (CPSU) took custody of the organization's records. The Comintern archives constitute an important resource for the study of world history during the inter-war period and early years of World War II. The archives also contain interesting biographical material from the Cold War era, when the International Department of the CPSU continued to add personal files.

The formerly secret Comintern archives were opened to the public in late 1991. Until recently, access to the collections required a trip to the Russian State Archives for Social and Political History (RGASPI) in Moscow, where researchers faced an endurance test to locate specific information among more than twenty million pages of documents. Extensive finding aids to the collections existed, but they were in the Russian language only. Researchers, regardless of language capability, required staff assistance to determine whether personal files on given individuals even existed.

On June 6, 1996, after three years of discussions, the Council on Archives and the Federal Archival Service of Russia (Rosarkhiv) signed an agreement that would make the Comintern archives more accessible to researchers around the world. The agreement set up the International Committee for the Computerization of the Comintern (INCOMKA). Partners in this effort included Rosarkhiv; RGASPI; the Archives of France; the Federal Archives of Germany; the State Archives of Italy; the National Archives of Sweden; the Federal Archives of Switzerland; the Ministry of Education, Culture, and Sport of Spain; the Open Society Archives of Hungary; and the Library of Congress.

ROLE OF THE LIBRARY OF CONGRESS IN INCOMKA

In the winter of 2004, the European Division of the Library of Congress loaded onto a dedicated terminal in its reading room more than 580 CDs containing the entire catalog of the Comintern archives and more than a million pages of digitized documents. This was the culmination of a multinational effort stretching over several years.

In addition to a significant financial contribution as a partner institution, the Library of Congress invested many staff hours to help bring the INCOMKA project to fruition. John Van Oudenaren, chief of the European Division, attended several INCOMKA planning and coordination conferences in Europe and hosted a two-day meeting on linguistic issues in February of 2001. John E. Haynes of the Manuscripts Division also attended meetings, provided expertise in the selection of materials for digitization, served as liaison with 154 historians in fifty-four countries, and reviewed the lists of Romanized personal names and English translations of keywords.

The Library of Congress assumed responsibility for converting some 175,000 personal names from Russian Cyrillic to the Latin alphabet and translating from Russian to English close to 20,000 descriptors (keywords or subject headings) taken from Comintern archival finding aids. I was given the task of coordinating this linguistic effort. The goal was to make the INCOMKA database accessible to researchers with little or no Russian capability. The Library of Congress was well suited for this undertaking because of its vast collections of historical, biographical, and lexicographic works and the foreign-language diversity of its staff. Thirty-two staff members, most from the Area Studies Divisions, participated in the project.

In the summer of 2000, RGASPI sent to the Library of Congress a list of about 110,000 names taken from personal files (*lichnye dela*) maintained by the Comintern and, after 1943, the International Department of the CPSU. All names were in Russian Cyrillic as recorded over a period of many decades by clerks with highly divergent levels of foreign-language competence. Our task was to convert the Cyrillic version of the names to their standard American English spelling.

The Comintern had files on persons from essentially all the countries of the world as it existed during the inter-war years, including some, like Tannu Tuva, that no longer exist. Many of the persons listed, such as Palmiro Togliatti, were prominent party members, while others were staunch anti-communists, e.g., Harry Truman. There were files on writers, painters, actors, civic leaders, and religious leaders. There even was a file on Karol Wojtyła, Pope John Paul II. But a large share of the persons were unknown functionaries, whose names could not be attested in published sources. The Library of Congress did not have access to the files themselves, which might have provided a Latin spelling for some of the names.

The name-conversion process involved four stages. First, using a computer macro devised by our European Division colleague Michael Neubert, we produced a phonetically based transliteration from Russian according to Library of Congress Romanization rules. We arranged the names into more than 100 country tables and distributed them to Library of Congress staff with native or near-native competence in given languages.[1]

In the second stage, Library of Congress linguists analyzed the computer transliterations and converted sequences of letters into meaningful, language-specific combinations. For example, from the Mexican list, *KHUAN* became *Juan*; from the Polish list, *IATSEK* became *Jacek;* from the Moroccan list, *KHADZH* became *Haj.* Library staff attempted to identify individuals and provide the standard American English spelling of their names, e.g., *DZHON RID* was identified as *John Reed,* as opposed to *John Read* or *John Reid.* Identifying individuals turned out to be an especially daunting task in the case of the tens of thousands of names originally written in neither Cyrillic nor Latin alphabets. To proceed from the Library of Congress phonetic transcription of a Russian phonetic transcription of a name originally recorded in a third writing system and arrive at the "correct" spelling in American usage was a challenge we were not always able to meet.

In the third stage, John Haynes sent the lists to foremost authorities in the histories of the respective countries for "vetting." In most cases, two or three specialists reviewed each list. The lists were in the form of multi-column tables presenting the original Cyrillic, the computer transliterations, and the spellings produced by the Library staff. The specialists confirmed or corrected the spellings, sometimes adding aliases, and returned the lists to the Library of Congress.

The final step was incorporating the experts' inputs and delivering the finished tables to the Spanish software company El Corte Inglés, which loaded the information into the special version of ArchiDOC it developed for the INCOMKA database.

Just as we were nearing the completion of the name-conversion project, we received a revised list from RGASPI, which created a whole new set of complications. The revised list included tens of thousands of additional names extracted from collective personal files and from the detailed finding aids compiled by RGASPI archivists. Most unfortunately, the revised list merged the additional entries with the original set of 110,000 names. El Corte Inglés, after considerable effort, eventually sorted out most of the new names for us. We completed the name conversion in house, but time did not allow us to send the additional names to outside experts for correction. Meanwhile, RGASPI sent us several long lists of Russian descriptors taken from the Comintern archival *opisi* (finding aids). Harold Leich, Russian area specialist in the European Division, and I translated these terms into English, and John Haynes edited them.

CONTENTS OF THE DATABASE

The INCOMKA project digitized more than a million document pages. Although this is not a small amount of material, it is only a fraction of the Comintern archive of more than twenty million pages. Perhaps more importantly, the project made available to off-site researchers the entire catalog of Comintern archival collections. Even when researchers find that documents of high interest are not among those digitized, the database provides detailed bibliographic descriptions of every *delo* (file) in the archive, which will enable them to judge whether it is worth traveling to RGASPI or having someone photocopy the material for them.

Below is a list of the *Fondy* (collections, abbreviated F.) and *opisi* (inventories/finding aids, abbreviated op.) scanned during the INCOMKA project. It is immediately apparent that the focus was *Fond* 495, the files of the Executive Committee of the Communist International (ECCI). *Fond* 495 accounts for 57 of the 86 *opisi* and 7,049 (just over 75%) of the 9,366 files that were scanned. Nearly 85% of the files in these 86 *opisi* were scanned. The figures in parentheses indicate the number of files scanned and the number of digital images, respectively.

1. F. 488, op. 1. First (founding) Congress of the Comintern (18 / 922)
2. F. 489, op. 1. Second Congress of the Comintern (66 / 5,965)
3. F. 495, op. 1. Comintern Executive Committee (ECCI) (112 / 12,195)
4. F. 495, op. 2. ECCI Presidium (287 / 50,319)
5. F. 495, op. 3. ECCI Political Secretariat (341 / 84,072)
6. F. 495, op. 4. Political Commission of the ECCI Political Secretariat (463 / 71,741)
7. F. 495, op. 6. ECCI Small Commission (50 / 2,497)
8. F. 495, op. 7. ECCI Permanent Commission (37 / 4,028)

9. F. 495, op. 11. Secretariat of ECCI Secretary W. Pieck (357 / 27,675)
10. F. 495, op. 12. Secretariat of P. Togliatti (171 / 14,564)
11. F. 495, op. 13. Secretariat of K. Gottwald (74 / 4,563)
12. F. 495, op. 13a. Secretariat of K. Gottwald (15 / 2,251)
13. F. 495, op. 14. Secretariat of A. Marty (393 / 49,561)
14. F. 495, op. 15. Secretariat of W. Florin (266 / 28,482)
15. F. 495, op. 16. Secretariat of O. Kuusinen (100 / 13,314)
16. F. 495, op. 17. Secretariat of D. Ibarruri (355 / 12,825)
17. F. 495, op. 18. ECCI Secretariat (1,196 / 131,302)
18. F. 495, op. 24. ECCI Presidium (71 / 7,538)
19. F. 495, op. 26. ECCI Orgbureau (31 / 4,037)
20. F. 495, op. 27. Illegal Commission of the ECCI Orgbureau (17 / 920)
21. F. 495, op. 28. Central European Regional Secretariat of the ECCI (200 / 21,996)
22. F. 495, op. 29. Communist Party of Brazil (144 / 11,402)
23. F. 495, op. 31. Scandinavian Regional Secretariat of the ECCI (183 / 24,002)
24. F. 495, op. 32. Latin Regional (France, Italy, Belgium, Switzerland) Secretariat of the ECCI (232 / 31,942)
25. F. 495, op. 35. Austrian Commission of the ECCI (11 / 777)
26. F. 495, op. 36. Agrarian Commission of the ECCI (21 / 2,424)
27. F. 495, op. 37. American Commission of the ECCI (61 / 9,813)
28. F. 495, op. 38. English Commission of the ECCI (32 / 3,235)
29. F. 495, op. 39. Bulgarian Commission of the ECCI (6 / 498)
30. F. 495, op. 40. Hungarian Commission of the ECCI (16 / 1,215)
31. F. 495, op. 41. Dutch Commission of the ECCI (9 / 436)
32. F. 495, op. 42. Indian Commission of the ECCI (15 / 1,837)
33. F. 495, op. 43. Italian Commission of the ECCI (16 / 1,278)
34. F. 495, op. 44. Chinese Commission of the ECCI (18 / 1,577)
35. F. 495, op. 45. Korean Commission of the ECCI (28 / 1,506)
36. F. 495, op. 46. ECCI Reorganization Commission (19 / 892)
37. F. 495, op. 47. German Commission of the ECCI (22 / 4,329)
38. F. 495, op. 48. Norwegian Commission of the ECCI (20 / 2,301)
39. F. 495, op. 49. Polish Commission of the ECCI (38 / 3,715)
40. F. 495, op. 50. ECCI Program Commission (17 / 1,094)
41. F. 495, op. 51. ECCI Trade Union Commission (26 / 3,686)
42. F. 495, op. 52. Romanian Commission of the ECCI (46 / 3,051)
43. F. 495, op. 53. Scandinavian Commission of the ECCI (13 / 616)
44. F. 495, op. 54. Ukrainian Commission of the ECCI (10 / 955)

45. F. 495, op. 55. French Commission of the ECCI (27 / 4,213)
46. F. 495, op. 56. Czechoslovak Commission of the ECCI (23 / 1,629)
47. F. 495, op. 57. Swedish Commission of the ECCI (12 / 793)
48. F. 495, op. 58. Yugoslav Commission of the ECCI (22 / 815)
49. F. 495, op. 59. Japanese Commission of the ECCI (9 / 669)
50. F. 495, op. 60. Various ECCI Commissions (278 / 12,913)
51. F. 495, op. 61. Polish-Baltic Regional Secretariat of the ECCI (120 / 21,635)
52. F. 495, op. 72. Anglo-American Regional Secretariat of the ECCI (178 / 18,272)
53. F. 495, op. 77. Correspondence and Work among POWs in WWII (56 / 6,089)
54. F. 495, op. 78. ECCI Publishing Department (191 / 21,677)
55. F. 495, op. 79. Latin American Regional Secretariat of the ECCI (203 / 15,699)
56. F. 495, op. 101. Latin American Regional Secretariat of the ECCI (45 / 5,153)
57. F. 495, op. 102. Secretariat of D. Ibarruri (11 / 756)
58. F. 495, op. 155. Negro Section of the ECCI Eastern Department (73 / 5,468)
59. F. 495, op. 292. German Communist Party Representation in the ECCI (114 / 14,118)
60. F. 495, op. 293. ECCI Materials on the Communist Part of Germany (159 / 14,138)
61. F. 496, op. 1. Editorial Board of the Journal "Communist International" (99 / 10,071)
62. F. 497, op. 1. Press bulletins and materials of the Amsterdam Bureau (11 / 982)
63. F. 497, op. 2. Correspondence between the Amsterdam Bureau and the Leadership of the Communist Parties (11 / 1,000)
64. F. 498, op. 1. Vienna (Southeastern) Bureau of the ECCI (52 / 4,431)
65. F. 499, op. 1. West European Bureau of the ECCI (51 / 6,164)
66. F. 500, op. 1. Caribbean (Central American) Bureau of the ECCI (19 / 1,029)
67. F. 502, op. 1. Southern Bureau of the ECCI (22 / 3,108)
68. F. 504, op. 1. Statistical Information Institute of the ECCI in Berlin (the Varga Bureau) (259 / 56,584)
69. F. 506, op. 1. Cooperative Section of the ECCI (181 / 22,746)

70. F. 508, op. 1. Protocols of Sessions of the All-Union Communist Party (Bolshevik) in the ECCI (134 / 3,940)
71. F. 508, op. 2. Correspondence between the All-Union Communist Party (Bolshevik) delegation and the Russian Communist Party (Bolshevik) Central Committee (13 / 484)
72. F. 508, op. 3. Correspondence between the All-Union Communist Party (Bolshevik) delegation and the Russian Communist Party (Bolshevik) Central Committee (14 / 2,251)
73. F. 526, op. 1. E. Thälmann's Personal *Fond* (81 / 7,704)
74. F. 531, op. 1. International Lenin School: Orders, Correspondence, Documents of Sections and Regional Groups (283 / 21,417)
75. F. 531, op. 2. International Lenin School: Documents of Party, Komsomol, and Trade Union Organizations (129 / 7,972)
76. F. 538, op. 1. International Workers Relief: Congresses and Conferences (13 / 1,762)
77. F. 538, op. 2. International Workers Relief for the Hungry in Russia (115 / 15,974)
78. F. 538, op. 3. International Workers Relief: Documents (202 / 32,318)
79. F. 540, op. 1. International Federation of Revolutionary Theaters (120 / 13,790)
80. F. 540, op. 3. International Federation of Revolutionary Theaters (3 / 392)
81. F. 541, op. 1. International Federation of Revolutionary Writers (133 / 2,806)
82. F. 542, op. 1. Committee of the Anti-imperialism League (80 / 7,831)
83. F. 543, op. 1. International Anti-fascist Organizations (31 / 5,448)
84. F. 543, op. 2. International Anti-fascist Organizations (44 / 4,749)
85. F. 551, op. 1. Leipzig Trial (8 / 5,848)
86. F. 615, op. 1. Personal Papers of W. Z. Foster (114 / 11,168)

SEARCHING THE DATABASE

The Comintern database delivered to INCOMKA partners in winter 2004 uses ArchiDOC 2.3.7.17 Unicode software. Although searching is rather cumbersome, the software accomplishes its primary purpose–enabling scholars to search the large database in either Cyrillic or Latin alphabet, identify files of interest, retrieve bibliographic information, and in some cases, view digital images of actual documents. The software provides excellent image-enhancement tools, and readers often will find the digitized documents more legible than the originals. Researchers can print pages of manuscripts for their own use, and the software inserts the bibliographic citation at the bottom of each page–a very useful feature.

The database home page presents four menu choices: CLASSIFICATION, DESCRIPTORS (keywords), PHYSICAL *FOND* (bibliographic citations, listed in ascending numerical order), and LANGUAGES.

CLASSIFICATION organizes the vast Comintern archive into eleven thematic sections, shown below. All researchers who can read Russian, especially first-time users of this resource, will profit from a quick look at the eleven sections. It would enhance database accessibility if the sections and subsections were presented in English as well as Russian, but to make searching via CLASSIFICATION truly bilingual, at least the titles of the 521 inventories (*opisi*) should be translated.

Clicking on the plus symbol before each CLASSIFICATION heading opens a list of subheadings, which, in turn, open sub-subheadings, then *opisi,* then specific files. Wherever a camera icon appears, a double click will bring up the digital image of an actual document. The CLASSIFICATION sections in English are:

- Comintern Congresses and Plenary Sessions of the Comintern Executive Committee
- The Comintern Executive Committee and Its Administrative Departments
- Communist Parties and Sections of the International
- Comintern Institutions of Higher Learning
- International Revolutionary Organizations
- Personal files and documents
- Personal files by country
- The international socialist movement
- International brigades of the Spanish Republican Army
- International Trotskyite Organizations
- Other Comintern documents

Section 1 might serve to illustrate the logical structure of CLASSIFICATION. Under the heading "Comintern Congresses and Plenary Sessions of the Comintern Executive Committee" there are three subheadings. The first, entitled "Congresses of the Comintern," lists seven *Fondy*, namely:

- *Fond 488.* First (Founding) Congress of the Comintern, 1919
- *Fond 489.* Second Congress of the Comintern, 1920
- *Fond 490.* Third Congress of the Comintern, 1921
- *Fond 491.* Fourth Congress of the Comintern, 1922
- *Fond 492.* Fifth Congress of the Comintern, 1924
- *Fond 493.* Sixth Congress of the Comintern, 1928
- *Fond 494.* Seventh Congress of the Comintern, 1929

Each of the *Fondy* lists two or more *opisi*, which in turn list specific *dela*. For example, *Fond 488, opis' 1* lists 18 *dela*, the first being "Address on Convening the First Congress of the Comintern, 24 January 1919." It happens that this twenty-page file was among those digitized, and the researcher can view the document on the screen or print it off. *Fond 488, opis' 2* does not subdivide into *dela*; it is a collection of seventy-six photographs, which were not digitized. Altogether, the subheading "Congresses of the Comintern" comprises 15 *opisi*, and 2,618 *dela*. Subsection 2, entitled "Plenums of the Executive Committee of the Communist International," comprises 14 widely scattered *opisi* of *Fond 495* and totals 3,130 *dela*. Subsection 3, "International Control Commission of the Comintern, ICC," contains two *opisi* totaling 216 *dela*. Each *delo* contains, on average, several dozen pages and occasionally can be hundreds of pages in length.

CLASSIFICATION provides the most direct path to bibliographic records: a double left click on a title at any level in the CLASSIFICATON hierarchy brings up the bibliographic record in the opposite window of the split-screen display. Bibliographic information becomes more detailed as one proceeds from the section to the *delo* level. On the section and subsection levels, the record provides a title, the name of the RGASPI archivist who processed the material, and a brief contents note, which generally duplicates the title but occasionally provides a little more information. For example, Section 9, entitled "Interbrigades of the Spanish Republican Army," has the contents note "International formations and brigades of the Spanish Republican Army." On the *opis'* level, the record additionally provides an information start date and shows the number of *dela* contained therein. On the *delo* level, the record contains a contents note (typically a short paragraph in length), and information start and end dates; indicates the number of pages and the languages of the documents; and provides a list of descriptors. The list of descriptors can be several pages in length.

Comintern database users with poor or no Russian capability are at a severe disadvantage. Although the bibliographic field names can be displayed in English, the contents note is in Russian only. And since it is the contents note (not the actual text of the digitized documents) that is searched by the so-called text-search function, persons not knowing Russian do not have access to this useful tool. The researcher without Russian capability who does not have a specific citation to access directly through the third menu option, PHYSICAL FOND, has only one way to identify and retrieve files, the second menu option, DESCRIPTORS.

Based on a review of Comintern archival documents, RGASPI staff identified essential terms and grouped them in ten categories of descriptors. The lists of descriptors can be viewed in either Russian or English. Several of the categories are imprecisely delineated and often overlap. The SUBJECTS list is particularly fuzzy, and many terms are so generic it seems doubtful that a researcher would ever think of searching for them, e.g., *Domestic and international situation*. Terms within a list are not arranged in any hierarchy of specificity, i.e., there are neither general headings nor increasingly specific subheadings. The distinction between the categories of SOCIAL LEVEL and STATUS is especially vague. The apparent difference seems to be that terms in SOCIAL LEVEL are in the plural form, e.g., *graduate students*, and entries in STATUS are either singular, e.g., *architect*, or corporate bodies, e.g., *Bulgarian delegation*.

The descriptor category labels in Russian are not very descriptive, and their English equivalents (supplied by RGASPI) are even more mysterious. The fuzziness of categories is not a minor inconvenience. Since the software cannot search all descriptor lists simultaneously, the researcher must explore each one separately to have an acceptable level of confidence in the search results. The only apparent advantage of breaking the descriptors up into separate thematic lists is browsability. The inconvenience of having to search several lists should be addressed in future versions of the Comintern database.

Descriptors are listed alphabetically, which facilitates browsing. To move rapidly down the long lists (with more than 175,000 entries, the personal names list is the longest), the researcher highlights any descriptor and begins typing a word or phrase–as much or as little as desired–and hits Enter. Within an instant, the desired descriptor (or the space where it should appear in the alphabetized list) appears. This Hot

Search function is a great time saver, but it has one major limitation: it is left-anchored. The software does not offer a simple Find In Document function, which would locate any term regardless of its position within a descriptor.

The ten descriptor categories (Russian equivalents are in parentheses) are:

- SUBJECTS (TEMA)
- ORGANISMS [sic] (ORGANIZATSII)
- GEOGRAPHICS [sic] (GEOGRAFIIA)
- PERSONS (IMENA)
- SOCIAL LEVEL (SOTSIUM)
- PRESS (NAZVANIE IZDANIIA
- STATUS (STATUS)
- CONGRESS (FORUM)
- DOCUMENT TYPES (VID DOKUMENTA)
- COUNTRY CODES (KODY STRAN)

Having located and highlighted the desired descriptor, the researcher right clicks to find the option Show Related Documents. Left clicking on this option will bring up a list of all *dela* that include the descriptor in their bibliographic records. Double left clicking on a *delo* title will display the complete bibliographic record. If the *delo* was digitized, a camera icon appears before the title. Double clicking on the icon will bring up the document image.

If Show Related Documents displays too many (or too few) *dela,* the researcher can search two or more descriptors simultaneously. This is accomplished by selecting the Search Assistant option on the toolbar, which displays a search form on the opposite half of the split screen. The researcher left clicks on the descriptors (one at a time), and drags them across the screen into the bottom window of the search form. Selecting the option All of Them activates the Boolean AND operator, while Some of Them engages the OR operator. The search form also allows one to specify a range of dates or a specific date.

The third option on the database menu is labeled PHYSICAL FOND. For researchers who already have specific archival citations, this is the quickest path to the files. Citations are arranged in ascending numerical order, beginning with the Fond number. As with other sections of the menu, one expands or collapses lists by clicking on the plus sign at the beginning of each entry.

Part four of the database menu is LANGUAGE. This alphabetic list of all the document languages functions in the same way as a descriptor for searching purposes. A researcher who can read only Norwegian, for example, would click on Norwegian and drag the term over to the search window to limit search results to documents written in that language.

Researchers who can work with Russian have the option of keying terms directly into a search window and, by toggling to the Latin keyboard, using truncation (the percentage sign) and Boolean operators AND, OR, NOT. ArchiDOC misleadingly calls this function text searching. What the software is searching are file titles and/or file abstracts only a few lines in length. Considering that files often are hundreds of pages long and consist of dozens of documents, the odds are high that a search will show no hits. And even when a search is successful, i.e., one or more files are identified, the researcher's work has just begun. He/she still must page through the file to identify the manuscript(s) where the search terms occur.

CONCLUSION

The INCOMKA project, one of the most ambitious international archival digitization efforts to date, has achieved many, but not all, of its goals. In the near future the database will be available free of charge to researchers through the World Wide Web, although access to actual digital images will require a paid subscription. We hope the online version will be more user-friendly than the version delivered to INCOMKA partners on CDs. A Search This Site window that would allow users to search simultaneously all ten categories of descriptors and to find individual terms regardless of position within a descriptor is a badly needed improvement.

The conversion of about 175,000 personal names to Latin alphabet and the translation of almost 20,000 descriptors into English were a major undertaking. On the whole, we are pleased with the results. Nevertheless, researchers are certain to discover errors, and we hope the online version will enable them to send corrections and suggestions to the database administrators for updating. Researchers also will soon discover that none of the personal files have been, and probably never will be, digitized–ostensibly for privacy considerations. But, thanks to the INCOMKA project, researchers now can go to RGASPI with specific citations in hand and request the personal files.

The INCOMKA project has made the Comintern archives more accessible, to be sure. But researchers who cannot read Russian still face special challenges and have fewer search strategies than those who can work with Russian. The CLASSIFICATION menu option is available only to researchers able to work in Russian. In an ideal world, the titles of the 521 *opisi* and 230,000 files would be translated into English. At the Library of Congress, we have observed that nearly half of the Comintern database users have had limited or no Russian capability. It bears emphasizing that a large share, perhaps more than half, of the actual documents in the Comintern archives are in languages other than Russian, and that German, French, Spanish, and English account for most of these. These shortcomings nothwithstanding, the research community should welcome the Comintern database enthusiastically.

NOTE

1. The German, French, and Swiss INCOMKA partners handled the name conversions for their respective countries. Because of the special problems posed by the Chinese names, Dr. Haynes hired the services of historians at the State Archives Administration of China to identify persons and provide the standard Pinyin transliteration of their names. The Chinese experts, however, were unable to recognize close to half of the entries.

The Comintern Archives Online

Tatyana Doorn-Moisseenko

SUMMARY. Access to the Comintern archives has been virtually impossible for many years. In 1992, the Project for Computerization of the Comintern Archives was launched. This resulted in the creation of a comprehensive database with an inventory to the complete Comintern archives and scanning of 1,200,000 pages from the records of the central bodies of the Comintern. The recently started Joint Venture RusAR Publishers is making the database, as well as the scanned images, available online. *[Article copies available for a fee from The Haworth Document Delivery Service: 1-800-HAWORTH. E-mail address: <docdelivery@haworthpress.com> Website: <http://www.HaworthPress.com> © 2005 by The Haworth Press, Inc. All rights reserved.]*

KEYWORDS. Comintern archives, Communist International, CPSU, Communist Party of the Soviet Union, Communism, political history, Slavic studies, labor history, digitization, microform, RusAR Publishers, IDC Publishers, INCOMKA, RGASPI

THE HIDDEN ARCHIVES

The Communist, or Third, International (Comintern) and its archives, kept hidden away for many years, have been shrouded by rumor,

Tatyana Doorn-Moisseenko, PhD, is Project Manager for Slavic Studies, IDC Publishers BV, P.O. Box 11205, 2301 EE Leiden, The Netherlands, (E-mail: tmoisseenko@idc.nl).

[Haworth co-indexing entry note]: "The Comintern Archives Online." Doorn-Moisseenko, Tatyana. Co-published simultaneously in *Slavic & East European Information Resources* (The Haworth Information Press, an imprint of The Haworth Press, Inc.) Vol. 6, No. 2/3, 2005, pp. 37-44; and: *Virtual Slavica: Digital Libraries, Digital Archives* (ed: Michael Neubert) The Haworth Information Press, an imprint of The Haworth Press, Inc., 2005, pp. 37-44. Single or multiple copies of this article are available for a fee from The Haworth Document Delivery Service [1-800-HAWORTH, 9:00 a.m. - 5:00 p.m. (EST). E-mail address: docdelivery@haworthpress.com].

doi:10.1300/J167v06n02_04

conjecture, and myth. The semi-legal and clandestine activities coordinated by the Comintern made this one of the most cloistered societies in recent centuries. Its influence was heavily felt even in countries where it could operate only in semi- or total illegality, through secretive activities, yet it is impossible to write twentieth century history without these archives. However, access to this indispensable source of information–fifteen linear kilometers of shelving–was virtually impossible for many years. After Stalin dissolved the Comintern in 1943, the documents testifying to its decisions were classified as top secret and held in the inaccessible repositories of the Central Party Archive in Moscow. In 1992 the archives were opened to the public, but were still difficult to access, due to its vastness (fifty-five million pages) and complexity (more than ninety languages).

PROJECT OF COMPUTERIZATION
OF THE COMINTERN ARCHIVES

Several initiatives were undertaken to answer the challenge of making the holdings of the Comintern archives accessible to the international scholarly community. In 1992, the Project of Computerization of the Comintern Archives was launched when several parties decided that an international project should be undertaken to facilitate access to the Comintern archives through computer technology. The project was carried out under the aegis of the Council of Europe as part of the program for the democratization and modernization of the archives in post-Communist Europe. It was managed by an international committee, INCOMKA (International Computerization of the Comintern Archives), composed of representatives of the Council of Europe, the Archives of Russia (Rosarkhiv), and the International Council of Archives and Partner Organizations sponsoring the project: the Federal Archives of Switzerland, the Federal Archives of Germany, the Archives of France, the State Archives of Italy, the Ministry of Education, Culture, and Sport of Spain, the National Archives of Sweden, The Library of Congress, and the Open Society Archives of Hungary.

The work resulted in the creation of a comprehensive database with an inventory to the complete Comintern archives and the scanning of 1,200,000 pages from the records of the central bodies of the Comintern. The Library of Congress offered a substantial addition to the database. Under the supervision of John Earl Haynes, some 200,000 personal names were transliterated from Cyrillic to Latin script (whenever necessary, by restoring the original spelling), and all descriptors were translated from Russian into English. To assist with the difficulties of translating the names from Russian into Latin-alphabet English, 167 scholars from fifty-four countries were called upon. At the end of the INCOMKA project in summer 2003, stand-alone configurations of this dataset have been installed in the Russian State Archive of Social and Political History (RGASPI) in Moscow and at the premises of each of the eight partner organizations, where the database and the digitized images are freely accessible.

The Joint Venture RusAR Publishers–which combines the complementary expertise of IDC Publishers, a Dutch academic publisher, and its Russian partner, Electronic Archives (ELAR)–made the next step in providing online access to this dataset. They developed *COMINTERN Online* at <http://www.comintern-online.com/>. *COMINTERN Online* consists of two components: a freely available online inventory of the complete Comintern archives of 55,000,000 pages, plus 1,200,000 digital images of the most frequently used documents, which are accessible by subscription. This unique cooperation makes the archives, held by RGASPI in Moscow, accessible now worldwide for research.

STRUCTURE OF THE COMINTERN ARCHIVES

The structure of the Comintern archives is hierarchical. RGASPI holds the documents from the Comintern archives in separate storage groups, called *fondy* (singular *fond*). The detailed contents of each *fond* are registered and described in a master inventory (or several inventories) called an *opis* (plural *opisi*). Each *fond* and each *opis* is identified by a number. The *opisi* contain individual numbered entries; each of these describes a single storage unit in the archive (e.g., typescript, dossier, folder, album, box). This storage unit is sometimes referred to as an item (Russian *delo*; plural *dela*). Each item in the archive is therefore defined by three identifying numbers: *fond, opis,* and individual *delo* numbers. The *COMINTERN Online* website represents the hierarchy as a tree structure, which enables the user to browse through the archives.

The documents of the Comintern Archives, arranged in 66 *fondy* and within these in 521 documentary units, comprise more than 220,000 files from seven Congresses, thirteen Executive Committee Communist International (ECCI) Plenums, and over 70 communist, socialist, and other international organizations. Finding aids (*opisi*) for the various sections themselves total more than 20,000 pages and are written in

Russian. Consequently, it was not easy to explore this archive, even for professional archivists. The frequent reorganizations of the Comintern headquarters in Moscow and the conspiracy-laden norms of illegal activity abroad created even more confusion within the structure.

ONLINE INVENTORY
TO THE COMINTERN ARCHIVES

COMINTERN Online includes a free online database that provides researchers user-friendly access to the complete inventory of the Comintern archives (the 55,000,000 pages of the trackless forest of documents written in more than ninety languages). This database reflects the structure of the entire Comintern archives and gives an idea of this content and organization in series and sub-series. The database contains 220,000 records, which are based on the original inventories of the archives in RGASPI.

The online inventory provides the possibility to search through the complete Comintern archives in both Cyrillic-alphabet Russian and Latin-alphabet English. (Figure 1 illustrates the Latin-alphabet English version.) There are two ways to find documents: through the hierarchical "rubricator" and through full-text search. The rubricator consists of three sections: CLASSIFICATION, DESCRIPTORS, and PHYSICAL *FOND*. In the CLASSIFICATION section documents are grouped by themes and are organized as a tree structure. DESCRIPTORS contain the documents' keywords, arranged by types (organizations, names, etc.). The structure of the physical storage in the archive is represented in the PHYSICAL *FOND* section. The full-text search functions on all fields of the document. The advanced search function allows the user to specify the query, e.g., to search exclusively among the descriptors, or to specify particular branches of the tree structure.

ONLINE DOCUMENTS
FROM THE COMINTERN ARCHIVES

After subscribing, it is possible to access about 1,200,000 scanned pages online. These images are material from the central bodies of the Comintern and represent the most frequently used and historically significant documents. These pages cover 59 sub-series, which were selected by INCOMKA, drawing upon the expertise of leading Comintern historians. The sub-series concentrate on the commissions, secretariats,

FIGURE 1

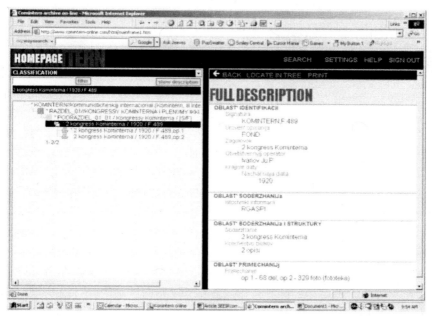

Reprinted with permission.

and departments that operated under the ECCI, the *Ländersekretariats* and regional bureaus, the party delegations with the Communist International, and other units of special interest such as the Lenin International Schools, International Workers Relief, and the International Federations of Writers and Theatres. Entire sections (*fondy*) were chosen for digitization, not just individual documents. The scanned pages are part of the general sections of the Comintern Archives. The total number of pages of these general sections is estimated at 3,000,000. Thus since the launch of *COMINTERN Online*, about forty percent of this most frequently used part of the Comintern archives has been available online. There is a clear intention to double the available number of pages within a period of two years after launch.

The available data can be divided into the metadata describing the inventory of the complete Comintern archive and the images of the pages themselves (see Figure 2). Access to the database with the inventory is free. Anyone interested in the content of the archive can query the data-

FIGURE 2

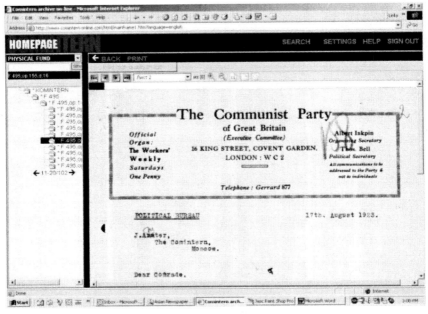

Reprinted with permission.

base. However the user needs to register at <http://www.comintern-online.com/> before searching the database. Access to the available images of pages is only possible after subscription. Subscription is based on IP address, enabling instant access from any computer in a defined IP range.

OTHER PUBLICATIONS FROM THE COMINTERN ARCHIVES

About 700,000 pages of other sections of the Comintern archives are already available on microform carriers through IDC Publishers. In 1994, IDC Publishers and RGASPI started a large project to publish the records of the seven Congresses and 13 Plenums of the ECCI, including preparatory and working commissions. The complete records were published on 14,569 microfiche. They include transcripts and minutes of the meetings, lists of delegates, mandates, and questionnaires filled out by delegates, etc.

Following this successful release, IDC Publishers is expanding its offering of materials from the Comintern archives. A new initiative was devoted to the publication of the files of national Communist parties on analog carriers (microfiche/microfilm). The Comintern ruled over the international Communist movement through its seventy partner organizations in Europe, Asia, America, and Africa for almost a quarter of a century (1919 -1943) and deeply influenced the political life of many countries worldwide. These Communist parties have always been secretive organizations. Many documents in these collections are unique because of the party's practice of hiding or destroying records. In addition to records produced by national Communist parties, these files also contain documents created or gathered in Moscow by parties' representatives to the Comintern.

This extensive project started in 2002 when RGASPI granted IDC Publishers the exclusive right to distribute the microfilm collection of the Communist Party of the USA (*fond* 515). It includes 4,313 files (326 microfilm reels), largely the original headquarters records of the CPUSA shipped to Moscow many decades ago. (A sample frame can be seen in Figure 3.) John Haynes, from the Library of Congress, prepared a finding aid to this collection. In early 2004, the material of the Communist Party of Japan (616 files from *fond* 495) was released on 132 reels. These files cover the period 1919-1941 and include extensive documentation on the relations between the Communist Party of the Soviet Union and its counterparts in Japan, the Far East, Europe, and America. Collections on the Communist Party of Mexico (*fond* 495) and other Asian and Latin American countries are currently being prepared. In the near future, there is no intention to scan the national party archives and make them available through the online service mentioned above. Relevant data of the analog publications (such as fiche and reel numbers) will be added to the inventory of the complete Comintern archives and will thus be available to scholars worldwide.

EXPANDING THE COLLECTION

This offering will grow by means of international cooperation. Rosarkhiv, the former INCOMKA partners, and the International Council of Archives are represented in the supervisory board of RusAR

FIGURE 3

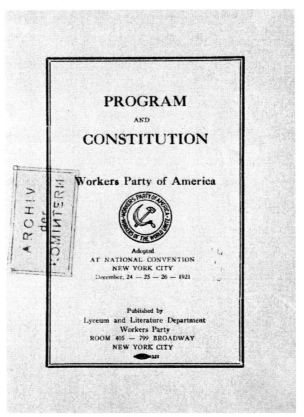

Reprinted with permission.

Publishers and consider new projects on opening up the Comintern archives using both online and analog publications. If you are interested in these initiatives and need more information or if you have any comments or suggestions, please contact IDC Publishers at <info@idc.nl>.

Academic Digital Libraries Russian Style: An Introduction to *The Fundamental Digital Library of Russian Literature and Folklore*

Joseph Peschio
Igor Pil'shchikov
Konstantin Vigurskii

SUMMARY. This article provides an overview of *The Fundamental Digital Library of Russian Literature and Folklore* (FEB-web). The intersection of philology and information technologies at FEB-web is considered in the context of Russian culture and the Russian academy. Topics discussed include: the FEB-web process for creating digital scholarly editions, the structure of FEB-web, new developments in the

Joseph Peschio, PhD, is Editor of the English-language version of FEB-web and Slavic Languages Coordinator, University of Wisconsin-Milwaukee, Department of Foreign Languages and Linguistics, Milwaukee, WI 53201-0413 USA (E-mail: peschio@feb-web.ru).

Dr. Igor Pil'shchikov, K.Fil.N., is Editor-in-Chief of FEB-web and Leading Researcher, Moscow State University, Institute of World Culture (E-mail: pilshch@feb-web.ru).

Dr. Konstantin Vigurskii, K.T.N., is General Director of FEB-web and Department Chief, The Informregistr Center for Scientific Research and Development, Russian Ministry of Communications and Informatization (E-mail: vigur@feb-web.ru).

[Haworth co-indexing entry note]: "Academic Digital Libraries Russian Style: An Introduction to *The Fundamental Digital Library of Russian Literature and Folklore*." Peschio, Joseph, Igor Pil'shchikov, and Konstantin Vigurskii. Co-published simultaneously in *Slavic & East European Information Resources* (The Haworth Information Press, an imprint of The Haworth Press, Inc.) Vol. 6, No. 2/3, 2005, pp. 45-63; and: *Virtual Slavica: Digital Libraries, Digital Archives* (ed: Michael Neubert) The Haworth Information Press, an imprint of The Haworth Press, Inc., 2005, pp. 45-63. Single or multiple copies of this article are available for a fee from The Haworth Document Delivery Service [1-800-HAWORTH, 9:00 a.m. - 5:00 p.m. (EST). E-mail address: docdelivery@haworthpress.com].

doi:10.1300/J167v06n02_05

45

FEB-web collections, plans for the future, copyright issues, digitization processes, inter-library cooperation, and the place of digital libraries in constructing civil society in Russia. *[Article copies available for a fee from The Haworth Document Delivery Service: 1-800-HAWORTH. E-mail address: <docdelivery@haworthpress.com> Website: <http://www.HaworthPress.com> © 2005 by The Haworth Press, Inc. All rights reserved.]*

KEYWORDS. Digital libraries, Russia, *Fundamental Digital Library of Russian Literature and Folklore, Fundamental'naia elektronnaia biblioteka "Russkaia literatura i fol'klor,"* FEB-web

The Fundamental Digital Library of Russian Literature and Folklore (FEB-web) is the first major academic library on the Internet to specialize in Russian folklore and literature of the tenth to twentieth centuries, satisfying an urgent scholarly and public need for editorially-reliable, bibliographically-documented texts and the tools for studying them.[1] FEB-web is a digital, multi-functional, full-text information system with advanced analytical instrumentation. This system is geared toward the compilation, preservation, and dissemination of Russian verbal art, as well as the scholarly, bibliographical, and other works needed to understand it. In addition, FEB-web is designed to provide the user with a set of technical tools for the analysis of its holdings. FEB-web is a totally non-commercial enterprise, making the canon of Russian literature available, free of charge, to anyone with Internet access.

A joint project of the Institute of World Literature (Russian Academy of Sciences) and the Russian Ministry of Communication and Informatisation, FEB-web has been in development since the mid-1990s. Since FEB-web launched its online version in July 2002, it has been recognized by the Russian Academy of Sciences as the most promising electronic resource for the study of Russian literature and has received two major prizes and two nominations as the best digital library on the Russian Internet. One online publication, *Lenta.ru*, called FEB-web "the largest and most ambitious of all the known humanities projects on the Russian Internet."[2] In the spring of 2003, FEB-web had approximately 500 visitors per day; within a year, that number grew to 2,000 visitors per day, and it is expected to continue growing at this pace in subsequent years. Since it went online, FEB-web has been visited over one million times by approximately 300,000 users–approximately half of them from inside Russia, twelve percent from other C.I.S. countries, twenty percent from European countries, and twelve percent from the United States.

It was designed in such a way as to expand organically, and FEB-web continues to grow at a steady pace. In summer 2004, its holdings included the full texts of over 50,000 works, 60,000 bibliographical annotations, and hundreds of illustrations. The overall volume of the information in FEB-web exceeds one gigabyte. With monthly updates, the FEB-web holdings continue to grow at a rate of approximately 3,000 pages of text per month, not to mention new graphic material and, now, audio files. FEB-web continues to develop its technical-analytical tools as well, constructing massive indexes, integrating an array of concordancing and other tools, and linking the mass of literary works at the center of its collections to an extensive reference and bibliographical apparatus.

FEB-web IN THE RUSSIAN CONTEXT

Any discussion of FEB-web must take as its starting point the Russian specifics–ranging from the theoretical to the geographical and economic–which conditioned the form FEB-web originally took, and which continue to shape its development.

The first issue to consider here is the dire need for free digital libraries in Russia. Access to information is a basic human right, and, contrary to overly-optimistic expectations at the beginning of the post-Soviet era, the Russian public finds its access to information more and more limited. Ironically and sadly, this is particularly true as regards the nation's own literary heritage. The Russian library and archival system is in a state of collapse (witness the closure and possible destruction of the Pushkin archive at The Institute of Russian Literature in St. Petersburg), and the Russian book market remains extremely primitive.

Over the last fifteen years, the Russian library system has come dangerously close to disintegrating altogether. The Russian State Library in Moscow, for example, has not operated at full capacity since 1998. This reflects a nationwide trend of neglect and collapse. Of the major state research libraries, only the National Library in St. Petersburg is fully functional and continues to build its collections in a systematic manner, albeit on a modest scale. The library situation is particularly acute for humanistic disciplines, especially literary scholarship. For example, the thousands of student philologists and professional researchers in the nation's capital are compelled to limit their primary materials to the woefully inadequate holdings at relatively small institutions like the State

Public Historical Library, where they often have to stand in line for several hours during examination periods to gain access.

Meanwhile, the commercial publishing business in Russia has failed to develop in any meaningful way over the last decade. Due to deficiencies in storage and distribution, as well as shoe-string publishing budgets, books–except, of course, the ever-popular *detektiv* and romance novel–are still published only in limited print runs which are guaranteed to sell out. This ensures that consumers outside the capitals have practically no access to new publications of literary scholarship, canonical Russian authors, works of philosophy, etc., and in the provinces it is often difficult to obtain even poor-quality copies of the most central works of the Russian canon. Almost all of the Russian book distribution system is controlled by a handful of companies such as AST, which have served the vast provincial markets exceedingly poorly. As a result, Russian students and scholars all over the country have been turning more and more to the Internet in order to obtain fundamental texts.

Amateur digital libraries, such as *Maksim Moshkov's Library* <http://lib.ru>, have been growing at an astounding rate to meet the demand for the most basic works of Russian literature and foreign literature in translation. Nonetheless, the growth of Russian-literature resources on the Russian Internet is not keeping pace with the overall growth of the sector, and the humanistic disciplines in Russia have yet to fully embrace the possibilities offered by digital text resources.[3] This has partly to do with the culture of these disciplines in Russia, where they remain highly conservative and, due partly to a devastating brain drain since 1990, extremely isolated from global developments in the humanities. It also has to do with the overall paucity and dismal quality of Russian Internet resources for scholars in these disciplines. Most Russian scholars have been hesitant to delve into the quantitative and so-called "exact" methods that digital texts make possible for the simple reason that there are too few digital texts available, and those that are available are often unreliable. FEB-web's main objectives include increasing the availability of fundamental texts, as well as inculcating information culture into the disciplinary culture of Russian philology.

This brings us to another purely Russian phenomenon that has played a large role in the formation of FEB-web: philology. In Russia, the term *philology* refers to a unique set of theoretical and disciplinary orientations. In conventional usage, philology is ". . . the commonwealth of disciplines–linguistics, literary scholarship, history, and others–that study history and explicate the essence of human spiritual culture through the linguistic and stylistic analysis of written texts. The text with the entire conglomeration of its internal aspects and external connections is the fundamental reality of philology."[4] Generally speaking, the specialists at FEB-web follow the formulation of Maksim Shapir: "The main object of philology is the text and its meaning"; only philology is interested in "the text as a whole . . . that is, a unique and unrepeatable unity of meaning in all the totality and in any details of its material embodiment in a form that can be apprehended by the senses."[5] Whereas Western literary scholarship has devolved of late into a fairly amorphous grouping of individual researchers who each feel entitled (and even compelled) to approach literature in increasingly idiosyncratic and interdisciplinary ways, Russian philology sees itself as an autonomous and self-contained scholarly discipline with fairly concrete objectives and standards.

FEB-web is a thoroughly philological enterprise in that it focuses on making its collections suitable for philological research: texts are assiduously vetted and checked for accuracy of representation, and full bibliographical annotations accompany every text. Furthermore, its analytical tools are geared toward making possible the kind of detailed analysis (stylistic, poetic, orthographic, textological, etc.) that philology centers on, but on a much larger scale than has been possible in the past. For instance, textological projects that once would have consumed years, reams of paper, and hundreds of pencils can now be completed in a matter of days or weeks using FEB-web. To date, sadly, FEB-web is one of only a handful of Russian literature resources on the Internet that is sufficiently accurate for such purposes.

As rooted as FEB-web is in the Russian context, it also has the aim of becoming an international resource for the study of Russian verbal art and Russian philology. The state of Russian library collections is certainly dire, but such collections are often non-existent outside Russia. It would ill behoove us to dwell on the trite catchwords of globalism, but the obvious fact remains that, as Internet availability continues to expand worldwide, free digital libraries will serve an increasingly important role in humanities education. Given its orientation toward the professional philologist and educator, FEB-web is especially valuable to students and scholars of Russian literature all over the world. Not only in the Russian provinces, but also in the United States, where dozens of research libraries house estimable Russian literature collections, key publications are often difficult or impossible to access. For example, FEB-web makes available an extremely rare edition of Griboedov, without which it is quite simply impossible to undertake any serious study of this author. FEB-web also provides access to the eleven-volume *Literaturnaia entsiklopediia* (1929-39), which is one of the field's great bibliographical rarities–few libraries have a copy, and it is nearly impossible to buy. As our collections continue to grow, more and more of the materials that scholars used to travel across the world in order to study will be only a mouse-click away.

Furthermore, FEB-web, so to speak, opens the window onto the East for scholars in related disciplines. The twentieth century saw major developments in literary theory and literary history emerge from Russian philology–from Moscow and Petersburg Formalism to Bakhtin to Tartu semiotics–but always with a lag time of forty years or more. Obviously, Russian philology was forcibly isolated from Western humanities scholarship in the Soviet era. As noted, however, it continues to be rather isolated. Worse yet, it remains mostly inaccessible to non-Russianists in the West, primarily because of the idiosyncrasies of Soviet and Russian editorial practice. FEB-web aims to make it easier for scholars in related disciplines, especially those with a limited knowledge of Russian, to get the information they need–in order to trace subtexts, for example. FEB-web also hopes to become a useful resource for foreign undergraduate students with intermediate Russian-language skills. Toward this end, FEB-web launched an English-language version last fall. At present, the English-language version is a limited, parallel version: the texts are the same, and all in the original language(s), but the interface is in English, making it easier for non-Russianists to navigate. For the future, a collection of English-language translations is planned. This collection will, in some respects, parallel the Russian-language collections, but it will also serve as an ideal resource for the study of the theory and practice of literary translation.

We hope that the English-language version will also make it easier to integrate the FEB-web holdings into electronic catalogs worldwide, thus providing a gateway to FEB-web for all the potential users who have not yet encountered it. One important feature of the English-language version is that all the bibliographical descriptions are transliterated (according to the Library of Congress transliteration scheme), which will facilitate the integration of these descriptions into library catalogs in the United States and, eventually, into WorldCat, RLIN, and other global catalogs. Another significant step in this direction is the opening of the FEB-web Bibliographical Database described below. Finding a way to formulate MARC records for the FEB-web holdings is a major priority.

PHILOLOGY AND INFORMATION TECHNOLOGIES

At the root of many philological methods lie two basic tasks: the search for text fragments which are relevant in one respect or another, and the comparison of text fragments. The analytical instrumentation of FEB-web is being developed, first and foremost, to aid researchers in locating and comparing data. The first step in the development of this instrumentation was the creation of the FEB-web search systems. FEB-web uses its own version of the Yandex search engine, which is modified to accommodate both contemporary and pre-Revolutionary Russian orthography. FEB-web supports three basic kinds of searches:

1. The attribute search makes it possible to find works and editions by running searches of *author*, *title*, or *publication date* attributes. Attributes can be assigned multiple meanings (e.g., author = Pushkin AND Griboedov), and searches can be performed simultaneously on multiple attributes (e.g., author = Pushkin, title = Monakh). When selecting attribute meanings, users are presented with a list of authors, titles, or publication dates to select from.
2. The lexical search is a full-text search that allows users to find any word or phrase in the text of works or bibliographical annotations (this function works only for words with Cyrillic or Latin characters). Lexical searches in Russian are sensitive to morphology (i.e., changes in case, number, etc.) in both pre-Revolutionary and contemporary orthography.
3. The combined search allows for simultaneous lexical and attribute searches–that is, to narrow the search field for lexical searches to only those works with a given author, title, or date.

At present, full-text searches can be performed only within an individual digital scholarly edition, but it will soon be possible to search the entirety of the FEB-web holdings.

The next step will be the creation of digital concordances. (Concordances, for example, of Griboedov's oeuvre and Dostoevsky's journalism will become available online in the near future.) Full-text search capabilities and digital lexical indexes put the location and recording operations so central to philology on a whole new level of sophistication and quality. The new generation of concordances has an immeasurably greater degree of precision and volume than concordances created using the old pencil-and-index-cards technology (which, unfortunately, is still in use in Russia). That said, these new concordances are better than the old ones only when the automated linguistic analysis from which they spring is applied to philologically sound corpora. Hence FEB-web's dedication to presenting texts that meet the most stringent demands of contemporary philology.

Technological solutions to a number of more specific philological issues are also being pursued at FEB-web. A few examples: automatic morphological analysis of text; grammatical and prosodic markup; mechanisms enabling researchers to compare texts or groups of texts according to user-defined parameters; the construction of indexes and lists; the issue of fonts; etc. Many such issues not only remain unresolved, but have not yet been properly conceptualized. In order to find the right approach to such issues in the Russian context, it will be necessary to conduct a great deal of basic research, which must be carried out by philologists in concert with experts in programming and information technology. The FEB-web corpora are well suited for such research, and it is to be hoped that they will prove useful for Russian scholars who seek to improve the quality and standards of research in the discipline.

THE STRUCTURE OF FEB-web

Due to the sheer volume and variety of material on FEB-web, its architecture is rather complex. However, from the user's point of view, it may be seen as a hierarchical structure. The first level of this structure consists of four groups of sections: (1) general information about FEB-web (static and interactive sections designed to help the user work with the system); (2) thematic sections devoted to four chronological periods of Russian literature and to Russian folklore; (3) reference sections, which contain materials on the history of Russian philology, philological encyclopedias, dictionaries, and other reference information; and (4) indexes of authors and works, including the Bibliography Database. This hierarchical structure can be accessed by users on the site's main page as well as the main pages of each section. At the heart of all these sections, in turn, lies a number of digital scholarly editions (DSEs).

FEB-web started out primarily as an experiment in encoding, structuring, and presenting massive collections of text. Once issues of digitization and encoding were more or less resolved (no small feat in the mid-1990s; FEB-web was compelled to invent its own process), the real question became one of structure. How to decide what should go in the collections? And how to structure and present the collections such that they will be useful to scholars and students? The real trick here is to devise a structural element that is not closed, to speak, but open; one which can be developed and expanded continuously over the years without any changes to the fundamental principles of its structure and function. The answer that FEB-web hit upon was the digital scholarly edition. DSEs form the foundation of FEB-web. They are developed by teams of scholars, editors, and computer scientists as independent units, each with its own database, software, and internal system of hypertext links, and each containing information which has been thoroughly vetted in terms of its scholarly and editorial content.

The FEB-web DSEs are devoted to a single topic: an author, a genre, or an individual work. They are primarily an instrument for collecting and reproducing in digital form existing editions of literary and scholarly works. FEB-web DSEs bring together the most authoritative editions of folklore and Russian writers, memoiristic and critical literature, the most significant works of literary scholarship and biography, comprehensive bibliographies, audio-visual material, and reference resources.

Though it reproduces existing editions in full (with front matter, etc.), FEB-web is an essentially new kind of information resource, primarily because its fundamental unit is the work (as defined in modern literary theory), and its basic structural unit is the DSE. In this sense, it differs from traditional (and many electronic) libraries, which structure their collections on the level of the book–e.g., one can locate books in library catalogs, but not individual poems, novels, essays, etc. FEB-web also differs from critical editions, which provide only one critical text of a given work and do not give a full representation of work's editorial and textological history. FEB-web seeks to provide the most comprehensive array of texts available for each work in its holdings, making it possible to trace shifts in the representation of a given work. At the same time, FEB-web differs from the collections of texts (often rather haphazard) one finds in traditional and electronic libraries because the DSEs are actual editions: the print editions which form the foundation of each DSE are compiled in such a way as to present the fullest possible collection of an author's works. For example, the FEB-web DSE of M. IU. Lermontov contains, among hundreds of other texts, four academic editions of Lermontov's complete collected works, the editorial strengths and weaknesses of which complement each other. The FEB-web DSEs also include existing critical commentaries and bibliographies, along with a host of other materials: chronicles of a given author's life and works; the standard works of basic research on an author, genre, or work; etc. (To remedy obvious lacunae, new bibliographies are often commissioned especially for particular DSEs.) The result is a comprehensive facsimile-compilation–an ideal starting place for assembling new critical editions, as well as a valuable resource in itself for researchers, educators, and students. Finally, the FEB-web DSEs differ from traditional and electronic editions in that they provide built-in tools for textual analysis. First of all, FEB-web is fully searchable, which allows users to locate the text fragments and texts they need for their research. Work is underway on more indexes and concordances like the ones available (for now, only partially) in the FEB-web DSE of A. S. Griboedov–the most comprehensive and reliable edition of this important author available in any format. These tools are being developed and integrated into the FEB-web DSEs by and for specialists in Russian literature in concert with computer scientists, computational linguists, designers, etc. This is another major advantage that FEB-web has over the vast majority of existing Russian literature resources on the Internet, most of which are run either by philologists *or* computer scientists, and most of which are therefore either technologically primitive or editorially unsound, and often both.

At present, the FEB-web holdings include ten functioning DSEs (bold type in Table 1) in its five topical categories: Old Russian Literature, 18th-Century Russian Literature, 19th-Century Russian Literature, 20th-Century Russian Literature, and Folklore. Sixteen more DSEs in these categories are projected and will be online within the next two to three years. (See Table 1.)

In addition, the FEB-web reference sections contain DSEs of several reference works, such as encyclopedias (e.g., *Lermontovskaia entsiklopediia* [*Lermontov Encyclopedia*] and the five-volume *Entsiklopediia "Slova o polku Igoreve"* [*Encyclopedia of "The Lay of Igor's Campaign"*], among others) and dictionaries. Users will also find DSEs that present material created wholly by and for FEB-web. For example, the Personalia DSE (in the Scholarship section, <http://feb-web.ru/feb/feb/science.htm>), is a collection of biographical entries on Russian philologists and folklorists. One of the most exciting DSEs to open on FEB-web in 2004 will gather all the volumes of *Izvestiia Rossiiskoi akademii nauk: Seriia literatury i iazyka* (Annals of the Language and Literature Division of the Russian Academy of Sciences) <http://feb-web.ru/feb/izvest/>. In existence for over 150 years, this journal is the single most important serial in Russian philology, but it is impossible to find online for free. (At least one site is now making recent issues available for exorbitant fees.)

TABLE 1. Topical Categories and DSEs Within Them

Old Russian Literature	18th-Century Russian Literature	19th-Century Russian Literature	20th-Century Russian Literature	Folklore
"The Primary Chronicle" **"The Lay of Igor's Campaign"** "The Life of Archpriest Avvakum"	Lomonosov Derzhavin Karamzin	**Pushkin** **Griboedov** **Batiushkov** Zhukovskii **Boratynskii** **Lermontov** **Tiutchev** Gogol **Leo Tolstoy** Dostoevsky	Blok Mayakovsky Mandelstam **Esenin** Gorky Sholokhov	**Byliny** Songs Spells Fairy tales

FEB-web's catalog of Internet Russian-literature resources <http://feb-web.ru/feb/feb/sites.htm> is presented as a separate structural unit within the overall structure of the library. This catalog, which is regularly updated, is organized into ten categories, with over 600 links to digital libraries of Russian literature and Internet projects that deal with Russian philology and folklore. At present, the catalog lists all Russian-language resources of any significance alongside a select list of foreign-language resources for the study of Russian literature and folklore. In the near future, we plan to expand the foreign-language portion of the catalog.

HOW FEB-web CREATES DSEs

To give the reader an idea of what goes into making one of the core FEB-web DSEs, we should describe the process in some detail. The projected DSE of Nikolai Karamzin, now in its initial planning stages, is an illustrative example. At the turn of the nineteenth century, Karamzin revolutionized the language and institutions of Russian literature, and no scholar would deny that Karamzin was one of the most important Russian writers of all time. Yet, to this day, we do not have an edition of Karamzin's complete works. As source materials disappear and disintegrate due to neglect, corruption, and age, the lack of such an edition grows more and more critical, both for literary scholarship and for the cultural legacy of Russia. As such, in this case, as with the DSE of Griboedov, the objective is not so much to reproduce an existing edition in digital form, but to create a fundamentally new collection of texts in order to remedy a massive lacuna.

The FEB-web digital scholarly edition of Karamzin will include the following works:

- all three editions of Karamzin's collected works published during his lifetime
- two posthumous editions of his collected works (Smirdin 1834-35 and Makogonenko 1964)
- both editions of his poetry and prose collection *Moi bezdelki* (My Trifles), 1794 and 1797
- the almanachs compiled and edited by Karamzin (*Aglaia* [Aglae] I–II, 1794-1795; I–II*bis*, 1796; *Aonidy* [Aonides] I–III, 1796-1799)
- the journals edited by Karamzin (*Moskovskii zhurnal* [Moscow Journal], 1791-1792, 2 editions; *Vestnik Evropy* [Herald of Europe], 1802-1803)
- publications of his poetry in the periodical press during his lifetime
- the first (and only) volume of the Russian Academy's edition of Karamzin's works (1917)
- Iurii Lotman and Boris Uspenskii's edition of *Polnoe sobranie stikhotvorenii Karamzina* (The Complete Collected Poems of Karamzin), 1965
- all editions and variants of Karamzin's *Pis'ma russkogo puteshchetvennika* (Letters of a Russian Traveler)
- the edition of Karamzin's *Istoriia Gostudarstva Rossiiskogo* [History of the Russian State] published during his lifetime, the facsimile edition (1843/1991) with its commentary, and the new edition published by the Russian Academy
- Grot and Pekarskii's *Pis'ma N. M. Karamzina k I. I. Dmitrievu* (N. M. Karamzin's Letters to I. I. Dmitriev), 1866, with its rich commentary, supplemented by a collection of Karamzin's letters gathered from various print and archival sources to present the fullest possible collection
- Karamzin's translations from French, English, German, and other languages, along with the foreign originals
- a selection of the fifty or so of the most important books and articles written about Karamzin

- exhaustive bibliographies of Karamzin's works as well as the secondary literature from the 1790s to the present
- an exhaustive scholarly chronology of Karamzin's life and works
- a full concordance of Karamzin's works

The projected size of the edition is approximately 40,000 pages of text. Creating the edition can be broken down into three basic projects: conceptualization, compilation, and digitization. In other words, we need to figure out how to structure the edition, do the bibliographical research and gather all the needed texts, and then put them through the digitization process. Some of our objectives can be accomplished only after the bulk of the edition has been assembled. For example, the chronology will be based on the materials gathered for the edition, and the concordance will be the result of processing the entire corpus for use with FEB-web's search systems.

A number of factors make this DSE a formidable conceptual challenge. FEB-web DSEs are typically structured around a single existing print edition. Other editions are then added, which supplement the core edition in terms of content (works and texts that are absent in the core edition), textological precision, scholarly apparati (indexes, commentaries, etc.), and so on. Karamzin presents a somewhat unique case in that there is no such base edition. His complete works have never been compiled, and nearly 300 of his texts have never been included in any edition of his collected works. Most of Karamzin's works have never been published with a proper textological apparatus, and many important variants have remained practically unknown as a result.

The first task is to develop a framework that can accommodate such a mass of such disparate material. We will tackle these issues, in part, by constructing a series of experimental versions of the DSE. As available texts are digitized, these data will be entered into the experimental versions, which we will post on FEB-web. This approach serves two purposes. First, it makes these texts available to users right away. Second, the more texts we get up on the experimental versions, the better our picture of what works and what does not in terms of design and structure.

Compiling this DSE will be no simple task. In order to determine a final list of all the texts to be included in the edition, a significant amount of bibliographical research must be completed. The results of this research, of course, will later become part of the bibliographical component of the edition. Existing bibliographies must be cross-referenced, and new bibliographies must be created. The new bibliographies, in turn, will be based by and large on the materials we compile for the edition. Some components of this bibliographical research require significant textological and literary-historical work. For example, a great many of Karamzin's works were published anonymously in the serial publications he edited. Using stylometric software, literary-historical expertise, and knowledge of Karamzin's oeuvre, FEB-web specialists will establish attribution for approximately fifty such texts. Another example: many of Karamzin's works were published in several different versions. In many cases, the basic textological work on Karamzin's shorter works–determining which versions are primary, comparing variants, etc.–has yet to be done. These textological issues, of course, bear directly on Karamzin's bibliography.

As we progress with this bibliographical work, we will set about finding and obtaining all the texts we need. A host of Russian libraries regularly make their holdings available to FEB-web on special arrangements. Depending on the condition of the source materials, we will either arrange to borrow them for scanning or commission library staff to photocopy or scan them for us. Finally, as this preliminary work moves forward, the massive project of digitizing 40,000 pages of text also begins.

THE FEB-web DIGITIZATION PROCESS

The FEB-web digitization process is uniform for all the texts in our holdings. This process consists of ten basic steps:

1. scanning and recognition
2. proofreading
3. preparation for markup
4. quality control of the prepared text
5. markup
6. formatting the bibliographical annotations
7. formatting the object
8. indexing
9. assembling preprints and final quality control checks
10. uploading the information into FEB-web

We use a professional version of OCR ABBYY FineReader for scanning and recognition. MS Word is our base software for a number of operations. For processing and storage, we use the markup language Argo, which is the original Russian version of SGML; for the online version, files are converted into HTML. Deriving the HTML files from the deeper Argo files allows FEB-web to remain flexible. As new web languages are developed–for example, new versions of HTML–FEB-web will not have to redo the entire markup. Instead, we will be able to produce an updated markup on the basis of the Argo files. To automate the digitization process, we use a set of specialized, in-house applications. To make it possible to extend the network of people contributing to FEB-web, this technology has been developed from the start in such a way that it can function on any scale, regardless of the amount of material or the number of people working. The fundamental issue in automation is to strike a balance between the quantity and the quality of the material. Every operation in this process–from putting together the initial plan to uploading the material–is monitored at all levels of FEB-web. Regardless of who formats the information, there are two quality-control checks: once before markup, and once before uploading.

COPYRIGHT ISSUES AND CONDITIONS OF USE

It goes without saying that intellectual property issues pose a number of major problems for America-based digital libraries. These issues are somewhat less complicated for FEB-web because it is based in Moscow. In the formation and use of its bank of information, FEB-web adheres to international and Russian copyright laws as they apply to librarianship (to wit: the 1971 version of the Universal Copyright Convention, and the relevant sections of the Codex of the Russian Federation). FEB-web follows the official position of the International Federation of Library Associations and Institutions: library users must be provided free and unfettered access to materials available on the open market and protected by copyright, be that remote electronic access or access to paper copies.

The exclusive copyright of the author (or other copyright owner) is preserved for all materials on FEB-web. FEB-web grants users the right to search, view, and collect all the materials in the Library according to their needs. Users do not have the right to use any of the materials they get from FEB-web for any commercial purpose.

FEB-web does not object to the republication in any form of any FEB-web materials, as long as such republication does not violate any laws, is approved by the FEB-web directors, and is accompanied by a citation of *The Fundamental Digital Library of Russian Literature and Folklore*, as well as the URL of the text used.

The user has sole responsibility to ensure that he or she is compliant with copyright law and with the requirements above, as well as the intellectual property law of his or her home country.

THE PRESENT, THE NEAR TERM, AND THE LONG TERM AT FEB-web

As with any endeavor on this scale, project management is key at FEB-web. Work at all stages and levels of creating the DSE is broken into individual tasks and planned out to the day months in advance. Each team of specialists on the FEB-web staff is asked to hit certain production targets in order to ensure that the project as a whole can move along in an orderly fashion and with all possible speed.

As we noted above, FEB-web is growing at a very fast pace. The bulk of this growth is directed toward completing the existing sections and DSEs, as well as opening all the projected sections and DSEs. New material is still added nearly every month, for example, to the nineteenth century DSE that FEB-web started with (Pushkin and Griboedov), as well as to the DSE that opened more recently (Tolstoy, Tiutchev, etc.). Likewise, new DSEs continue to be added: the Fairy Tales DSE in the Folklore section will be opened by the end of 2004; the Sholokhov DSE will open in early 2005 in time for the Nobel laureate's hundredth birthday; other DSEs slated to open in the near term include Avvakum, Lomonosov, and Blok. Compilation, editing, and digitization work has long been underway for all the projected DSEs, each of which will be opened as soon as a critical mass of materials is assembled in a basic structural and conceptual framework. As these DSEs continue to open over the next few years, new DSEs will be projected, outlined, and started.

One exciting new addition to FEB-web is the Lermontov in Music section of the Lermontov DSE <http://feb-web.ru/feb/lermont/>. At present, the section contains a dozen musical works (with scores in PDF format and MP3 files of famous recordings) based on Lermontov's poetry. Similar musical sections are planned for the FEB-web DSEs of Pushkin, Batiushkov, Griboedov (a composer of waltzes as well as a great poet), Boratynskii, and Esenin. The intersection of music and literature in Russia has garnered more and more scholarly interest in recent years, and FEB-web has enlisted leading musicologists to aid in providing the materials, some of them very difficult to find, needed to pursue this kind of research.

Another new addition is the FEB-web Bibliography Database <http://feb-web.ru/biblio/>. This database integrates tens of thousands of bibliographical entries in four categories: entries corresponding to works in the full-text holdings of FEB-web; entries corresponding to works that will be included in future FEB-web holdings; entries from the bibliographies on FEB-web (e.g., the bibliographies of secondary literature on Pushkin from the Pushkin DSE); and entries from the Personalia section. This resource is designed not only for bibliographical purposes, but also as a navigation tool–users can access the full text of the FEB-web holdings directly from the database.

In fall of 2004, FEB-web is focusing a great deal of energy and resources on restructuring and expanding the Reference section. Several new dictionaries, for example, will come online by spring. Eventually, this section will house a number of different kinds of resources: encyclopedias, dictionaries (of Russian in general and of the language of particular authors), concordances, etc. A variety of searches will be possible at three different levels: the entire section, one particular category of reference work, or one particular work. The entire section will be fully linked to the texts in the DSEs so that users can simply click on a word in a given text to form a query in the reference section. One major long-term goal is to integrate all the reference materials on FEB-web in such a way that they can be used to optimize the FEB-web search systems.

Another major integration project underway at FEB-web has to do with chronologies. A chronology (*letopis' zhizni i tvorchestva* in Russian) is a comprehensive, documented timeline of the life and career of a given writer–when works were started or completed, when significant social, political, or intellectual encounters took place, when reviews of a given work were published, etc. These chronologies are very popular research tools among scholars and students of Russian literature, and many important chronologies (of Pushkin, Chekhov, Tolstoy, and many other writers) were published in the twentieth century. Existing chronologies are included in the structure of FEB-web DSEs devoted to individual authors. Perhaps more importantly, given the nature and the scope of the information in the FEB-web DSEs, they provide an ideal information base for constructing new chronologies. Since its inception, FEB-web has been working on ways to integrate all the chronologies in its holdings. The end product–itself a dynamic, organically-expanding system–will be an overarching chronology of Russian literary, cultural, and social life since the eighteenth century. This will be a fundamentally new kind of information resource with no print or electronic analogs anywhere.

FEB-web AND THE FUTURE OF DIGITAL LIBRARIES IN RUSSIA

In some respects, FEB-web is conceived as a practical antidote to the poor quality that is the inevitable by-product of decentralized information systems like the Internet. Standards like TEI and SGML are certainly not recognized worldwide; indeed, many of them are all but completely unknown in Russia. In the end, one must admit that, for the time being, such standards are little more than theoretical prescriptions. In the standards vacuum that is the Russian Internet, FEB-web has taken it upon itself to create and adhere to its own standards, ones which very few American digital libraries meet. Moreover, it has done this on a massive scale. In doing so, FEB-web states the case for standards in the most eloquent fashion possible: by demonstrating what standards make possible.

FEB-web not only teaches by example, however. It makes its processes and resources available to associated groups of qualified scholars. For example, the FEB-web DSE of Dostoevsky is under construction hundreds of miles from Moscow at Petrozavodsk State University. Its editorial, information-technology, and project-management models are available to any organization that wants to collaborate with FEB-web and work toward the common goal of providing philologically-sound representations of the Russian canon to anyone with Internet access.

Certainly, given its connections to various bodies within an increasingly authoritarian Russian state–the Academy of Sciences, the Ministry of Communication and Informatisation–the growing centrality of FEB-web (in Russia, at least) might well raise certain questions. If the political situation in Russia grows worse, are projects like FEB-web likely to be subject to the arbitrary whims of the regime, or to suffer under a new iron fist? This is, of course, a question for future historians. A related question: is there a danger that such a massive resource will discourage others from initiating new (and sorely needed) digital libraries? The answer to this question is fairly clear: in a free and functional society, a resource like FEB-web can only inspire and aid new projects.

For now, the most urgent problem facing academic digital libraries in Russia is a much more banal one: funding. It goes without saying that an operation like FEB-web, which employs over thirty highly qualified specialists (which is possible purely due to the state of the Russian economy), has a sizable annual budget. In years past, FEB-web has been the recipient of substantial grants from the Soros Foundation, as well as the Russian Foundation for Basic Research and the Russian Foundation for Humanities Scholarship. Since Soros pulled out of Russia in 2003, times have gotten extremely hard for digital libraries in Russia. Other, smaller projects are in a much more difficult position than FEB-web. It is to be hoped that FEB-web will provide needed leadership in this arena by demonstrating to potential sponsors that the confluence of philological and information-technology expertise that is unique to Russia makes Russian digital libraries a fruitful laboratory for developing new techniques for the preservation and study of cultural heritage.

NOTES

1. <http//:feb-web.ru> For the English-language version of FEB-web, see: <http://feb-web.ru/indexen.htm>. For a full, up-to-date bibliography of scholarly works about FEB-web, see: K. Vigurskii and I. Pil'shchikov, "Fundamental'naia elektronnaia biblioteka 'Russkaia literatura i fol'klor': sostoianie i perspektivy," in *Filologiia i informatika* (Moskva, forthcoming). For a sampling of popular press pieces on FEB-web see: <http://feb-web.ru/feb/feb/media/index.htm>.

2. "Otkrylas' novaia versiia Fundamental'noi elektronnoi biblioteki," *Lenta.ru: Internet* (Feb. 28, 2004), <http://www.lenta.ru/internet/2004/02/28/feb/index.htm> (accessed August 15, 2004).

3. See: K. Vigurskii and I. Pil'shchikov, "Filologiia i sovremennye informatsionnye tekhnologii: k postanovke problemy," *Izvestiia Akademii Nauk. Seriia literatury i iazyka* 62, no. 2 (2003): 9-16; K. Vigurskii and I. Pil'shchikov, "Informatika i filologiia: (Problemy i perspektivy vzaimodeistviia)," *Elektronnye biblioteki* 6, no. 3 (2003), <http://www.elbib.ru/index.phtml?page=elbib/rus/journal/2003/part3/VP> (accessed September 12, 2004).

4. *Bol'shaia sovetskaia entsiklopediia*, 3rd ed., s.v. "Filologiia" (by S. Averintsev).

5. M. Shapir, "Filologiia kak fundament gumanitarnogo znaniia: ob osnovnykh napravleniiakh issledovanii po teoreticheskoi i prikladnoi filologii," *Antropologiia kul'tury* 2003, no. 1:56-57.

The Central Eurasian
Interactive Atlas Project:
A Progress Report

Alexander Perepechko
Eileen Llona
Dmitry Sharkov
Michael Hunt
Michael Biggins

SUMMARY. Since 2000, researchers and staff at the University of Washington have been developing a unified Geographic Information Systems database of Russian Federation socioeconomic, demographic,

---

Alexander Perepechko, PhD, has served as Research Associate, Central Eurasian Interactive Atlas project, University of Washington, Seattle (E-mail: perepea@u.washington.edu).

Eileen Llona, MLS, is International Studies Computer Support Librarian, University of Washington Libraries, Seattle (E-mail: ellona@u.washington.edu).

Dmitry Sharkov, PhC, has served as Research Associate, Central Eurasian Interactive Atlas project, University of Washington, Seattle (E-mail: sharkov@u.washington.edu).

Michael Hunt, MAIS, has served as Data Technician, Central Eurasian Interactive Atlas project, University of Washington, Seattle (E-mail: mhunt42@u.washington.edu).

Michael Biggins, PhD, MS, is Head, Slavic and East European Section, University of Washington Libraries, Seattle (E-mail: mbiggins@u.washington.edu).

Address correspondence to: Slavic and East European Section, Suzzallo Library, Box 352900, Seattle, WA 98195, USA.

[Haworth co-indexing entry note]: "The Central Eurasian Interactive Atlas Project: A Progress Report." Perepechko, Alexander et al. Co-published simultaneously in *Slavic & East European Information Resources* (The Haworth Information Press, an imprint of The Haworth Press, Inc.) Vol. 6, No. 2/3, 2005, pp. 65-78; and: *Virtual Slavica: Digital Libraries, Digital Archives* (ed: Michael Neubert) The Haworth Information Press, an imprint of The Haworth Press, Inc., 2005, pp. 65-78. Single or multiple copies of this article are available for a fee from The Haworth Document Delivery Service [1-800-HAWORTH, 9:00 a.m. - 5:00 p.m. (EST). E-mail address: docdelivery@haworthpress.com].

65

and political information at the *raion* and city (*gorsovet*) level. The Central Eurasian Interactive Atlas (CEIA) that has grown from this effort serves both to archive and to provide access to annual progressions of standardized geographic and tabular data covering the entire Russian Federation at a level of geographic detail not readily available elsewhere. As the CEIA grows, it will serve as a curricular and research focus of the UW's Russian, East European, and Central Asian Studies program. *[Article copies available for a fee from The Haworth Document Delivery Service: 1-800-HAWORTH. E-mail address: <docdelivery@haworthpress.com> Website: <http://www.HaworthPress.com> © 2005 by The Haworth Press, Inc. All rights reserved.]*

KEYWORDS. Russian Federation, former Soviet Union, *raion*-level, *rayon*-level, GIS, socioeconomic data, electoral data, quantitative area studies research, Central Eurasian Interactive Atlas, University of Washington

The Central Eurasian Interactive Atlas (CEIA) originated at the University of Washington (UW) in the late 1990s as part of an effort to assemble large, coordinated sets of demographic, socioeconomic, and political spatial data for the Russian Federation. It was designed to facilitate more systematic quantitative social science research on contemporary Russia and the former Soviet Union by faculty and students in UW's multidisciplinary Russian, East European, and Central Asian Studies program (REECAS). Development of the CEIA figured as one facet of a larger proposal to develop a Central Eurasian Information Resource (CEIR), which the UW and several nearby academic partners submitted to the Department of Education in 1999 under its program for Technological Innovation and Cooperation in Foreign Information Access (TICFIA). Funding from that program from 1999 through 2003 made it possible to create a CEIA pilot database, which now encompasses all of the Russian Federation (see <http://green.lib.washington.edu/website/ceir/>). Substantial headway has also been made in developing comparable coverage for selected Central Asian countries and Ukraine.

Traditionally, quantitative research on Soviet and post-Soviet topics has depended on data aggregations at the national level, while nuances of geographical variation within the country have been largely neglected. In part, this has been due to the outright unavailability of data at any but the national or, at best, provincial (*oblast'*) level. However, throughout the 1990s, Russian provincial statistical agencies published regular compilations of data, much of which was organized by counties (*raion*s) and cities (*gorsovet*s). These compilations were often published in no more than a hundred copies and were poorly distributed. Moreover, there was no apparent coordination of their format, so that the data categories (variables) presented in an oblast' compilation one year might differ vastly from the indicators published by another oblast', or even by the same oblast' in the following year. In the mid-1990s, the Russian federal statistical agency Goskomstat began coordinating data collection countrywide in a more consistent way, making the development of a comprehensive socioeconomic spatial database for Russia feasible at last.

At present, the CEIA pilot consists of a web-accessible Geographic Information Systems (GIS) map of the Russian Federation which allows the user to generate visualizations of up to 700 demographic and socio-economic indicators in annual progressions over a number of years. These map visualizations are presently accessible to any Internet user worldwide. In the near future, UW faculty and staff will also be provided with the option of downloading customized subsets of the tabular data comprised in the atlas for use in specific research projects. Substantial elements of geographic and tabular databases for Ukraine and parts of Central Asia have already been assembled, and the long-range plan for the CEIA includes the release of resources for these regions comparable to what CEIA will offer for Russia. A for-credit practicum at the UW in the use of spatial data for social science research in area studies will draw on the CEIA as a primary data resource, and is intended to equip students in the REECAS and international studies programs with quantitative research skills and background that will complement the program's more traditional qualitative methods.

PROJECT DEVELOPMENT AND SPECIFICATIONS

The CEIA brings together tabular and geographic information within a GIS framework. The spatial characteristics of socioeconomic information–such as population data, wage earnings, and industrial production–allow it to be combined geographically to enable the utilization of a geographic interface for visualization of the data. Most electronic information systems, such as library catalogs or commercial databases, rely on textual methods of search and retrieval, requiring the user to communicate verbally with the system, using keywords or controlled vocabularies. However, accessing information that has a geographic component compels the use of a visual approach for search and retrieval, such as the use of maps. Use of maps as an organizing tool, both for searching and information retrieval, allows the geographic dimension of data to be conveyed. If a user is vague about search criteria, he or she can use a map to select a region of interest without having to know the exact naming convention applied to the region. Conversely, utilizing maps to display search results can increase the user's awareness of the geography of an area, and does a more efficient job of conveying the geographic context and spatial distribution of the retrieved data.

Using GIS technology to create interfaces to textual and tabular data is becoming easier through the ongoing development and availability of GIS and web technologies. Integration of large datasets, such as those found in the CEIA, into a GIS system provides flexibility in maintaining the resources, and provides geographic searching capability. Once the underlying geography is generated (such as through the digitization of existing paper resources; see section on coverage development), adding new tabular data or other information becomes relatively easy, provided there is a way to link the data to the maps. While GIS software is often complicated to use, and requires a non-trivial amount of support and training, one of the goals of the CEIA is to make some degree of data access, visualization, and manipulation possible in an easy-to-use, online GIS-based resource, without requiring the user to have specialized GIS software or training. At the same time, more advanced users can download datasets for use in their locally-available software.

In order to make the CEIA map visualization interface as easy to use as possible, several issues needed to be addressed during the development of the resource. Problems encountered during the development stage included data format inconsistencies, changes in administrative boundaries across time, and the need for English translations of Russian-language labels, as well as such technological issues as support for Cyrillic script, support for large numbers of columns in spreadsheet software, and the best format for presenting the combined data and maps for search and display. While GIS and database software provided solutions to some of these problems, a large amount of human effort, including some amount of trial and error, was required to move data smoothly from its original formats to the current CEIA resource. In the sections following, we describe the various components that make up the current version of the CEIA: statistical data, geographic coverages, and the online interface. In summary, the resource was developed from statistical data that originated as Russian word-processed documents, obtained from numerous statistical agencies, and Russian government-issued paper maps. The development of the web interface required combining the results of digitization and normalization of the data and maps, utilizing commercial GIS software and open-source scripting technologies. As the project progressed over the past three years, technologies have improved, allowing us to modify our processes and structures to take advantage of new software. As we move forward in the project, we continue to evaluate new software and delivery mechanisms to simplify data maintenance and interface design.

Statistical Data Development

Only within the past several years have the national statistical agencies of some of the individual Soviet successor states begun to enforce uniform standards for data collection at all administrative levels within their jurisdictions, including local levels; but even in 2004 this process remains incomplete and, in some important respects, methodologically flawed. However, precise data describing each region–and the entire country–down to the raion (county) and city level often remain in the possession of the corresponding local branches of the national statistical agency, where they are available for consultation onsite but are not actively disseminated for broader use or coordinated with similar data of peer agencies. For example, in the Russian Federation, the Central Statistical Agency (Goskomstat) started collecting raion-level statistical data only in 1996. Moreover, these data are still much less available in database-compatible tabular formats.

The CEIA team was responsible for assembling, organizing, and converting raw data from a variety of official sources–ranging from national to provincial statistical agencies, and electoral commissions–to GIS-ready format. The team was also responsible for the labor-intensive task of data cleaning, i.e., proofing, verification, and standardization of data emanating from different statistical authorities, which at first often enumerated and presented those data in diverse and incompatible ways.

The validity and reliability of received (or locally compiled) tabular data were verified using a two-step method: (1) aggregating raion/city-level data ("study data") to the level of oblast', for comparison against separately-published oblast'-level data; (2) obtaining separately-published oblast'-level data (statistical handbooks, journals, etc.) for the same variables from different sources ("comparison data"). Manual checking was also a significant part of data validation. This was done by experienced data technicians familiar with the source languages.

Data were converted into database-compatible formats and provided with metadata including geographic codes, translations of statistical labels, and data codes. The use of database technologies ensured that errors were minimized. Inconsistencies in data were corrected using semi-automated normalization procedures to create a unified data set. Normalization involved the application of data dependency to a data model to avoid inconsistencies by prohibiting redundancy. Value-added data normalization includes converting units of measurement to a single type (i.e., some indicators will be measured by 1000s in some areas, while the same indicator will be measured by 100s in other areas) and eliminating redundant data and duplicate data. The normalization process required programming and manual editing.

In its present state, this database provides access to a table with more than 700 records on demography, social infrastructure, economics, and elections for 2,463 administrative units of the Russian Federation in an unbroken annual progression from 1996 through 2000. For urban areas, however, the pilot CEIA still provides these data only at the city-wide level. Fields in the table include geographic identifiers (cascading from the country down to the economic/federal region, to the oblast', to the raion and city), data values (in both English and the source language), date (year), and notes from the primary sources.

Since the data were transformed and standardized for display in the atlas, tabular data sources were documented and cited from the Central Eurasian Interactive Atlas interface, allowing users to identify and retrieve source data if desired. Standard annotations were made during the data standardization process, documenting modifications of source data, such as instances of data disaggregation and reaggregation for raions/city-level units, or adaptations to units of measure and enumeration. Metadata for attribute data included source data, changes in administrative boundaries for enumeration units over time if applicable, and the date of creation. Attribute data also included name variants.

Once the data were prepared, they were incorporated into the atlas with physical geographical layers. Each geographic region (rural raion, city) was assigned a code, based on data-derived coding schemes which are utilized in the tabular data sets. The tabular data sets were then joined with the digital geographical data to produce thematic digital maps.

Geographic Coverage Development

At the time the project started, detailed digital maps with the second level of administrative divisions (raion/city-level) for the Russian Federation were either unavailable or inconsistent. The decision was made to digitize recent government-published maps. A large digitizer was used, and the work required several thousand hours for digitizing and correcting. Every paper map that was digitized had raion-level administrative boundaries for the corresponding oblast' or republic. Even though each map was in a different geographic projection, they all varied in scale. Each map was digitized, georeferenced, transformed to a geographic coordinate system, and then matched with the digitized maps of adjacent territories. Each raion/city was assigned a unique code to be matched with its corresponding tabular dataset. For areas where no administrative printed maps were available, alternate sources were used to determine the location of administrative boundaries. These included web sources, magazine publications, digital maps, and sometimes Landsat images. All boundaries were corrected to reflect of the administrative division of the country for a predetermined date. City boundaries were checked using satellite images (when available). Special consideration was given to the fact that place names were changed for a significant number of administrative units since the dissolution of the Soviet Union. Moreover, some administrative units for which tabular data were available were not even shown on published maps (primarily the so-called secret cities. Their locations were determined though extensive web searching and referenced through satellite images. To enhance the visual component we also used some components from the Digital Chart of the World (DCW), generalizing them to match our geographic database.

Technical Aspects of Building the GIS

In the CEIA database, geographic coverage is presented at the raion/ gorsovet and oblast' levels. Many large gorsovets (cities) have their own administrative divisions (districts or prefectures). At the raion/ gorsovet level, the internal boundaries of those gorsovets that have them are not shown.

The Russian Federation coverage has both location and attribute levels of information. The spatial level of information in the coverage is represented as label points, tics, nodes, chains, and polygons. Oblast' boundaries are extracted from the raion "base" coverage. Oblast' thematic attributes (e.g., permanent_population) for 1998 are statistical aggregates of raion thematic attributes. If, for instance, an oblast' has the attribute *null* for "synthetic ammonia" (not every oblast' has a synthetic ammonia plant!) all attributes are removed in this oblast' object.

In a GIS database, spatial data are structured using coordinates and topological relationships. The coordinate data (such as longitude and latitude), based on principles of geometry are used to identify geographic feature locations and to support various properties of spatial location, including measurement. The topological data are used to identify relationships between geographic features' primitives–nodes, arcs, and polygons.

A database management system lets one create and manage non-spatial data–geo-referenced tables of statistical and thematic information. These geographic matrixes, in which rows (records) are raions and oblasts, and columns (fields or items) are characteristics of these places linked to geographic features in the topologically structured spatial database. Separation of space and attributes permits the graphics engine to connect with alternate external relational databases.

Hybrid architectures have some limitations. For example, spatial data cannot benefit from such standard database functions as concurrent access management, integrity, security, and reliability. In the case of large spatial and non-spatial data on Russia's demographic behavior and social-economic activities, these disadvantages were obvious; a few times they resulted in a partial loss of information. This loss resulted in having to reconstruct work that had already been done. Future generations of GIS software will, we hope, solve this technical glitch.

Web-Compatible Interface Development

While considering the design for providing access to the data and maps, several decisions had to be made. We knew we wanted to present the data in a web-accessible application, preferably utilizing a GIS software package, and while there were some open-source solutions available three years ago, we decided to use a commercial system. At this time, there are more open-source solutions available for web-enabled GIS, such as TimeMap from the University of Sydney,[1] MapServer from the University of Minnesota,[2] and other techniques such as using Flash and XML technology. These systems seem promising, and from a sustainability point of view (at least in an academic setting), implementing open-source software is often promoted as a desirable solution. Future development of the CEIA will consider migrating to open source technologies.

Web-Compatible Interface Development: Technical Aspects of Combining Data and Maps

Since the data correspond to geographic regions defined in the digitized raion coverages, it was combined with this geographic layer using GIS software. The original versions of the normalized statistical data files were in spreadsheet format, which is not a feasible format for on-going maintenance. To ease future data additions and modifications, these files were converted into a database format. Thematic shapefiles were then created based on the type of data value (demography, social indicators, industrial production, etc.). As of 2004, there are nineteen published data categories in the CEIA, representing over 700 variables.

There are over 1,000,000 separate data values contained in the CEIA, representing three years of data for Russia's 2,463 administrative regions (two additional years' worth of data are nearly processed and can soon be added to the database). Presenting this amount of information in single interface presented some design challenges. The team decided to use categorical coding for the statistical variables, which provides a mechanism for indicating that any given variable belongs to one of about twenty categories, ranging from demographics and social indicators to manufacturing indicators. These categorical codes were used to produce thematic shapefiles, which are used in the interface, and form the basis for grouping the large amount of statistical information available through the resource.

Web-Compatible Interface Development: Graphic Design Considerations

Given the power of a GIS system and the amount of information CEIA has collected, designing an interface that accommodates many typical GIS features (zooming, panning, showing tabular information, showing features, etc.) without confusing a non-GIS-trained user has been a challenge. Since we wanted the information contained in the statistical data to be visualized, the team decided to use a graduated color quantile classification method to present the data. This method allows values to be color coded on the underlying map, so that a gross indication of high or low values can be quickly ascertained.

The large geographic area that the Russian Federation covers presented another design challenge. The amount of data for the entire country is quite large, and sending a large amount of information round trip from a web browser to the spatial server can significantly impact a user with a slow Internet connection. In order to improve the access time and the resolution of the geographic features, we divided the map into three broad regions. This allows users to select a less-than-full country study area if appropriate, and allows for features to be more fully visible. An option for querying values for the entire country is also available.

Color schemes, as well as font styles and types, were used to unify aspects of the interface. The interface relies heavily on client-side scripting (Javascript) and cascading stylesheets (CSS), which makes it most compatible with newer versions of web browsers. Our decisions to use these technologies were based on their capabilities for utilizing as much screen space as possible without cluttering it. The incorporation of hidable menus and mouseover instructions is an example of using scripting and stylesheets to maximize the amount of information available to the user on demand, rather than "on" at all times. User studies of the website showed that most users found the site intuitive, although those with previous GIS experience were able to intuit tool actions (such as zooming and panning) more quickly than novice users.

Data visualizations are presented as a series of thematic maps. These are generated on the fly by the spatial server, depending on the variable selected by the user. Values are color-coded on the map to represent value ranges, with a thematic key available for reference. Individual data values are viewable by zooming in on an area, and by selecting an Info button that shows all data values for the selected category. Figures 1 and 2 show examples of visual and tabular presentations of data by CEIA.

Web-Compatible Interface Development: Future Plans for Interface Development

One of the main problems of presenting the data is that while there are over 700 variables, many of them occur only in a small geographic area. As a result, it is often difficult to find on the map where variables are displayed as a result of a request. Future modifications to the interface will include a way to zoom automatically to the parts of the map that have the values. We would also like to integrate more of the advanced GIS features available through the spatial server, such as creating Boolean queries for the data values (e.g., show me urban areas with

FIGURE 1. Sample Display from CEIA Interface, Providing Visualization of Average Monthly Wages in Central Russia in 1998

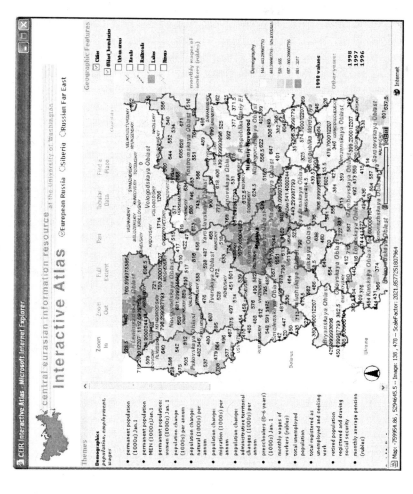

FIGURE 2. Tabular display of a selected region and data

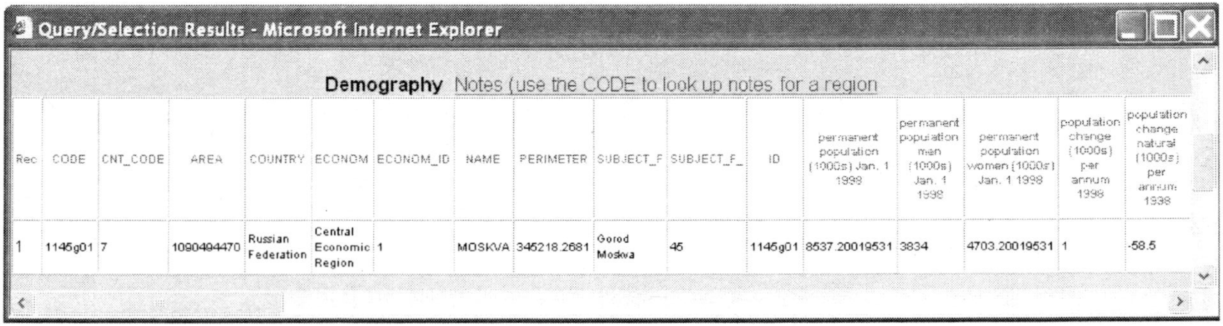

Query/Selection Results - Microsoft Internet Explorer

Demography Notes (use the CODE to look up notes for a region)

Rec	CODE	CNT_CODE	AREA	COUNTRY	ECONOM	ECONOM_ID	NAME	PERIMETER	SUBJECT_F	SUBJECT_F	ID	permanent population (1000s) Jan. 1 1999	permanent population man (1000s) Jan. 1 1998	permanent population women (1000s) Jan. 1 1998	population change (1000s) per annum 1998	population change. natural (1000s) per annum. 1998
1	1145g01	7	1090494470	Russian Federation	Central Economic Region	1	MOSKVA	346218.2681	Gorod Moskva	46	1145g01	8537 20019531	3834	4703 20019531	1	-58.5

a population greater than 1,000,000 AND an unemployment rate under 10%). This can be achieved using a textual database interface, but it is more difficult to program using the spatial server software and the visualization prototype we have developed.

Currently the atlas displays values as provided by the data providers only after very substantial normalization. Some values are relative to an area or population (e.g., incidence per 1,000 people) though many are raw numbers, which have limited meaning without some kind of contextual analysis. Future development of the atlas will include providing the user with a choice of displaying the values as they are, or combining a category of values with another to provide a relational analysis.

Besides socioeconomic data, the project has experimented with incorporating other types of data into the atlas, such as encyclopedia entries, background information about geographic features and administrative units, and text and images. Developing separate digital resources, but making them available communally through a single interface using geospatial referencing would enhance interconnectedness across the resources, and should make a valuable resource for research and teaching. We hope to continue this development as future funding allows.

CONTINUED DEVELOPMENT OF THE CEIA

In its early stages, work on the CEIA has involved vast amounts of data encoding, proofing, standardization, and organization. With these main tasks now completed, and with data workflows and matrices now in place, the CEIA stands ready to expand in several dimensions: longitudinally, by adding new years of data coverage; geographically, by extending coverage to more areas of Eurasia; and functionally, by incorporating new kinds of data and by developing a scholarly communications module that will archive research produced using CEIA resources.

As the other CIS regions of greatest academic interest at UW, Central Asia and Ukraine are priority areas for continued CEIA development. The challenges of obtaining data for these regions at the raion and gorsovet level differ significantly, on a continuum extending from Ukraine (where data is most readily available) through Kazakhstan, Kyrgyzstan, Tajikistan, and Uzbekistan (where obtaining data is a challenge), to Turkmenistan (where data may simply be impossible to obtain). Partnerships with agencies and academic institutions in most of these countries can help overcome obstacles to data access and result in the creation of useful, jointly-owned and -developed research tools.

A further resource enhancement planned for the next phase of project development is the inclusion of a GIS layer of English-language text describing each country's cities, large towns, administrative units, and other significant geographical features. This information will be derived from recent, authoritative encyclopedic sources produced in each country, by agreement with the publishers. The clarification of the geographical context provided by this layer of text will play an important role in expanding the user group for the CEIA, productively drawing in K-16 teachers and students, who can adapt the resource to their instructional needs, even as the resource continues to support the needs of advanced researchers.

So far, CEIA resource development has focused entirely on assembling and providing source data. As this body of material reaches critical mass and becomes useful for research, CEIA resources will expand to include instructional materials to support the inculcation of research applications, as well as full text, abstracts, and citations of research produced by students, faculty, and other scholars on the basis of data from the CEIA.

To date, the UW library has functioned as the locus of most CEIA activity, although GIS-based projects can and do occur almost anyplace on university campuses. For CEIA, the library offers essential infrastructure, data acquisition, data security, data archiving, and information architecture support which can be significantly harder to obtain elsewhere. GIS technologies, though not traditionally part of most libraries' systems repertory, are steadily gaining expert advocates among library staff. Still, collaborative, interdepartmental sponsorship is important for broadly interdisciplinary social science projects such as the CEIA. At UW, these include the Russian, East European, and Central Asian Studies Program and its affiliated departments; the Center for Statistics in the Social Sciences; and the Center for Studies in Demography and Ecology.

NOTES

1. TimeMap <http://www.timemap.net/> (accessed August 13, 2004).
2. MapServer <http://mapserver.gis.umn.edu/> (accessed August 13, 2004).

Collision or Coexistence?
Copyright Law in the Digital Environment

Janice T. Pilch

SUMMARY. Digital technology and global economic trends present fundamental challenges to copyright law in the twenty-first century. On a practical level, librarians need to understand the particulars of current laws in order to make responsible decisions and to utilize to the fullest extent the possibilities that copyright law affords them in their missions. This article will identify the major copyright issues associated with library digital activities, and will discuss copyright protection in the digital environment of material originating in the Slavic, East European, and Eurasian nations. It covers use of Slavic and East European material in the U.S. in various contexts, including Internet activity, preservation and replacement, interlibrary loan, electronic reserves, classroom and educational use, text encoding, digitization of print and microform materials, and creation of digital content and databases. *[Article copies available for a fee from The Haworth Document Delivery Service: 1-800-HAWORTH. E-mail address: <docdelivery@haworthpress.com> Website: <http://www.HaworthPress.com> © 2005 by The Haworth Press, Inc. All rights reserved.]*

Janice T. Pilch, MA, MS, is Assistant Professor of Library Administration and Slavic and East European Technical Services Librarian, Slavic and East European Library, 225 University Library, University of Illinois at Urbana-Champaign, 1408 West Gregory Drive, Urbana, IL 61801 USA (E-mail: pilch@uiuc.edu).

[Haworth co-indexing entry note]: "Collision or Coexistence? Copyright Law in the Digital Environment." Pilch, Janice T. Co-published simultaneously in *Slavic & East European Information Resources* (The Haworth Information Press, an imprint of The Haworth Press, Inc.) Vol. 6, No. 2/3, 2005, pp. 79-116; and: *Virtual Slavica: Digital Libraries, Digital Archives* (ed: Michael Neubert) The Haworth Information Press, an imprint of The Haworth Press, Inc., 2005, pp. 79-116. Single or multiple copies of this article are available for a fee from The Haworth Document Delivery Service [1-800-HAWORTH, 9:00 a.m. - 5:00 p.m. (EST). E-mail address: docdelivery@haworthpress.com].

KEYWORDS. Copyright, intellectual property, international copyright, digital technology, digitization, Slavic, Eastern Europe, Central Europe, Eurasia

INTRODUCTION:
DIGITAL TECHNOLOGY, ECONOMICS,
AND COPYRIGHT

The digital age is one of interesting contradictions. Even as information has become more readily available in the last twenty years, we have begun to see new legal, technical, economic, and social barriers to that information.[1] More strikingly, in an age that places an unprecedented value on information as property, and aggressively advances the economic value of that information,[2] libraries are relinquishing their property assets in information and becoming renters of information resources, as they turn toward temporary access to expensive electronic formats as the basis for their services. In addition, even as copyright law grants broad privileges in the form of exemptions to libraries and educational institutions in support of their missions that benefit individuals and society, these privileges are being passed up for digital products with licensing terms that restrict the privileges, and subscription costs that shrink the purchasing power for tangible assets of libraries; the digital products are generally seen as an improvement to society and culture.

While there is no question that copyright has been strengthened with the advent of new laws designed to extend protection to the digital environment and to enforce compliance globally for longer periods of time, the opposite is also happening: copyright is disappearing. It is being bypassed by licensing models, based on contract law, that supersede rights granted in federal copyright law, and by security encryption that disables its effective application; and it is threatened by database legislation that, if enacted, will erode the fundamental principle that factual information is not subject to copyright. Extreme approaches to control involve encryption devices built into hardware that prevent the use of unrecognized or illegal software programs, even in cases when it would be perfectly legitimate to use the content for transformative purposes such as scholarship, criticism, and teaching, or even for personal use. They are often associated with efforts to wipe out music and film piracy in the international arena.

It is no wonder that people are confused about the role of copyright today, and the stand they should take in acting in the best interest of the library profession. Current trends–the drive toward a pay-per-use business model for information, the growing use of digital rights management systems, the gradual elimination of hard, analog copies that cannot effectively be controlled in the digital world of the future, and longer copyright terms–all create a tenuous situation for information access. The very preoccupation with form over content often appears at odds with the ideal, so prevalent in the 1980s and early 1990s, of a digital age flourishing in cultural enrichment and universal access to information.[3]

At the center of the issue confronting both technology and copyright law today is the notion of dematerialization of the physical work. The physical format was a basic assumption behind the creation of copyright law in the early eighteenth century. The physical format by its nature permits limited copying. Current intellectual property regimes, which arose in an age of printing, have been, and to some extent are still, based on the idea that there are practical limits on acts of copying and distributing copyrighted works. Advances in digital technology and the computer networks, on the other hand, allow for easy replication and broad distribution of works over the Internet. The web has been called "one of the world's largest libraries and surely the world's largest copying machine."[4] Some conclude that the concept of the copy may no longer be a logical basis for copyright law in the digital age, because making copies is such an integral function of computers and networks.[5]

Alongside the notion of dematerialization of the physical work is the dematerialization of territories and borders in the global environment. Copyright originated in a time when courts easily determined where works originated and were distributed. The integrity of national borders was reinforced with the development of the international copyright regime, associated with conclusion of the Berne Convention in 1886. The concept of national sovereignty is a basic tenet underlying international copyright. But in the twenty-first century, global networks make works available simultaneously in many different locations, and their origins are sometimes traceable to many different physical localities. The overarching link between technology and copyright is the rise of global economics. As scholars note, "Territoriality and physical space are the pivot around which the concept of national sovereignty is structured. When territoriality comes up against the virtual spaces of cyberspace, the rigour of the concept is weakened. . . . A sort of extraterritorial realm is coming into being whose only sovereign is commerce and trade."[6]

Copyright has clearly been thrust into the spotlight as a consequence of a global push toward private profit from forms of information and creativity, a trend that shakes the foundations of an intellectual property system founded on the idea that creative and intellectual works should exist for the benefit of people in society as a whole. Digital technology is one of the means being used toward these aims. A rift has been created in the longstanding balance between the twin purposes of copyright, diminishing socially expansive aspects and skewing the system toward a narrower range of private interests. Thus the digital networked environment presents a fundamental dilemma to the international copyright regime that has developed for well over a century.

Copyright law in the past has been flexible enough to withstand the evolution of new technologies. The large issues raised by the link between digital technology, the global economy, and copyright will require adaptation in the twenty-first century. On a more practical level, we need to understand the particulars of current laws and work within the longstanding traditions that have encouraged scientific progress, intellectual development, and artistic creativity. That tradition still makes it possible for libraries to fulfill their role in serving the scholarly community and the public with works manifesting those efforts. This article is an attempt to synthesize the realities of copyright today into practical advice for librarians, so that they can make responsible decisions about copyright and utilize to the fullest extent the possibilities that copyright law affords them in their missions.

A PRACTICAL APPROACH TO COPYRIGHT FOR SLAVIC AND EAST EUROPEAN MATERIAL

A basic knowledge of the structure and application of international copyright legislation is essential to librarians using foreign works. This article will discuss copyright protection of material originating in the Slavic and East European sphere, and will identify the major copyright issues associated with the digital environment. It concentrates on the use of foreign works in or by U.S. libraries, and digital works created and used in the U.S., but does not attempt to discuss the protection afforded to U.S. authors in Slavic, East European, and Eurasian countries.

Libraries engage in digital copyright issues both as users of the content of other copyright holders and as creators of their own copyrighted works; generally they are more concerned with the former than the latter. The range of activities undertaken by libraries involving copyright is broad: reproduction, display and distribution of digital resources on the Internet; archiving and preservation of digital materials; interlibrary loan; electronic reserves; classroom and educational use of digital materials; text encoding to enable display and scholarly analysis of texts; creation of metadata; digitizing of print and microform materials; and creation of born-digital materials and database compilations. The digital environment and laws related to it are complex and constantly changing. There are still many questions related to digital copyright that will be answered only with the continued development of legislation addressing those issues.

The use of Slavic and East European materials presents a particular challenge. Literature on the international aspects of copyright for libraries is still limited, and the topic is inherently complicated by the array of instruments governing copyright in any given country or region. Copyright practices are governed by national laws, regional treaties, and international copyright conventions and trade agreements, all of which need to be considered in any copyright scenario. Being an expert on Czech copyright law does not necessarily qualify one to make judgments about Hungarian law. Much depends on the particulars of the country and region in question.[7]

The most important thing to know generally in approaching copyright is that U.S. copyright law governs use of eligible foreign materials being used in this country. Eligible works are, generally speaking, copyrightable works originating in, first published in, or created by an author who is a national of a country that has reciprocal copyright relations with the U.S. under an international copyright convention. If reciprocal relations exist between the U.S. and the country of origin of the copyrighted work, one needs to look at U.S. law to determine how the work may be used in the U.S. The statutory framework for U.S. copyright law is set out in Title 17 of the *United States Code*, and is just over 200 pages long.[8] The current law, the Copyright Act of 1976, went into effect on January 1, 1978. The previous law, the 1909 U.S. Copyright Act, could be useful for historical purposes, but since the statute of limitations in copyright cases in the U.S. is three years after a claim accrues,[9] practically speaking only the current law will be relevant in most cases. Some parts of past law have been incorporated into the current law; of particular note in this regard is the scheme of copyright duration. U.S. copyright terms are complex, and are not uniformly based on the current term of life of the author plus seventy years, as many often assume.[10]

It is easy to know whether a country has reciprocal copyright relations with the U.S. International copyright for Slavic and East European materials today is governed largely by the Berne Convention.[11] The reciprocal relations that exist between the U.S. and nations in Eastern and Central Europe and Eurasia by virtue of membership in that convention are the basis for copyright protection in this country. To a lesser degree, the fact of past or current membership in the Universal Copyright Convention (UCC) can come into play, but the effect of the UCC has been eclipsed by the membership of nations of Central and Eastern Europe and Eurasia in the Berne Convention, and the UCC is regarded today as largely obsolete. Likewise, bilateral copyright agreements that once existed between the U.S. and nations of Eastern Europe are of little practical relevance today in light of membership of these nations in the Berne Convention.

Today the U.S. holds reciprocal copyright relations under the Berne Convention with all the nations of Central and Eastern Europe and Eurasia with the exception of Uzbekistan and Turkmenistan. Between 1991 and 2000, twenty-one of these nations joined the Berne Convention; four had become members in the 1920s. The Berne Convention is the starting point for any discussion of copyright law today, because it figures in all of the new global legislation and has retroactive effect. Uzbekistan and Turkmenistan have not yet signed the Berne Convention, but there is reason to hold that they remain bound by the UCC from their obligations as former members of the Soviet Union.[12]

DETERMING WHETHER A FOREIGN WORK IS COPYRIGHTED IN THE U.S.

Most of the information in this article is written under one very basic assumption: it applies if work is under copyright protection. If the work has never been copyrighted, or if it has entered the public domain, the exclusive rights may be exercised without seeking permissions.

How does one know if a foreign work is copyrighted? The process for making that determination is not always easy. It has been treated in considerable detail in other sources.[13] One must consider the date of creation or first publication of the work, distinguishing between them; note whether the work is published or unpublished; confirm the place of first publication and know whether the work is a first or later edition; make a judgment on the nature of the work, and make distinctions for works produced as part of employment, and for anonymous and pseudonymous works; identify the legal author and ascertain the author's nationality and date of death; and consider a number of other factors. Then one must consider the issue of copyright restoration under Article 18 of the Berne Convention. This provision has restored copyright in the U.S. to a vast number of eligible works from Slavic and East European countries created and published since 1923. This development is important for librarians embarking on digital projects. For example, prior to January 1, 1996 it was understood that all pre-1973 Soviet works were in the public domain. That is no longer the case.

THE ISSUE OF COPYRIGHT RESTORATION

On January 1, 1996 the Agreement on Trade-Related Aspects of Intellectual Property Rights (TRIPS Agreement) became effective for the U.S., and this carries an important obligation with respect to foreign works being used in the U.S. On that date the U.S. was obliged by its adherence to the Berne Convention and the TRIPS Agreement to restore copyright protection to eligible works of Berne member nations. Article 18 of the Berne Convention requires member nations to restore copyright to works that have not entered the public domain in fellow member nations on the date that Berne comes into force with respect to those nations. It states, "This Convention shall apply to all works which, at the moment of its coming into force, have not yet fallen into the public domain in the country of origin through the expiry of the term of protection." The date that copyright restoration comes into force in the U.S. with respect to foreign nations is the earlier of January 1, 1996, or the date after January 1, 1996 on which the other country joined the Berne Convention or the World Trade Organization (WTO), or signed one of the 1996 copyright and neighboring rights treaties administered by the World Intellectual Property Association (WIPO), or was granted restoration by a presidential proclamation. In the U.S., copyright was restored automatically on January 1, 1996 to literary and artistic works that were not in the public domain in nineteen East European nations but were in the public domain in the U.S. due to expiry of copyright protection, lack of fulfillment of formalities, or lack of national eligibility.[14] It was restored on later dates as other nations joined the Berne Convention or WTO or signed the above-mentioned instruments. The duration of copyright in the U.S. for restored works is the full U.S. term for a work created or published on that date.

Copyright restoration for the CIS nations in particular is more complex. The new copyright laws of the CIS nations are considered in those nations to apply to pre-existing works created or published prior to the effective dates of the post-Communist laws. This situation amounts to retroactive protection for some works on which copyright expired under Soviet copyright laws, which had shorter terms than the current laws. Copyright specialists agree that there is legal uncertainty as to whether works that expired in the country of origin, such as under the Soviet term, and then were "extended" in national copyright legislation providing for longer terms, are protected by the copyright restoration provisions of the Berne Convention and the TRIPS Agreement.[15] Until a legal precedent has been set, the uncertainty is likely to remain. It is in the best interest of librarians to treat works as though these provisions apply, and calculate the term of duration as though the copyright had been restored.

The process for determining whether a work was restored is to consider the date on which copyright restoration became effective for the U.S. with respect to the foreign country in question. If the work was protected in the country of origin on that date, it is protected in the U.S. for the full U.S. term for a work created or published on that date. If it was not protected in the country of origin on that date, it is not currently protected in the U.S. Works created or published in Slavic and East European countries after that date are protected in the U.S. for the full current U.S. term.

The effective date of copyright restoration in the U.S. with respect to Slavic, East European, and Eurasian nations is January 1, 1996 for Albania, Bosnia and Herzegovina, Bulgaria, Croatia, Czech Republic, Estonia, Georgia, Hungary, Latvia, Lithuania, Macedonia, Moldova, Poland, Romania, Russia, Serbia and Montenegro, Slovakia, Slovenia, and Ukraine. The effective date for the other nations is: Armenia–October 19, 2000, Azerbaijan–June 4, 1999, Belarus–December 12, 1997, Kazakhstan–April 12, 1999, Kyrgyzstan–December 20, 1998, and Tajikistan–March 9, 2000.

Two examples may make this situation easier to understand. The works of the Russian writer Mikhail Sholokhov, who died in 1984, were protected in the Soviet Union throughout his life, and are still protected in the Russian Federation, for 54 years after his death, through 2038. This is because the 1928 copyright law of the USSR established copyright duration for written works as life of the author plus fifteen years; in 1973, that was extended to life plus twenty-five years. In 1992, the Russian Federation extended the term for life of the author plus fifty or fifty-four years, and adopted that term in its new copyright act of 1993 which remains in effect today. Thus Sholokhov's works never fell into the public domain in the Soviet Union or Russian Federation, and were protected in Russia on January 1, 1996 when the TRIPS Agreement became effective for the U.S. There is no question that Sholokhov's works originating in the Soviet Union are protected in the U.S. today. In the U.S. they are protected for the full U.S. term. His epic novel *Tikhii Don*, first published from 1928-40, is protected in the U.S. for 95 years from publication, or through 2023-2035.

The works of literary theorist Mikhail Bakhtin fall into the same scenario. Bakhtin died in 1975; thus his works never fell into the public domain in the USSR or Russian Federation. They would have been protected in the USSR through 2000, and their term was further extended by the law of the Russian Federation. There is no ambiguity in that they were eligible for copyright restoration in the U.S. His work *Problems of Dostoevsky's Poetics*, published in 1929, was protected in Russia on January 1, 1996 and is therefore protected in the U.S. through 2024.

There is more ambiguity in the situation of a work on which copyright expired under Soviet law and was later extended by the law of the Russian Federation, or another CIS nation, such as for the Russian literary historian and theorist Boris Eikhenbaum, who died in 1959. His *Literature: Theory, Criticism, Polemic* was first published in 1927. It entered the public domain in the USSR in 1984, twenty-five years after his death, but is protected in the Russian Federation through 2009, fifty years after his death. There is some question as to whether the work was restored in the U.S. on January 1, 1996, but it is in the best interest of librarians to take this approach until case law resolves the question. The U.S. term for this work is ninety-five years from publication, through 2022.

Once one has established that a work is protected in the U.S., the provisions of U.S. law apply with respect to any use of the work. It is important to know that digital works are entitled to copyright protection, as are print works, providing that they fulfill the requirements of originality; fixation in a tangible medium of expression (written, printed, drawn, recorded, videotaped, etc.); and that they are minimally creative. Copyright is extended automatically upon creation of a work. There is no requirement for formal registration or formalities for works created in the U.S. or works created in countries of the Slavic, East European, and Eurasian sphere, by virtue of their membership in the Berne Convention.[16]

EXCLUSIVE RIGHTS OF COPYRIGHT HOLDERS

In approaching U.S. law, one must relate the rights of the copyright holder with particular activities planned for the copyrighted works. As is well known, computer technology allows for easy reproduction, display, distribution, and at least as far as text is concerned, editing and mark-up of works. As it turns out, each of those activities involves one or more of the exclusive rights of copyright holders in U.S. law, as set out in Sections 106 and 106A of the law. U.S. law sets out six specific exclusive rights, defining actions that the author or copyright holder has the sole right to perform in relation to the work; those rights enable authors or copyright holders to benefit economically from their works, and are commonly referred to as *economic rights*. They will be discussed in detail below.

Beyond this, the U.S. law contains a provision for respecting *moral rights*, those rights upholding recognition of the author's identity, individuality, and of the integrity of the work, apart from its economic value. U.S. protection for moral rights is considered to be insufficient in comparison with the protection accorded by many other nations of the Berne Convention, particularly those of the civil law tradition, which generally provide substantial protection for moral rights for all categories of works. U.S. copyright law extends protection only to the rights of attribution and integrity for works of visual art, in Section 106A. Works of visual art are a limited category of works based on images existing in a single copy or in a limited edition of two hundred signed and numbered copies or fewer. It is understood that the U.S. compensates for its slim protection of moral rights in federal law through its protection of derivative works, and through provisions of state laws dealing with unfair competition, defamation, and privacy, but that is a separate issue.

Copyright holders hold exclusive rights for a limited period of time, as defined in the Sections 301-305 of the law. Any action involving an exclusive right requires permission of the copyright holder unless there is an exemption in the law permitting such use. In U.S. law there are fifteen limitations and exceptions that exist to benefit individuals or society without harming the economic or moral rights of the author or copyright holder. The limitations most relevant for libraries and educational institutions ensure adequate public access and use of information: Section 107 (fair use), an open-ended limitation; and three categorical, or specific, limitations, Section 108 (reproduction by libraries and archives), Section 109 (first sale doctrine), and Section 110 (performance or display of works for classroom use and in distance learning). It is important to understand that these limitations, so critical for the operations of libraries, can only be forfeited by voluntary submission to licensing terms that restrict them, and it is not in the best interests of libraries to accept contractual terms of rightholders to this effect.

Digital library activities may entail any of the six economic rights in Section 106: reproduction, preparing a derivative work, public distribution, public performance, public display, and public performance by means of a digital audio transmission. These rights are valid until the term of copyright has expired and the work has entered the public domain. After works enter the public domain, they may be used freely.

Right of Reproduction

Section 106(1) of the U.S. Copyright Act establishes the exclusive right "[t]o reproduce the copyrighted work in copies or phonorecords." The reproduction right for digital library projects might involve scanning of material; or storage of a file on a hard drive, back-up drive, disk, CD-ROM, or in RAM; or reproduction for the purpose of encoding text or supplying metadata. Any copy made in the process of reformatting would also involve the reproduction right. Until the Digital Millennium Copyright Act (DMCA), digitization was considered to be reformatting, rather than reproduction, and it fell outside the bounds of permitted uses in the copyright law.[17] The law allowed for copying for library preservation as an exemption under Section 108, but digitization was not considered to be copying, so it did not fall under this exemption. The U.S. copyright law was amended in 1998 to implement the DMCA and allows for digital preservation copies to be made as a limitation to the reproduction right under certain conditions. They will be discussed below. In short, whenever a work is digitized, the reproduction right is involved.

Preparing a Derivative Work

The right "[t]o prepare derivative works based on the copyrighted work" under Section 106(2) is implicated in library activities in many different ways. Derivative works involve activities such as making a translation, or editing a work to produce an abridgement, annotated version, or revised version. It essentially involves the creation of a new work, bearing original characteristics, from an older one. This is true in the print world as in the digital world. Digital activities involving derivative works might include digital alteration of an original image or sound recording so as to produce an original work; or placement of original material in a new arrangement that constitutes an original work. Editing a work by routine mark-up of text, such as HTML or XML coding, does not typically result in a derivative work because text encoding is a technical, not a creative process, and does not result in alteration of the essential content.

Right of Public Distribution

Section 106(3) involves the right "[t]o distribute copies or phonorecords of the copyrighted work to the public by sale or other transfer of ownership, or by rental, lease, or lending." This right is implicated when the work is made available by some type of transfer to the public by any means. This would include public distribution on the web, or in any electronic form available to the public, or through file sharing that involves actual distribution to users that make up the public. Case law has treated the question of whether uploading copyrighted works to a server to make them available for downloading constitutes distribution, or whether an actual transfer of copies must take place. The answer appears to be that the action of uploading to a server, without retrieval of files by users, does not constitute public distribution. However, when uploading copyrighted material to a server is intended to facilitate public distribution, and distribution occurs, such distribution must be authorized. It is generally understood that electronic transmission constitutes public distribution in peer-to-peer file sharing situations when someone makes files on a server available to others, and the distribution occurs.[18] The public distribution right is heavily implicated in classroom teaching, distance education, and interlibrary loan.

Public Performance

Section 106(4) of the U.S. Copyright Act covers the right "[i]n the case of literary, musical, dramatic, and choreographic works, pantomimes, and motion pictures and other audiovisual work, to perform the copyrighted work publicly." The definitions of public performance or display, transmission, and digital transmission are further delineated in Section 101. Digital library activities involving the public performance right would include public viewing of a motion picture on DVD, digital audiovisual work, or streaming video. There is a separate right for public performance by digital audio transmission that applies to digital transmissions of sound recordings, to be discussed below. It is important to know that the public performance right involves a moving sequence of images and sounds, and does not apply to pictorial, graphic, or sculptural works that are not "performed." The public display right is considered adequate to cover use of those works.

Public Display

Section 106(5) covers the right "[i]n the case of literary, musical, dramatic, and choreographic works, pantomimes, and pictorial, graphic, or sculptural works, including the individual images of a motion picture or other audiovisual work, to display the copyrighted work publicly."

As mentioned, there is an important distinction between public performance and public display. Public performance entails a moving sequence of images or sounds such as in the showing of a motion picture, playing of an audiovisual work, streaming video, or sound recording. Public display involves non-sequential display of an image, as in a still shot. Digital library activities involving public display would include placing images or text material on a server or on the Internet for public viewing, displaying still shots from a digital film or video, or showing still digitized images in an area for public viewing.

Public Performance by Means of Digital Audio Transmission

Section 106(6) involves the right "in the case of sound recordings, to perform the copyrighted work publicly by means of a digital audio transmission." This is a more specific provision than Section 106(4). It was added to the statute by the Digital Performance Right in Sounds Recordings Act of 1995.[19] Streaming audio transmissions involve moving digital sound transmitted to an audience that qualifies as "public." Individual reception of a streaming audio recording from a computer does not qualify as a public performance.[20]

Why is it important to differentiate the above rights? Performing any of these activities to a copyright-protected work requires permission of the copyright holder unless the activity is covered by a limitation or exception. In seeking permissions, one should specify each of these rights in a request. With digital material, the reproduction right, public distribution right, public display right, and public performance right are closely intertwined. Many kinds of electronic transmissions involve all four rights. When seeking permission to use copyrighted material, it is often wise to include all of these rights in a request. If there is reason to believe that a limitation or exception applies to use of the work, this should be considered before seeking permissions.

LIMITATIONS AND EXCEPTIONS
TO THE EXCLUSIVE RIGHTS OF COPYRIGHT HOLDERS

There are four major sections in the law that allow for lawful use for special cases relating to libraries, archives, and educational institutions. They allow library and archival staff to perform certain activities lawfully for the internal use of the institution or for the benefit of users without seeking permission from the copyright holder under certain conditions.[21]

Section 108

Section 108 of the Copyright Act covers several different aspects of copyright for libraries and archives. It deals with preservation and re-placement, reproduction for staff use, reproduction for library users, photocopying services, and interlibrary lending. Amended by the DMCA to include digital reproduction, it allows libraries and archives that are open to the public or that allow access to their collections to those doing research in a specialized field to reproduce and distribute copies, for non-commercial purposes, provided that the copies include a notice of copyright or a legend indicating that the work may be protected by copyright.

Up to three copies of an unpublished work may be reproduced and distributed for purposes of *preservation or security or for deposit for research use* in another library or archive of the same type, if a copy of the work is currently in the collections of the library or archive. If the preservation copies are digital, they may not be otherwise distributed in that format, and may not be made available to the public in that format outside the premises of the library or archive. Up to three copies of a published work may be made for the purpose of *replacing* works that are damaged, deteriorating, lost, or stolen, or if the existing format has become obsolete, if, after reasonable effort, the library or archive has determined that a replacement copy cannot be obtained at a fair price. If the replacement copies are digital, they may not made available outside the premises of the library or archive in lawful possession of the copies.

Section 108 also allows for reproduction and distribution of material from the collection of a library or archive *for the benefit of users*. This section of law is what makes possible interlibrary loan of journal articles. One copy of (a) an article or other contribution to a collection or periodical issue, or a small part of any other work, or (b) an entire work, or a substantial part of it, may be reproduced at the request of a user or another library, if the copy becomes the property of the user, and if the library or archive has no knowledge that the copy will be used for any purpose other than private study, scholarship, or research; and if the library or archive prominently places a warning of copyright at the place where orders are accepted and on its order form as prescribed by the Registrar of Copyrights. An entire work may be reproduced only if after reasonable effort, the library or archive has determined that a replacement copy cannot be obtained at a fair price.

The limitation for reproduction and distribution *for the benefit of users* does not apply to musical works, pictorial, graphic, or sculptural works, or motion picture or audiovisual works other than audiovisual works dealing with news. However, it does apply to pictorial and graphic works published within a work, such as illustrations and diagrams.

Section 108(g) clarifies that reproduction and distribution rights described in the provision extend to the "isolated and unrelated reproduction or distribution" of a single copy "of the same material on separate occasions" but not to "related or concerted reproduction or distribution of multiple copies," or the "systematic reproduction or distribution of single or multiple copies." It further stipulates that interlibrary activities exercised under the terms of the provision must not involve "such aggregate quantities as to substitute for a subscription to or purchase" of a work. As a benefit to libraries, Section 108 stipulates that a library or archive or its employees cannot be held liable for copyright infringement for unsupervised use of reproducing equipment on its premises, provided that the equipment displays a notice that copying may be subject to the copyright law.

Section 108 was amended by the Sonny Bono Copyright Term Extension Act of 1998 to include another important provision, applying to the rights of reproduction, distribution, display, and performance. It allows libraries, archives, and nonprofit educational institutions to treat certain published works in their last twenty years of protection more freely for purposes of preservation, scholarship, or research, subject to certain conditions: that the work is not subject to normal commercial exploitation (not being marketed), that a copy cannot be obtained at a reasonable price, and so long as the copyright holder has not notified the Registrar of Copyrights that either of these conditions applies. If the copyright owner provides notice that either of those conditions applies, use of the work must stop.

Section 109: First Sale

Section 109 of the Copyright Act is known as the first sale doctrine. Codified in Section 27 of the 1909 U.S. Copyright Act, it enables libraries to lend, resell, or otherwise dispose of lawfully obtained materials without seeking permissions. This section of the law makes possible interlibrary loan of books and other physical materials. The first sale doctrine does not apply to the rental, lease, or lending of computer programs or sound recordings for commercial use (it does, however, apply to videos). Nonprofit libraries may lend computer programs, but a copyright warning prescribed by the Registrar of Copyrights must be placed on the software package. Nonprofit libraries and educational institutions may also rent, lease, or lend phonorecords, a category that includes records, audiotapes, and CDs. Section 109 also allows the owner of a copy of a work to display it publicly, thus implicating the exclusive right of public display. This permits libraries to display works in exhibits.

Consensus does not exist on whether first sale, commonly referred to in other countries as the exhaustion principle, applies to digital works. The question hinges on the fact that in the U.S. "copies" are defined in Section 101 of the law as tangible objects. It states that copies are "material objects, other than phonorecords, in which a work is fixed by any method now known or later developed. . . ." The European Commission has explicitly excluded non-tangible copies from the scope of the exhaustion principle. Some argue that the first sale doctrine cannot apply to digital copies because the original copy is retained by its owner, and that for first sale to apply, the original copy would have to be destroyed. Others believe that the doctrine should apply in some way to digital copies as well.[22]

Section 110

Section 110 is a lengthy and complex provision, addressing exemptions for certain types of performances and displays of copyrighted works. As concerns libraries and educational institutions, it addresses performance and display of copyrighted works in face-to-face teaching activities of a nonprofit educational institution, in a classroom or similar place devoted to instruction. Section 110(2) was completely revised by the TEACH Act, which became law on November 2, 2002, to allow for use of digital works in the classroom, or for the purposes of distance education, without prior permission.

Section 110(1) allows for performance and display of copyrighted analog works in the face-to-face teaching situation in a classroom; it specifies that motion pictures and audiovisual works used under this provision must be lawful copies. Section 110(2) allows for use of copyrighted works transmitted through digital networks as part of "mediated instructional activities." It permits performance of nondramatic literary or musical works (such as excerpts from books, journal articles, songs, etc.), or "reasonable and limited portions of any other work" (such as charts, graphs, diagrams, operas, plays, audiovisual works, etc.), or display of a work "in an amount comparable to that which is typically displayed in the course of a live classroom session," provided that the copy used is lawfully made, or the institution should have reason to believe that it is lawfully made. The teaching must be done by an instructor as an integral part of a class session at an accredited nonprofit educational institution, and the use must be directly related to the teaching content of the transmission. The transmission must be limited to students officially enrolled in the course.

To benefit from Section 101(2), the institution must implement a number of policy and technical measures. It must institute copyright policies and provide informational materials to faculty, students, and staff that promote compliance with the copyright law, and it must provide copyright notice on materials being used for courses. It must also apply technological security measures that reasonably prevent retention of works in accessible form beyond the duration of the class session and unauthorized further dissemination of the work. In addition, the institution must not engage in conduct that could reasonably be expected to interfere with technological measures set up to prevent such retention or unauthorized further dissemination of works.

Section 110 further elaborates that the term "mediated instructional activities" in the digital environment refers to activities that use works in a manner analogous to performance and display of works in a live classroom setting. It does not refer to digital transmission of textbooks, coursepacks, or other materials that are typically purchased or acquired by students for their independent use. The TEACH Act also amended Section 112 of the copyright law to permit retention of content and student access to course materials for a limited time, provided that no further copies are made; and permits reproduction and retention necessary for technical purposes. In addition, it permits digitization of analog works for the purpose of classroom teaching, if the amount is appropriate pursuant to Section 110(2) and if a digital version of the work is not already available to the institution; or if available, it is restricted by technological protection measures that prevent its use under Section 110(2).

It is important to know that educational institutions are not obligated to implement the policy and technological requirements of the TEACH Act. TEACH offers an option for regulating digital use of copyrighted works in distance education that is reasonably defined. The benefits of TEACH are available if an institution complies with the implementation requirements of the law. Fair use remains an alternative option to educational institutions for handling performance and display of works in the classroom, although it leaves more questions open for use of materials in the digital environment.[23]

Section 107: Fair Use

The fair use doctrine is often viewed as the most important, as well as the most confusing, exemption in the copyright law. Unlike Sections 108, 109, and 110, the fair use doctrine is both broad and ambiguous, and is not based on a defined formula or set of rules. It applies to all types of works and all formats, provided there is no conflict with another part of the law (for example, with restrictions on circumvention of technological measures), but it does not guarantee protection from infringement. It is considered a defense to copyright infringement, rather than a right. It is based on the premise that, if accused of infringement, one could construct an argument weighing the relevance of four factors to prove that the use in question was lawful.

The fair use doctrine establishes that certain reproductions of copyrighted material–published and unpublished, in any format–are not infringing, and provides a non-exhaustive list of those uses: criticism, comment, news reporting, teaching (including multiple copies for classroom use), scholarship, and research. It then provides the well-known list of four factors to be considered to determine whether a use is fair: the purpose and character of the use, the nature of the copyrighted work, the amount of the work being used, and the effect of the use on the market for the work. The fair use doctrine is a complex exception because of its open-endedness, which allows for exceptions to be made on a case-by-case basis. There is no black-and-white answer to a copyright situation when it comes to fair use. One can only read about fair use in order to understand its logic, read cases on it, make an assessment based on consideration of the four factors, and consult with institutional counsel to estimate what a court might rule if a lawsuit were filed.

Section 117: On Computer Programs

Section 117 of the copyright law, on computer programs, allows the owner of a computer program to make a copy or adaptation of the computer program if this is necessary in order to use the program on a computer, provided that the copy or adaptation is for archival (back-up) purposes only and is destroyed when "continued possession of the computer program should cease to be rightful." Section 117 also allows for making a copy of a lawfully acquired computer program for purposes of maintenance or repair of a computer, if the copy is generated automatically by the computer containing it, and if it is destroyed immediately after the maintenance or repair is finished.

CONTRIBUTORY INFRINGEMENT BY AN ONLINE SERVICE PROVIDER

There is another important consideration for libraries in the online environment: assessing liability as online service providers (OSPs) for third-party copyright infringement. In 1998, Congress passed the Online Copyright Infringement Liability Limitation Act. It originated in the DMCA deliberations, and was incorporated as Title II of the DMCA, adding Section 512 to the copyright law, which, as amended, limits criminal liability for third-party infringement relating to material online. This means that service providers, and libraries that provide Internet services and access, cannot be held liable for infringement of copyright committed by someone using their services, providing that certain conditions are met. To avoid liability OSPs must comply with certain requirements.

A provider may be exempt from liability if it is merely acting as a "passive conduit" for the material: if the act has been initiated by someone else, if the provider has not selected the material or been involved in its transmission, or selected the recipients of the material, or maintained a copy on the system, or modified the content. The provider must not have actual knowledge of the infringement, or be aware of facts or circumstances from which infringing activity is apparent. An OSP must act expeditiously to remove or disable access to the infringing material. It must not receive a financial benefit from the infringing activity. The

OSP must not interfere with technical measures in place to protect and identify copyrighted works. It must implement a policy that terminates the accounts of repeat infringers, designate an agent to receive notifications of claimed infringements, and make the contact information for this agent available to the public and to the Copyright Office.

Section 512 contains an additional provision for public and nonprofit institutions of higher education. Section 512(e) stipulates that if a faculty member or graduate student infringes copyright in the course of teaching or research, the institution will not be liable in the following circumstances: if the infringing activities do not involve online access to instructional materials required for courses taught by that individual within the last three years; if the institution has not received more than two infringement claims concerning the individual within the last three years; and if the institution provides to its users information promoting compliance with U.S. copyright law.

LIBRARIES AS USERS OF OTHERS' CONTENT IN A DIGITAL ENVIRONMENT

Another way of looking at what is stake for libraries in the world of digital copyright is to view in more detail the activities they perform, and how these activities implicate copyright. It is important to remember that any use of licensed material, such as electronic journals and databases held by the library, must be handled according to the terms of the license. If the license addresses uses for interlibrary loan, reproduction for distance education, or other library activities, you must consider those terms, which are governed by state contract law, as preemptions of the terms of the U.S. Copyright Act.

Use of the Internet

Use of the Internet raises tricky questions with respect to the all of the exclusive rights, and in particular those of reproduction, public distribution, public performance, and public display.

Browsing

It seems odd that browsing the Internet could be a violation of copyright, but the question has been raised. Browsing the web creates temporary copies of pages and caches those copies either in RAM or on the computer's hard drive. At least two courts have held that RAM copies may indeed infringe copyright and some specialists think that it remains uncertain in case law whether temporary storage in computer RAM during browsing sessions qualifies as reproduction.[24] However, most agree that browsing does not implicate the reproduction right unless a substantial portion of the work is copied for more than a transitory period of time. The argument centers in the statutory requirement for "fixation" as a prerequisite for copyright protection. The definition of fixation requires that a work be fixed in tangible medium of expression to be "perceived, reproduced, or otherwise communicated for a period of more than transitory duration." Because the term "transitory duration" is not defined in the copyright law, questions remain as to whether RAM copies meet the vague statutory requirement of fixation for more than a transitory period. In any case, it hardly seems that in normal situations browsing would trigger a lawsuit, and so we need not worry that it is an infringement to read or to scroll through websites.

Linking

Linking is often divided into the categories of outlinking, deep linking, and inline linking, or framing. *Linking*, also referred to as *outlinking*, is not generally considered to cause infringement of copyrighted material because no content is reproduced on the linking site. Another common method of reasoning in the U.S. is that linking is allowed under the legal doctrines of "implied license" or fair use.[25] Some specialists have more reservations where images are concerned, and suggest that linking to copyrighted images without permission might make one liable for violation of the rights of reproduction, distribution, creation of a derivative work, and public display, because an image (illustration, photo, sketch, etc.) constitutes a whole work, and suggest that it is proper etiquette to ask permission before linking to anyone's image.

In the case of either text or images, as long as nothing is done to violate copyright blatantly, the question of violation should not arise. Questions might arise if there is excessive linking to other sites; linking in such a way as to affect the market for a work; linking that distorts or misuses the content or organization of the linked site (the selection and arrangement of material are copyrightable); willful linking and distribution of infringing copies; or linking that appears to create a derivative work from other copyrighted works. There is agreement among copyright specialists that it is indeed risky to link to trademarked logos, and that one should obtain permission, or use a textual description of the trademark instead of an image of the logo. Any link that contributes to the unauthorized reproduction of a copyrighted work when the linker knew or had reason to know of the unauthorized nature of the work many constitute contributory infringement.

Deep Linking

Deep linking is direct linking to interior pages in another site, and is problematic for several reasons: in commercial sites, advertisements are often displayed on the homepage and the operators of those sites may have objections to use of their sites that bypass the ads. In non-commercial sites, deep linking can distort the context and undermine the authority of the content. Deep linking is still an unresolved area in case law, but most agree that it is better to avoid, or to seek permission first. If one is unable to contact the owner of a website to obtain permission for a link, it is advisable to place a prominent disclaimer on the site to minimize liability for infringement.

Framing

Also known as inline linking, framing is bringing another image into one's own web page, or bringing other pages into one's frames. Framing is thought to involve a higher risk of liability than linking. Framing creates a composite web page from selected elements, not just a direct link to the linked site, thus implicating the reproduction right. Framing may also be considered to contribute to the creation of a derivative work, because it permits alteration of the original content. Framing could be viewed as a modification, transformation, or even distortion of an original work, thus violating Section 106(2). It is also possible that framing could violate the public display and performance rights. U.S. specialists do not agree whether framing is permitted under the copyright law, and the status of framing remains unclear. It is generally suggested that libraries avoid using frames or deep links of others' content in a way that might cause confusion in the mind of the viewer, and to avoid deep links that interfere with advertising.[26]

Caching and Mirroring

Exclusive rights have been called into question with respect to caching, the mechanism that automatically creates temporary copies on a computer's RAM (local caching) or on a server in the process of accessing websites, to enhance speed and efficiency in retrieving the site later during a session. Mirroring involves copying a substantial portion of the contents of an accessed server to facilitate prompt retrieval of the site by a service provider. Being standard functions of browsers, caching on a server, local caching on a user's RAM, and mirroring are generally considered not to infringe copyright. Specialists agree that there is "implied consent" on behalf of creators of websites or other online content to caching as an integral part of the functionality of servers and browsers.[27]

ARCHIVING AND PRESERVING DIGITAL MATERIALS

Creating a Digital Archive for Preservation

As discussed above, Section 108 of the copyright law provides an exemption for the purposes of preservation, security, deposit for research use in another library or archive, or replacement, subject to certain conditions. The provision was revised in 1998 to allow for digital preservation. It applies to published and unpublished works in any format–print works, musical works, pictorial works, graphic works, motion pictures and other audiovisual works, sound recordings, etc. This means that if all the conditions are met, one may copy works without seeking permissions from the copyright holder.

The provision allows for up to three copies of *unpublished* material to be duplicated for *preservation, security, and deposit for research use* in another library or archive; this includes reformatting for preservation. The work must be currently held in the collections of the library or archive (you may not use interlibrary loan to receive copies and then make copies of them); the digital copies may not be otherwise distributed in that format, and may not be made available to the public in that format outside the premises of the library or archive. The provision also allows for up to three copies of *published* material to be duplicated for *replacement* purposes.

It is important to remember that material must be in poor condition–damaged or deteriorating–lost, stolen, or in an obsolete format, for this exemption to apply. Digitization as preventive or anticipatory preservation is not allowed. Conditions are that the library or archive has determined after reasonable effort that an unused replacement copy cannot be obtained at a fair price, and the digital copies may not be made available to the public in the digital format outside the premises of the library or archive.

Section 108(h)(1) allows libraries, archives, and nonprofit educational institutions to treat published works in their last twenty years of protection differently for purposes of preservation, scholarship, or research, subject to certain conditions, as discussed above. It applies to the rights of reproduction, distribution, display, and performance. It *does not apply* to musical, pictorial, graphic, or sculptural works, motion pictures, or other audiovisual works other than audiovisual works dealing with news. This provision essentially applies to published textual material. It does not apply to subsequent users of the material, so it is advisable for the library or archive to include a notice to that effect on the digitized copies.[28]

> *A librarian notices that issues of the journal* Znanie–sila *from the 1950s and 1960s are disintegrating. She thinks that it would be a good idea to digitize them for preservation and make them available on a website open to faculty and students at the university. At the same time, she thinks it might be a good idea to digitize the more recent issues, to provide a complete run of the journal in digital form. May she do this?*

Determining which of the articles are still protected based on the lives of the individual authors would be very time-consuming. It is reasonable to assume that some, if not most, of the articles are still protected, and therefore the journal issues are not in the public domain. Up to three copies of each journal issue that is truly in deteriorating condition may be scanned, but they may not be made available to the public outside the premises of the library. A restricted website may be set up for display within the library, not to include access from other university workstations, or from the homes of faculty and students, or from any other location. The issues that are not deteriorating may not be digitized without seeking permission from the copyright holder. However, some of the issues may be in their last twenty years of copyright protection. If these issues are not subject to normal commercial exploitation (not currently being marketed), if the issues cannot be obtained at a fair price, and if there has been no notice to either of these conditions from the copyright holder, those issues may be scanned and placed on a website for public display, whether or not they are deteriorating. Works that are not deteriorating and not in their last twenty years of copyright protection may not be scanned, displayed, or distributed without permission of the copyright holder.

May a library make digital preservation copies of journal issues for another library that was flooded and lost its Slavic serial collection?

That is allowable under Section 108 as long as those materials were part of the collection of that library before the flood.

A university library's copy of an important bibliography published in 1985 was stolen, and all attempts to purchase it through book dealers in Poland have failed. The library borrows it from another library, makes a digital copy, prints it, and binds the printed digital copy as a replacement. The scanned version is retained in a file on the librarian's computer. Has the librarian acted within the law?

Yes, the librarian has acted within the law in making the digital preservation copy, and in printing a copy for replacement, providing he has met all the conditions of Section 108. Since three digital copies are allowed for replacement, it is lawful for the digital version to remain on the librarian's computer.

Creating a Digital Archive for Enhanced Access

It is common for libraries to seek ways of providing better access to material that is commonly used, difficult to find, or just interesting. But this is a very different thing as far as the law is concerned. There is no exemption to cover this type of situation.

A librarian receives a grant to digitize some rare photographs and posters illustrating artistic life in Prague in the twentieth century. The materials are in good physical condition. What are the copyright considerations?

Any of the works dating after 1923 may be still protected by copyright in the U.S. This type of digitization project implicates the rights of reproduction, public display, public distribution, and possibly creation of a derivative work if the library views the end result as a compilation, or if the works will be modified in any way. Because this project involves pictorial works, Section 108(h)(1) for works in their last twenty years of protection does not apply. The librarian would be free to digitize and display any of the works that were already in the public domain, but would need to seek permissions to use the works still protected by copyright.

INTERLIBRARY LOAN

Two separate sections of the U.S. copyright law are relevant to interlibrary loan. Section 109, the first sale doctrine, is the provision that permits lending of books, audiotapes, videotapes, and other whole works, under the conditions discussed above. This activity is governed by first sale because it involves transfer of an entire work to a user at another library; the reproduction right is not involved. Section 108 governs the activity of reproducing and distributing parts of works, such as journal articles, or small sections of books, when the loaning library does not lose access to the original work as a result of the loan.

Most libraries in the U.S. follow the guidelines for interlibrary loan established in 1978 by the Commission on New Technological Uses of Copyrighted Works (CONTU) after the U.S. Copyright Act was amended in 1976 to provide for new technology and communications media. Not being a part of Title 17, United States Code, the CONTU guidelines do not have the force of law, but they are widely accepted and are regarded as a national standard for interlibrary loan practices.[29]

The CONTU guidelines established the well-known "rule of five" to define limits to copying to comply with Section 108(g)(2). The guidelines apply to journals published within the last five years. They recommend that interlibrary loan copying be limited to no more than five copies of an article or articles of a journal title within a calendar year. Upon the sixth request, the borrowing library should pay copyright royalties for the copy, or purchase a subscription to the journal. For other works, for example, requests for excerpts from a book or pamphlet, no more than five copies per year should be made during the entire period for which the work is covered by copyright. Requests must contain a statement that the borrowing library is compliant with CONTU guidelines, and the borrowing library must keep records of filled and unfilled requests for three years after the requests are made. These limitations do not apply if the library has ordered a subscription to the periodical; if the library's copy of the work is lost, stolen, or unavailable; or if the library has ordered the title but it has not yet arrived.

There are currently no guidelines addressing interlibrary loan in the digital environment. The Conference on Fair Use (CONFU), convened by the Working Group on Intellectual Property Rights of the Information Infrastructure Task Force, met from 1994 to 1998 to establish guidelines for library applications of new technologies, but did not reach a consensus in many areas, including electronic interlibrary loan and document delivery. Libraries continue to rely on the CONTU guidelines established in 1978, and on careful reading of the statute, in some cases applying the fair use doctrine to questions concerning interlibrary loan.

If the library mentioned above receives an interlibrary loan request for the 1985 Polish bibliography, may it send a copy of all or part of its digital preservation copy through interlibrary loan to a patron?

The digital version may not be loaned. Section 108 states that a digital preservation copy may "not otherwise be distributed in that format." The library may loan only the printed version to the patron.

A library receives a special request for copies of selected portions of an important reference work published in Moscow in 1975, on behalf of a scholar who is teaching in a small town and does not have access to this edition. May the librarian scan the selected pages and send them in an electronic file as an attachment to an e-mail, or photocopy them and send them to the borrowing library by fax?

Either method would be appropriate, even if not standard, but the borrowing library should include on the work the CONTU compliance statement, and the borrowing library must keep a record of the request for three years.

ELECTRONIC RESERVES

There is still no copyright legislation in the U.S. covering course reserves, let alone electronic course reserves. It is one of the more confusing aspects of copyright for libraries. Various guidelines have been issued by organizations over the years, and institutions have dealt with guidelines for reserves in many different ways.

No consensus was reached on the 1998 draft CONFU guidelines, and the guidelines were never officially endorsed, but some libraries follow them. The guidelines, all the same, do not have the force of law.[30] The 1982 *Model Policy Concerning College and University Photocopying* of the American Library Association treats reserves in Section IIIC as an extension of the classroom, recommending that excerpts of a work may be copied and placed on reserve within limits: the copying may not occur every semester, and the number of copies should be "reasonable in light of the number of students enrolled." If one copy is requested, the library may photocopy one article, one chapter from a book, or one poem.[31] The *Guidelines for Classroom Copying in Not-for-Profit Educational Institutions with Respect to Books and Periodicals*, crafted by the House Judiciary Committee as part of the legislative history of the 1976 Copyright Act, do not address reserves specifically, but do address copying for the classroom, and could possibly be applied to course reserves as well. Their application to the digital environment is unclear.[32]

Some institutions treat reserves as fair use, since making multiple copies for classroom use is sanctioned in Section 107 of the copyright law. A new document was issued in November 2003 on electronic reserves and fair use, to resolve some of these questions in the absence of specific legislation. Endorsed by the major U.S. library organizations, the statement "Applying Fair Use in the Development of Electronic Reserves Systems" strongly asserts that fair use is the best way of making judgments about e-reserves.[33]

A faculty member requests that the latest print edition of Mikhail Bulgakov's The Master and Margarita, *first published posthumously in Moscow in 1966-67, be scanned and placed on electronic reserve because it is expensive and difficult to obtain, and he has a large number of students in his class who need the book immediately.*

To be safe, one should treat the novel as restored, and protected in the U.S. through 2062, because it was protected in Russia as a posthumous work, under a term of fifty years from publication, when copyright restoration took effect in the U.S. on January 1, 1996. Aside from access restrictions set by e-reserve systems, there is no great difference in the copyright issues involved for print reserves and e-reserves if the fair use approach is taken. It would not be permissible to reproduce or scan an entire textbook or coursepack for reserves, since the copy would be in direct competition with the original work; only a purchased copy of a textbook or coursepack should be placed on reserve. Allowing for *multiple* copies of an *entire fictional* work that is available in the publishing *market* to be reproduced, tips the balance toward unfair use. A purchased print copy of the novel could be put on reserve, but not a full electronic version. The professor should either recommend that the class use a more readily available edition of the work, or make allowances for the students to use one or a limited number of purchased print copies on reserve.

A faculty member who is an enthusiast of digital applications for research use, has scanned a copy of The Master and Margarita, *performed a textual analysis, and created a research version of the work in XML, which enables students to perform linguistic analysis of the text. He requests that the library place a scanned copy of his XML version on electronic reserve. Is this lawful?*

In order to have produced his research copy, the professor implicated the right of reproduction. It is possible that his own use of the work, since it was for *research* purposes, and arguably did not affect the *market* for the work, even though it reproduced a *fictional* work in its *entirety*, might be considered a fair use. But reproducing and distributing the work to students goes one step further, and might appear to go too far to some analysts. Others might consider this a fair use because the purpose of using the work is linguistic analysis and not ordinary reading, and there is no market for the XML version. There is no definitive answer when it comes to fair use. One can only make an educated judgment by carefully considering the four factors in the determination.

CLASSROOM USE OF DIGITAL MATERIALS, INCLUDING IN DISTANCE EDUCATION

Using copyrighted material in the classroom may implicate the rights of reproduction, public display, and public performance. As discussed above, Section 110 is a limitation permitting performance and display of copyrighted works in face-to-face teaching activities of a nonprofit educational institution, in a classroom or similar place devoted to instruction, and in distance education sessions. In the digital environment, questions arise in using the Internet or digital material in the physical classroom, or transmitting material electronically to students in distance education courses.

Three CONFU documents attempted to address issues related to educational use of electronic works and distance learning, but only one of them was adopted at the close of the conference in 1998. No consensus was reached on the "Proposed Educational Fair Use Guidelines for Distance Learning" or the "Proposed Educational Fair Use of Digital Images." The "Fair Use Guidelines for Educational Multimedia" were adopted by CONFU and are used at many institutions nationwide, but are not universally accepted by libraries and library organizations.[34] The TEACH Act, discussed above, became law in November 2002, offering an additional way of handling digital distance education in accredited, nonprofit educational institutions. Institutions deal with digital classroom displays and digital transmission for distance education in many different ways. All of the above guidelines are optional, the provisions of the TEACH Act also remain optional, and fair use continues to offer a viable approach.

For a distance education class could an instructor take advantage of the TEACH Act to distribute a scanned version of The Master and Margarita *as required reading?*

No, this is not lawful. The TEACH Act was designed to facilitate "mediated instructional activity" analogous to the kind of performance or display one would expect in the physical classroom, such as a Powerpoint presentation, or projection of transparencies or websites onto a screen. It is not about material that would substitute for coursepacks, textbooks, or required course material that students are expected to purchase for their courses. You wouldn't–couldn't–display the whole work in the face-to-face classroom, so this kind of use is not the subject of Section 110.

An instructor would like to make excerpts from a digital version of The Master and Margarita *to include in a course segment for a distance education class. Her institution has not implemented the provisions of the TEACH Act. May she do this?*

Fair use continues to offer a viable approach for handling use of copyrighted material in distance education. The instructor should carefully weigh the four factors. Reproduction of multiple copies for classroom use weighs toward fair use. The fictional nature of the work weighs against fair use. Copying a small amount of the work weighs toward fair use. Reproduction and distribution for classroom use of a substantial portion of the novel weighs against fair use. Reproduction that hurts sales of the novel weighs against fair use. Also the instructor should be aware that the digital version being used must be lawful for this activity to be permissible. Ultimately the instructor must make a decision based on a careful judgment of the four factors, keeping in mind that restricting access to the students in the class for a limited period of time is an important consideration weighing in favor of the use.

DIGITAL TEXT ENCODING AND METADATA

As mentioned above, text encoding to enable display of material and scholarly analysis of texts involves technical manipulation of texts, but does not normally involve an essential alteration of the content. Section 102(b) of the copyright law states that copyright protection does not extend to an "idea, procedure, process, system, method of operation, or discovery, regardless of the form in which it is described, explained, illustrated, or embodied in such work." It is generally considered that one cannot obtain copyright for a marked up text as a derivative work. However, the process of encoding text likely involves reproducing the original text, and possibly public display and performance, and therefore might implicate the exclusive rights of the copyright holder. If the text is encoded in such a way as to modify the text, the right of creating derivative works is also implicated. Fair use would be an appropriate way of approaching text encoding of a copyrighted work.

DIGITIZATION OF MICROFORMS

Questions sometimes arise on the viability of library digitization of microfilm and microform document sets. As a matter of preservation, this is allowed under Section 108 if all the conditions of the provision are met. However, if the intention of the digitization project is to provide enhanced access to microform material that is not deteriorating, this likely requires permissions. There are typically two sets of copyright in microform–copyright in the original works (unless they are in the public domain), and copyright in the set as a derivative work based on selection and arrangement of those works, and on any original content or elements added by the set producer, such as indexing information, tables of contents, and annotations. Copyright to the set as a whole is normally held by the institution or organization that has produced the set. The set may not be reproduced as a whole without obtaining permission from that entity.

If the original works are in the public domain, the framed copies produced on the microfilm or microfiche, so long as they are exact reproductions of the public domain works, are also in the public domain. Those exact reproductions of public domain material could be digitized, barring any license or agreement between the library and the set producer disallowing such use. But it would not be permissible to digitize the set as a whole, or in any way that reproduced the selection and arrangement of the set or its original elements, or its added elements, without obtaining permission from the copyright holder of the set.

If the original works are still copyrighted, one may not digitize them without permission from the copyright holder for any use that is not justified by fair use or another limitation in U.S. law. It is also not permissible to digitize the set as a whole, or in any way that reproduces the selection and arrangement of the set or its original elements, or its added elements, without obtaining permission from the copyright holder of the set.

LIBRARIES AS CREATORS
OF ORIGINAL DIGITAL CONTENT

Copyright in original materials produced by librarians, such as websites, databases, and course material for library instruction, is held by the person or entity that creates the work. In the U.S. when such works are produced on the job by library staff, they are generally regarded as "works for hire" and copyright is held by the employer. Section 101 of the law defines "work for hire" as "a work prepared by an employee within the scope of his or her employment. . . ." Section 201(b) establishes that "the employer or other person for whom the work was prepared is considered the author for purposes of this title, and, unless the parties have expressly agreed otherwise in a written instrument signed by them, owns all of the rights comprised in the copyright." Works produced on one's own time are not works for hire, and authorship and initial copyright in them are held by the creator. Faculty members are generally considered the authors and initial copyright holders in original works they create. The question of ownership of intellectual property in the academic environment is under discussion in many institutions at the present time.[35]

The creator of a database holds initial copyright in the database as a whole if its selection and arrangement demonstrate a minimum of creativity or originality, but does not hold copyright in any non-original facts or citations comprising the database. An alphabetically arranged electronic database of all the libraries in Ukraine with address and contact information is probably not copyrightable because it does not exhibit enough originality. But the *Annual Bibliography of Slavic and East European Studies* (*ABSEES*) is copyrighted because considerable intellectual work has gone into the selection and organization of the bibliographic citations. The individual citations are not copyrighted. Thus, copying individual citations is permissible, but reproducing the entire database or significant portions of it is not permitted. The U.S. has not passed database legislation that would extend copyright protection to facts, including bibliographic citations, effectively allowing for facts to be owned by private corporations, but lobbying efforts continue to be made in Congress as part of the larger trend toward privatization of access to information. Library organizations are actively involved in efforts to keep factual information in the public domain by opposing database protection legislation.

CONCLUSION

Because the treatment of copyrighted works originating in Slavic and East European countries in the digital environment is subject to the same provisions of U.S. law as domestic works, it is critical to read U.S. law carefully when undertaking digital initiatives. Given the rapid evolution of the digital networked environment, it is not surprising that a number of issues remain to be resolved in copyright law with respect to creation and use of electronic materials. Distribution of digital preservation copies, digital interlibrary loan, and electronic reserves are among the areas seeking clear resolution. We see from this discussion that the U.S. copyright law continues to evolve to meet the needs of libraries and educational institutions in handling digital material. By becoming familiar with the law, and by actively exercising exemptions designed to protect research, educational, and other uses of copyrighted works, libraries can play a part in steering copyright from a collision with the economics of information, and keeping copyright on course in manifesting the dual aims of fairness in protecting intellectual and artistic creations and promotion of social and cultural advancement internationally.

NOTES

1. Efforts to establish an intellectual property regime to protect copyrighted works globally, within the larger goal of market expansion and tighter control in the area of intellectual property, were advanced in the 1980s by the U.S. during the Uruguay Round of GATT from 1986-1994. These negotiations resulted in 1995 in the establishment at the same time of the WTO and the TRIPS Agreement, which aims at strict enforcement of copyright law globally. In 1996, the U.S. signed the WIPO Copyright Treaty which extended principles of the Berne Convention to adapt copyright to the digital age. It established protection for computer programs and databases, and introduced concepts dealing with digital technology. It also required member states to protect against circumvention of encryption technologies for copyrighted works and against interference with digital rights management systems. This treaty led to the DMCA of 1998. Its rigorous compliance measures are widely considered to threaten basic copyright limitations such as first sale, fair use, lending, preservation, and archiving in a very concrete way. In 1996, the U.S. also signed the WIPO Phonograms and Performances Treaty, which protects the rights of performers, phonogram producers, radio and television broadcasting and cable organizations under the sphere of neighboring rights in the digital environment. This treaty was also implemented in the DMCA. And in October 1998, Congress passed the Sonny Bono Copyright Term Extension Act, which extended the term of protection for copyrighted works for an additional twenty years, and whose constitutionality was upheld in the 2003 Supreme Court decision in *Eldred v. Ashcroft*. It is widely considered to inhibit the republication and dissemination of older works that have no commercial value but are of strong interest to the scholarly community and to the public good. The current stigma attached to music downloading is a social and psychological barrier to use of copyrighted material by young people. Notwithstanding the illegality of some types of copying, there are some basic permitted uses of music that are being denied in the drive to wipe out piracy.

2. In the 1990s, financial terminology penetrated the sphere of intellectual property. Intellectual property was once seen as a way of protecting intellectual creations; it is increasingly seen as a means for obtaining a favorable return on investments. See Bruce Berman, ed., *Hidden Value: Profiting from the Intellectual Property Economy* (London: Euromoney Institutional Investor, 1999); Kamil Idris, *Intellectual Property: A Power Tool for Economic Growth* (Geneva: World Intellectual Property Organization, 2002; and Ralph Oman, *Copyright: Engine of Development: An Analysis of the Role of Copyright in Economic Development and Cultural Vitality* (Paris: UNESCO Publishing, 1998). There are efforts to counteract this trend by making scholarly and creative works available electronically for broader use, through open source software models and open licensing approaches. Among the noteworthy efforts in this direction are: Scholarly Publishing and Academic Resources Coalition (SPARC), <http://www.arl.org/sparc> (accessed September 1, 2004), Create Change, <http://www.createchange.org/home.html> (accessed September 1, 2004), and Creative Commons, <http://www.creativecommons.org> (accessed September 1, 2004). A thorough discussion of current efforts to build an information commons based on open, democratic, and noncommercial access to information can be found in Nancy Kranich, *The Information Commons: A Public Policy Report* (New York: Brennan Center for Justice, 2004), also available online at <http://www.brennancenter.org> (accessed September 1, 2004).

3. In 1980, Congress amended Section 102 of the U.S. Copyright Act to include computer software under the category of literary works. This set the stage for develop-

ment of copyright law to adapt to new technology and communications media in an information-oriented society. The priority of the Clinton administration in the 1990s for creation of a National Information Infrastructure, as outlined in the Report of the Working Group on Intellectual Property Rights, also known as the NII White Paper, and resulting in the NII Copyright Protection Act of 1995, created a policy platform for the global information society. See Information Infrastructure Task Force, *Intellectual Property and the National Information Infrastructure: The Report of the Working Group on Intellectual Property Rights* (Washington, D.C.: U.S. Patent and Trademark Office, 1995), <http://www.uspto.gov/web/offices/com/doc/ipnii> (accessed September 1, 2004).

4. Committee on Intellectual Property Rights and the Emerging Information Infrastructure, *The Digital Dilemma: Intellectual Property in the Information Age* (Washington, D.C.: National Academy Press, 2000), 23.

5. Gretchen McCord Hoffman, *Copyright in Cyberspace* (New York: Neal-Schuman Publishers, 2001), 75.

6. Karim Benyekhlef, and Fabien Gélinas, "International Experience in Regard to Procedures for Settling Conflicts Relating to Copyright in the Digital Environment," *Copyright Bulletin* 35, no. 4 (2001): 7-9. See also Egbert J. Dommering, "Copyright Being Washed Away through the Electronic Sieve: Some Thoughts on the Impending Copyright Crisis," in *The Future of Copyright in a Digital Environment: Proceedings of the Royal Academy Colloquium (Amsterdam, 6-7 July 1995)*, ed. P. Bernt Hugenholtz, 1-11 (The Hague: Kluwer Law International, 1996); Paul Edward Geller, "Conflicts of Law in Cyberspace: International Copyright in a Digitally Networked World," in *The Future of Copyright in a Digital Environment*, 27-48; and P. Bernt Hugenholtz, "Adapting Copyright to the Information Superhighway," in *The Future of Copyright in a Digital Environment*, 81-102.

7. Practical approaches to copyright, with emphasis on how to determine whether a foreign work is copyrighted in the U.S., are discussed in detail in Janice T. Pilch, "Understanding Copyright Law for Slavic, East European, and Eurasian Materials," *Slavic and East European Information Resources* 4, no. 1 (2003): 75-101; and Janice T. Pilch, "International Copyright for Digital Collections of Russian Material: U.S. and U.K Law and Practice," *Solanus: International Journal for Russian & East European Bibliographic, Library & Publishing Studies* 17 (2003): 24-49. A three-part series of articles by this author on the principal features of the copyright laws of the CIS nations that bear on copyright determinations in the U.S. is in progress in *Slavic and East European Information Resources*, beginning with "Current Copyright Legislation of the CIS Nations and Its Relevance for U.S. Library Collections: The Laws of Russia, Ukraine, Belarus, and Moldova," *Slavic and East European Information Resources* 5, no. 1-2 (2004): 81-122; followed by "Current Copyright Legislation of the CIS Nations and Its Relevance for U.S. Library Collections: The Laws of Armenia, Azerbaijan, and Georgia," *Slavic and East European Information Resources* 6, no. 1 (forthcoming). This will be followed by a treatment of the laws of the Central Asian nations.

8. The law is available online on the website of the U.S Copyright Office at <http://www.copyright.gov/title17> (accessed September 1, 2004).

9. Section 507(b) of the statute is well known to give rise to different interpretations. It states, "No civil action shall be maintained under the provisions of this title unless it is commenced within three years after the claim accrues." Some courts hold that a copyright infringement claim accrues when the infringement occurs, and others maintain that an infringement claim accrues when the copyright holder knows or has

reason to know of the infringement. See Bart A. Starr, "Fixing Copyright's Three-Year Limitations Clock: The Accrual of an Infringement Claim under 17 U.S.C. §507(B)," *Washington University Law Quarterly* 78, no. 2 (Summer 2000): 623-43.

10. Two helpful charts summarizing U.S. copyright terms have been produced by Laura N. Gasaway, at <http://www.unc.edu/~unclng/public-d.htm> (accessed September 1, 2004), and Peter B. Hirtle, at <http://www.copyright.cornell.edu/training/Hirtle_Public_Domain.htm> (accessed September 1, 2004).

11. A current list of membership in WIPO conventions and treaties is available on the WIPO website, <http://www.wipo.int/treaties/en/ip/index.html> (accessed September 1, 2004).

12. Professor Peter Maggs of the University of Illinois at Urbana-Champaign concluded in 1991 that whether or not the former Soviet republics emerged from the dissolution of the USSR as a successor state under international law, or as sovereign states, they would be bound to the intellectual property treaties to which the USSR was a party. He cites Article 34 of the *Vienna Convention on Succession of States in Respect of Treaties*, which states that "[w]hen part or parts of the territory of a State separate to form one or more States, whether or not the predecessor State continues to exist: (a) any treaty in force at the date of succession of States in respect of the entire territory of the predecessor State continues in force in respect of each successor State so formed." Peter B. Maggs, "Post-Soviet Law: The Case of Intellectual Property Law," *The Harriman Institute Forum* 5, no. 3 (November 1991): 6-7. See also the *Vienna Convention on Succession of States in Respect of Treaties*, <http://www.un.org/law/ilc/texts/treasucc.htm> (accessed September 1, 2004).

13. Pilch, "Understanding Copyright," and "International Copyright."

14. 17 U.S.C. §104A.

15. Peter B. Maggs, "Mutual Restoration of Russian and United States Copyright," *Parker School Journal of East European Law* 3, no. 1 (1996): 305-24.

16. Registration is not mandatory for a work to be copyrighted, but it is a prerequisite for filing an infringement suit. One can sue for infringement or claim statutory damages in an infringement suit only if the work is registered.

17. *Digital Dilemma*, 118.

18. Bruce P. Keller and Jeffrey P. Cunard, "Copyright in the Digital Age," chap. 14 in *Copyright Law: A Practitioner's Guide*, Patents, Copyrights, Trademarks, and Literary Property Course Handbook Series (New York: Practising Law Institute, 2003), 308-9.

19. There is still no public performance right for analog sound recordings in the copyright law, with the effect that when recordings are broadcast on the radio, the copyright holder in the song receives a royalty, but the copyright holder of the sound recording does not. See David Nimmer, "Ignoring the Public, Part I: On the Absurd Complexity of the Digital Audio Transmission Right," *UCLA Entertainment Law Review* 7, no. 2 (Spring 2000): 189-265; and Matt Jackson, "From Broadcast to Webcast: Copyright Law and Streaming Media," *Texas Intellectual Property Law Journal* 11, no. 3 (Spring 2003): 447-82.

20. Keller and Cunard, "Copyright in the Digital Age," 312-13.

21. An extensive treatment of copyright exemptions for libraries and archives is found in Chapters 2-4 of Carrie Russell, *Complete Copyright: An Everyday Guide for*

Librarians (Washington, D.C.: Office for Information Technology Policy, American Library Association, 2004).

22. Eric Tjong Tjin Tai, "Exhaustion and Online Delivery of Digital Works," *European Intellectual Property Review* 25, no. 5 (May 2003): 207-11.

23. For an excellent practical treatment of copyright for performance and display in and outside of libraries and educational institutions, see Russell, *Complete Copyright*, 46-61. See also the report, prepared by Kenneth D. Crews, on "New Copyright Law for Distance Education: The Meaning and Importance of the TEACH Act," <http://www. ala.org/ala/washoff/WOissues/copyrightb/distanceed/distanceeducation.htm#newc> (accessed September 1, 2004).

24. Hoffman, *Copyright in Cyberspace*, 74; Keller and Cunard, "Copyright in the Digital Age," 302-305.

25. Ignacio Javier Garrote, "Linking and Framing: A Comparative Law Approach," *European Intellectual Property Review* 24, no. 4 (April 2002): 187-89.

26. Hoffman, *Copyright in Cyberspace*, 47-48, 65-67; Keller and Cunard, "Copyright in the Digital Age," 321-23; Garrote, "Linking and Framing," 194-95.

27. Keller and Cunard, "Copyright in the Digital Age," 316-18; Hoffman, *Copyright in Cyberspace*, 46-47.

28. Mary Minow, "Library Digitization Projects and Copyright," <http://www.llrx. com/features/digitization.htm> (accessed September 1, 2004).

29. "CONTU Guidelines on Photocopying Under Interlibrary Loan Arrangement," in *Final Report of the National Commission on New Technological Uses of Copyrighted Works, July 31, 1978* (Washington, D.C.: Library of Congress, 1979), 54-55. The text of the CONTU guidelines is available on the website of the Coalition for Networked Information, <http://www.cni.org/docs/infopols/CONTU.html> (accessed September 1, 2004).

30. The "Fair Use Guidelines for Electronic Reserve Systems" were among many draft proposals on library copyright that failed to reach consensus during the conference. They are available online at <http://www.utsystem.edu/ogc/intellectualproperty/ rsrvguid.htm> (accessed September 1, 2004). For a history of CONFU, see Bruce A. Lehman, *The Conference on Fair Use: Final Report to the Commissioner on the Conclusion of the Conference on Fair Use* (Washington, D.C.: U.S. Patent and Trademark Office, 1998), also available online at <http://www.uspto.gov/web/offices/dcom/olia/ confu/confurep.pdf> (accessed September 1, 2004).

31. Originally published as Mary Hutchings, *Model Policy Concerning College and University Photocopying for Classroom, Research and Library Reserve Use* (Washington, D.C.: American Library Association, 1982), the policy is available on the website of the Coalition for Networked Information, <http://www.cni.org/docs/infopols/ ALA.html> (accessed September 1, 2004).

32. "Agreement on Guidelines for Classroom Copying in Not-For-Profit Educational Institutions With Respect to Books and Periodicals," in House Committee on the Judiciary, *House Committee Report on the 1976 Copyright Bill*, House Report No. 94-1476 to accompany S. 22, 94th Cong., 2d Sess., September 3, 1976, 65-74. It is available on several websites, including that of the Music Library Association, <http:// www.musiclibraryassoc.org/Copyright/guidebks.htm> (accessed September 1, 2004).

33. The statement may be found on several websites, including those of the American Library Association, Washington Office, <http://www.ala.org/ala/washoff/WOissues/

copyrightb/fairuseandelectronicreserves/ereservesFU.htm> (accessed September 1, 2004), and the Association of Research Libraries, <http://www.arl.org/access/eres/eresfinalstmt.shtml> (accessed September 1, 2004).

34. The "Fair Use Guidelines for Educational Multimedia" are available in Lehman, *The Conference on Fair Use*, 49-59, and online at <http://www.utsystem.edu/ogc/intellectualproperty/ccmcguid.htm> (accessed September 1, 2004).

35. Ann Monotti and Sam Ricketson, *Universities and Intellectual Property: Ownership and Exploitation* (Oxford: Oxford University Press, 2003), 97-140.

Organizing Interpretive Text
for a Digital Library:
How User Testing Found the Lost Frontier

Sandra J. Bostian

SUMMARY. This paper looks at exercises done with user focus groups and how they have influenced the reorganization of *Meeting of Frontiers'* interpretive text content. *Meeting of Frontiers* is an international collaborative digital library project at the Library of Congress. Testing consisted of a user survey and card sorting exercises in order to refine the site hierarchy and identify problems with design proposals.

KEYWORDS. Card sorting, focus groups, usability, digital library, information architecture, Library of Congress, *Meeting of Frontiers*

One of the challenges currently facing the *Meeting of Frontiers* (MoF) collaborative digital library project is how to organize large quantities of interpretive text to best serve the user and also allow room for future growth. The *Meeting of Frontiers* production team has conducted two rounds of focus group exercises with American and Russian teachers (K-12) in an effort to answer this question and develop a new

Sandra J. Bostian, MA, is Digital Conversion Specialist, Library of Congress, Washington, DC 20540-4800 USA (E-mail: sbos@loc.gov).

The views and opinions expressed herein do not necessarily state or reflect those of the Library of Congress, United States Government, or any agency thereof.

[Haworth co-indexing entry note]: "Organizing Interpretive Text for a Digital Library: How User Testing Found the Lost Frontier." Bostian, Sandra J. Co-published simultaneously in *Slavic & East European Information Resources* (The Haworth Information Press, an imprint of The Haworth Press, Inc.) Vol. 6, No. 2/3, 2005, pp. 117-133; and: *Virtual Slavica: Digital Libraries, Digital Archives* (ed: Michael Neubert) The Haworth Information Press, an imprint of The Haworth Press, Inc., 2005, pp. 117-133.

Available online at http://www.haworthpress.com/web/SEEIR
doi:10.1300/J167v06n02_08

framework for the site, sometimes with surprising results (at least for the MoF team). This paper concentrates on the testing of the content structure and how that is shaping the long-term organization of the site's interpretive text.

The Library of Congress (LC) presents primary source historical materials via its *American Memory* and *Global Gateway* digital library sites. *Global Gateway* is a newer effort that includes collaborative bilingual digital library projects with foreign and U.S. partners. The "flagship" is the *Meeting of Frontiers* site <http://frontiers.loc.gov> that, as of September 2004, includes more than 580,000 digital items and over 15,000 library items. The site consists of 83 collections from 20 institutions in the United States, Russia, and Germany.[1] MoF "is a bilingual, multimedia English-Russian digital library that tells the story of the American exploration and settlement of the West, the parallel exploration and settlement of Siberia and the Russian Far East, and the meeting of the Russian-American frontier in Alaska and the Pacific Northwest."[2]

Global Gateway collaborative projects differ from *American Memory* in that there are two core content areas: the collections (presentation of digitized items) and the interpretive text. The inclusion of a significant amount of interpretive text material is more consistent with LC's exhibit approach.[3] The narrative provides historical background for the digitized materials and also presents another point of entry into the collections.

Currently, over 200 pages of static html text are organized into six categories: Exploration, Colonization, Development, Alaska, National Identity, and Mutual Perceptions.[4] The site focuses on the Siberian and American West parallels in the non-geographic categories (Exploration, Colonization, Development, National Identity, and Mutual Perceptions). The Alaska section uses the same themes found in the general categories but restricts interpretive text and digitized content to the Alaska geographic region. This, in effect, creates a geographic approach for one area and a thematic approach for the other two.

This architecture dates to the original pilot site of 1999. It fit well with the materials at that time, but the MoF team has noted increasing problems appropriately placing new materials within the pilot structure. The quantity of digital items and associated interpretive text has far outgrown what was originally anticipated during the start-up period. The team is now considering ways of reorganizing the static text content to improve site functionality, particularly for educational users, while also allowing for future growth.

Within each thematic category, pages fall into two types: module and gallery. Module pages introduce topics and usually have three examples of digitized items.[5] Gallery pages are subtopics in the site hierarchy and provide more specific information within a narrower scope. They most often take the form of short text followed by three to nine digitized items, each with a short explanation of that item's significance, but can also be illustrative maps, timelines, or "for more items" link lists.[6]

The first round of testing occurred in Nome, Alaska in 2003 at the Beringia: Bridging Knowledge summer institute. The program, sponsored by the Alaska Geographic Alliance and the US National Park Service, was for Russian and Alaskan history, geography, and social studies teachers. The participant group consisted of eighteen educators, eight from Alaska and ten from Russia, and three institute coordinators. Due to time constraints, limited Internet access in Nome, and the bilingual nature of the participant group, it was decided to use a user survey approach rather than traditional one-on-one usability testing.

Two sets of exercises were used to examine site structure and hierarchy. In the home page test, they were given a mock-up of a proposed *Meeting of Frontiers* home page (see Figure 1) and asked general questions about what they would expect to find in the top-level categories. Card sorting was used to look at how the participants organized and categorized MoF's module level topics and to compare that to the current site.

HOME PAGE SURVEY

Participants were asked to fill out a bilingual questionnaire based on a mock home page (see Figure 1). They were given a black and white hard copy, and a color version was shown on a large screen at the front of the room. The first question asked participants to look at the home page mock-up and indicate what they thought the site was about and why they thought that (see Table 1; participants who indicated they had previously visited the site are noted with an X).

What is most striking from the answers to the question "What is the site about?" is that most respondents missed the American West component completely. Participants recognized the Russian element because of the main graphic, which shows a map of Alaska and the Russian Far

120

FIGURE 1. Home Page Mock-Up

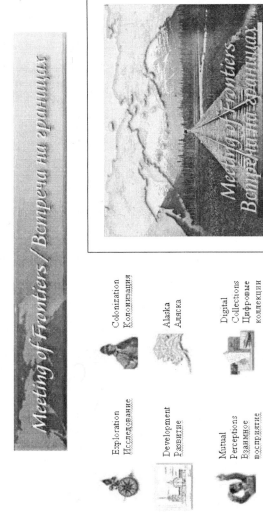

TABLE 1. What Is the Site About? Why Do You Think That?

Visited Site	Response
	No response/Don't Know (2)
	Socio-cultural connections between Alaska & the Russian North.
	About the history of Russia & America. I judge by the contents of the page.
X	Alaska & Russia & the interactions between them.
	About the friendship between the 2 countries of Russia-USA. Because this is very important.
	About the history & interrelationships of bordering territories. Name of the project and its sections.
	The meeting of 2 Western Frontiers. Because of the pictures and topics.
	Meeting of Russia/Alaska. People of the Beringia area.
	Explanation of Russian/Alaskan reunion after years of separation.
	Russian-Alaskan History. Exploration, colonization of geographical area.
X	It's about the history of Alaska & Russia's Far East. The themes on the main page suggest this conclusion.
	Alaska/Russia Frontiers. Pictures/Words
X	Alaska & Russia (Beringia). Because of the map in the background of the picture and the fact that it is written in Russian & English.
X	Historical document of Russian Far East & Alaska primarily–meeting of Russian & Amer Frontiers
	About the socio-cultural connections between the Russian North & American North
X	The similarities & differences of America's westward expansion & Russia's eastward expansion
	Russian-American history. Words like exploration, colonization.
X	Similarities between development/movement between Russia & U.S./Alaska. Westward expansion: U.S., Eastward expansion: Russia
	Perhaps about the various countries, which are separated by borders; independent of where the countries are located. Judging by the title of the site.
	About everything that touches on Beringia and its joint projects. Because of the name of the site & because I found out about it at the conference.

East, and the use of Russian language. They also recognized the Alaska focus from the main graphic and the "Alaska" category heading and icon. The American West focus is not specifically mentioned in text on the proposed home page and none of the icons visually depicted it. Also of interest is that three of the six respondents who had been to the existing site did not pick up on the American West component. In effect, the American West had become the "lost frontier" with the potential to confuse and frustrate users either looking for American frontier materials or wondering why such things were on a site about Alaska and Russia. The user survey had pointed out a serious problem with the new prototype home page.

This problem was further borne out in questions asking what the participants expected to find in the general top-level categories of Mutual Perceptions, Colonization, Exploration, and Development. The answers overwhelmingly cited Siberia, the Russian Far East, and Alaska, despite a separate section devoted exclusively to Alaska. And again, America's western frontier was nowhere to be found (see Tables 2-5).

The MoF team identified two major areas of concern from these results. The mixing of a very specific geographic category (Alaska) and broad themes (Exploration, Colonization, etc.) at the highest level was not a good combination. The participants clearly expected to find information about Alaska in the broad themes as well as in the Alaska section. The second problem was the lack of cues–either graphical or text–for the American West. This was a major factor to it being overlooked by the respondents.

The question then became what was the best organization to use at the highest level. Was it better to have a geographic-only (Alaska, Siberia, American West) or a thematic-only top level? Arranging the highest level geographically might help alleviate the "lost frontier" problem, while at the same time reinforcing the overall geographic orientation of the site. A downside to this would be that the module level (second tier) for this arrangement would have far too many sections per geographic area, making it potentially difficult for users to find the information they were seeking in a chaotic and lengthy list of topics. A thematic top level also presented the problem of too many topics at the second tier, with the additional problem of overlapping titles. Labeling would have to be very specific and clear (Old Believers in Russia vs. Old Believers in Alaska). Top-level labels would also need to be crafted carefully to ensure the user has a reasonable expectation of success in finding the information he or she is seeking from the home page.

TABLE 2. What Would You Expect to Find in a Section Called "Mutual Perspectives"?

Visited Site	Response
	No response (2)
	Interrelationships of various ethnic groups with native residents of Chukotka and Alaska during colonization and their further development
	General views between the peoples that settle Alaska and the Russian North.
	History and Description of contacts between native populations and newly arrived people. Also about the culture of ethnic groups.
X	What are the cultural perceptions of Alaskans of Russians and vice versa?
	Photographs of meetings, emotions, happiness between 2 continents
	Relations between residents of border territories
	What Russians & Americans thought/think about each other
	Things/Thinking in common.
	How each Native group (Alaskan & Natives of Russia) see or feel about topics. I would bet that a lot of the same ideals are shared.
	No clue—I'd open it to figure that out
X	Information on how people in Alaska view/think of/treat people of Russian Far East & vice versa.
	Perceptions/Ideas shared by both Russians & Alaskans
X	Perceptions on Beringia from both the Alaskan and the Russian point of view
	Tolerance of ethnic groups
X	Past/present views/perspectives on region
	About the interrelationships of people
X	Similarities (patterns) of expansion (colonization)
	Rus Amer cultural bias
X	Things that both cultures/sides regard to be important

TABLE 3. What Would You Expect to Find in a "Colonization" Section?

Visited Site	Response
	No response (1)
	The development of Chukotka and Alaska by various nationalities
	A story about how the colonization of Alaska happened
	The history of development and culture
	Information about the colonization of America and Siberia by Russians and Americans
X	How Alaska and Russia were colonized
	The history of colonization of Alaska by the Russians; the history of the colonization of Alaska by Americans after the sale
	The history of the settlement (seizure) of territory
	Info about how each area was settled
	How Russia colonized Alaska
	The gathering of people and/or animals into a confined environment
	Colonization history in both Siberia/Alaska
X	Facts on colonization processes in Alaska & Siberia
	Patterns of settlement, migration
X	Information on the colonization of both Alaska & Russia
	The state language and the national languages (daily life, folklore, ethnography, etc.)
X	Russia in the Far East; Amer./Rus. in Alaska; how colonization occurred; information base on econ, settle, people (diaries, reports)
	The history of the exploration and development of the territories in the area of forced colonization (conquest)
X	People/events
X	Material pertaining to both Russian & American movement to & habitation of Alaska (post-indigenous occupation)
	History of European powers

TABLE 4. What Would You Expect to Find in an "Exploration" Section?

Visited Site	Response
	Exploration of some sort of excavations [trans. note–archaeological]
	Scientific exploration of Alaska and Chukotka, geographic, economic, etc.
	Some kind of explorations which are being conducted?
	Scientific exploration of all branches and developments of ethnic, geographic, economic activities
	Historical materials about expeditions and explorers
X	Russian exploration of Alaska
	Searches, finds, exploration of the ethnic groups of the 2 northern continents
	Information about explorers and discoverers
	Discoveries, naming of areas, timelines
	How Alaska was explored and by whom
	Early historical data and pictures of Russia & Alaska
	Exploration of Siberia, Alaska, as a geographical region
X	The History of exploration; names of the famous explorers, their biographies; interactive maps with routes & historical places shown
	Exploration in terms of geography, technology, economy, etc.
X	Exploration of both countries as well as info on exploration of Beringia
	Information about research on various aspects of the life of ethnic groups, their places of residence; about the people who are conducting this or other research; about the reasons which compelled them to take up the given issues
X	Framework <u>maps</u> & charts to facilitate detailed info & reports
	Scientific and public materials about the explorations of the territories
X	People
X	Expansion of west
	Pre-colonization–maybe not–even current exploration of either side by scientists, "prospectors" (i.e., mineral extractors such as oil companies), tourism operators (looking for new destinations)

TABLE 5. What Would You Expect to Find in a "Development" Section?

Visited Site	Response
	How this or that country developed in various spheres
	Further development of interrelationships of Chukotkans and Alaskans, of Russia and America in all spheres of activities
	How the development of relations (native populations of Alaska and newer arrivals) occurred.
	Development of international relations
	About the development of cities and industry of seized territories
X	Economic development documents
	The settling of Alaska and development of ethnic groups and development of this site
	History of the use of the territory
	How we have progressed to develop our economies and cultures
	The development of the Beringia area; how it was influenced
	How people evolved with/were affected by outside influence
	Transportation, economics, infrastructure of each area; how areas are, will be tied together
X	Economic development, dynamics, figures, graphs; social development, ethnic groups, religion; land usage, resources (natural); hunting, fishing, housekeeping
	Development of a culture; economy, education, infrastructure, etc.
X	New sections under development that you need more information; development on both sides of Beringia
	How an ethnic group adapted to this or that circumstances? Stages or process of adaptation. This relates to economics, and culture and other aspects.
X	Natural resources development; transportation/communications; settlement and population development; impacts on area: human, environment; overview tables and maps for context
	Modern development of the economy, culture, education, health care, etc.
X	Cities/villages, infrastructure
X	Work in progress
	Growth of population centers, addition of amenities (sewer systems, water, etc.); industrialization, mass (or increased) transportation/access

CARD SORTING EXERCISES

The card sorting exercises looked at how users organized and categorized the site's module-level topics. Participants broke into five teams of three to five, and were asked to group forty cards into no more than six categories. The cards contained the current MoF module themes in both English and Russian. They were then asked to clip each group of cards to a blank sheet and write a category title on it.

Teams 1, 2, and 4 (see Table 6) had a strong geographic focus in how they organized the modules. Team 3 chose a mixed geographic and thematic approach and Team 5 picked a thematic approach. This led the MoF team to consider strongly using geographic categories at the top level.

An advantage to this approach is that a geographic focus on the home page is a very exact categorization. It presents the user with a clear choice of where to go to find information– Alaska, Siberia, or the American West. However, because of the large quantity of topics, the MoF team also began to consider whether it was better to move from a three-level hierarchy:

1. category
2. module
3. gallery

to a four-level version:

1. geographic
2. broad theme
3. module
4. gallery

or

1. broad theme
2. geographic
3. module
4. gallery

Both of these approaches would help keep the second tier uncluttered but would add a click to the process. The MoF team eventually decided that the 4-tier approach with a geographic top level (see Table 7) had a

TABLE 6. Card Sorting Results

Current Site Exploration Colonization Development Alaska National Identity Mutual Perceptions	Team 1 (3 Americans) Siberian Influences Russian Influences Eastern/Western Influences Alaskan Connection Inevitable Consequences	Team 2 (1 Amer., 2 Russians) Alaska–Before the Sale Alaska–After the Sale Western History Siberian History Other

Team 3 (1 Amer.,
   3 Russians)
Alaska History
Industries
Missionaries
Russian America
Explorers & Tourism
Migration
Culture
Russian North/Colonization
   of Siberia
	Team 4 (1 Amer., 2 Russians)
	Siberian History
	American West
	Alaska History
	Historical Facts
		Team 5 (1 Amer., 4 Russians)
		Exploration & Settlement
		Popular Culture
		Economics
		Travel, Transportation &
		   Tourism
		Religion
		None of the Above

number of advantages. The same broad themes could be reiterated in each geographic division, reinforcing the parallel aspect of the site. It would also make for easy cross-linking between geographic divisions with some sort of "see also" links (i.e., if the user is in the Exploration theme of the American West, there could also be links to Alaskan Exploration and Siberian Exploration). Expansion is also easier to implement at a secondary level. Themes can be added at that level without sacrificing specificity or cluttering the home page. *Meeting of Frontiers* has over 200 core content pages and sustainability of the hierarchy needs to be considered in light of anticipated growth.

In the 2004 Summer Institute in Anchorage, Alaska, the MoF team conducted another round of card sorting to determine better what broad themes users might give to the materials on *Meeting of Frontiers*. Participants were given 322 cards, each an existing or proposed module or gallery topic for the site. They were divided into their appropriate top-level categories (96 for Alaska, 118 for Siberia, and 108 for the American West), with each area constituting a separate exercise (see Tables 8-10). The participants were divided into three groups containing both Russians and Americans and asked to arrange the cards into groups and then attach a piece of paper with a title to each group. The

TABLE 7. Proposed Meeting of Frontiers Hierarchy

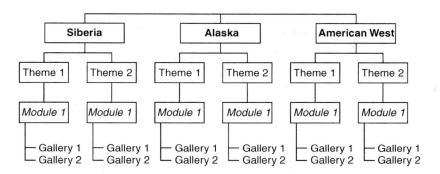

idea for the MoF team was to see if there were common themes chosen and, if not, what kinds of groupings were participants using. For purposes of trying to see trends and commonalities, the themes common to each team are lined up across the results. The final group of categories in each table are things that didn't seem to go together, each group's "other" category to a certain extent.

Although there was sometimes considerable variation in how things were organized, clear themes did seem to emerge from results within geographic areas and also across geographic areas. The common themes were:

- Cities & Towns;
- Exploration;
- Native Groups;
- Religion;
- Transportation;
- War & Conflict;
- Economic Development;
- Recreation & Tourism; and
- Popular Culture & Entertainment.

Part of the reason for the variations may be problems with labeling that is either too general or not reflective of the page's content. One example of this is "Malaspina," a proposed topic for the future. Most of the Alaskans assumed this referred to the Malaspina Glacier, a famous glacier in

TABLE 8. American West Card Sorting Exercise

Team 1	Team 2	Team 3
The 11 Largest Trans-Mississippi Cities, 1900	The 11 Largest Trans-Mississippi Cities, 1900	Largest Cities c. 1900
Exploration	Exploration	Exploration
Native American Studies	Native Americans	Native Americans: nations, conflicts
Religion	Missionary Activity	Religion, Missions, etc.
Transportation	American Transcontinental and Pacific Transportation	Transportation
Recreation & Entertainment	Entertainment Frontier Tourism	Entertainment Tourism Fiction
Army & War Dept.	U.S. Army in the West	
Mining & Industries	Business Opportunities	Mining Industry? Agriculture Fur
Settlement	Westward Expansion	
Immigration (?)		Laws, Exclusions and Background Info
Biographies	Mapping the West	Oregon Problem

Alaska. In fact, the MoF team had anticipated this topic to be about the Spanish explorer Malaspina's travels in the Pacific Northwest. Taken out of context, as it might be in a search engine result list, such labeling could be misleading. As part of the reorganization of content, the MoF team needs to pay particular attention to how pages are titled, making

TABLE 9. Alaska Card Sorting Exercises

Team 1	Team 2	Team 3
Native Groups	Native Groups	[Native Groups]*
Transportation	Transportation	[Transportation]*
Towns	"American" Towns "Russian" Towns	[Towns]*
Religions & Religious Groups & Their Material Culture	Religion	Russian Orthodoxy American Missionaries
Russian Exploration Exploration by the Spanish	Exploration & Settlement	
Economic Development	Industries	
Russian Colonization & U.S. Purchase	Russian-American Relations	The Alaska Purchase Transaction
World War II and Beyond		Wars
Popularizers (people and things that made AK part of imagination)	Literature	Alaska in American Popular Culture Newspaper Coverage Tourism Popular Literature
Gold Rush	Physical Features Alaska Today Biographies	

*Category was not titled but contents were analogous to those under the title in brackets

sure that the labels both fit into the whole and are able to stand on their own in isolation. Another point of interest in labeling is that all three participant teams used more region-specific terms for the "native groups" topic:

- some form of Native Americans for the American West;
- Native Groups for Alaska; and
- Nationalities/National Minorities for Siberia.

TABLE 10. Siberia Card Sorting Exercises

Team 1	Team 2	Team 3
Towns and Areas	Towns	Postcards of Siberia
Exile	Siberian Exile	Forced Tourism
Nationalities	Nationalities	National Minorities
Roads and Transportation Water Transportation	Transportation	Transportation Steamships
Expeditions Siberian Expeditions	Exploration & Expeditions	Expeditions
Religions Old Believers' Towns	Religion	Religion
Economy and Daily Life	Minerals & Industry	Resources
Russo-Japanese War Civil War	War & Conflict	Russo-Japanese War Civil War
Tourism and Photos by Visitors	Daily Life & Tourism	Private Travelers: 1760-1790
Jeannette Wreck	The Jeannette	
Timelines	The Cheliuskin Biographies	Cossacks Mapping of Siberia

This does point to the need at least to take into consideration regional variation in labeling, particularly in topics where cultural sensitivity is an issue.

Another reason for the variations is that there are some topics that are specific to a particular region. The sale of Alaska section does not have a counterpart in Siberia or the American West, at least within the scope of the site. The topic of exile has a much more specific meaning within the Siberia region and does not have as strong a parallel in Alaska and the American West. The MoF team feels the lack of parallel is not necessarily a reason to disqualify a topic from inclusion as one of the second tier themes. However, such inclusion should be examined closely in order to preserve clarity for the information seeker.

A good follow-up to this exercise might be a card sorting exercise that gives participants the main themes along with an "other" category and asks them to place the module and gallery topics with their appropriate theme. The MoF team could use this as both a test of new labels and conceptual organization.

The restructuring process for Meeting of Frontiers is still ongoing but the end product will be far better for the involvement of user focus groups. They have proven to be an integral part of site development, catching problems large and small. The results of surveys and card sorting exercises have also pointed out alternative paths of development not originally considered by the MoF team. With this feedback and guidance, we expect to restructure the hierarchy of the interpretive text on *Meeting of Frontiers* in a more usable and user-friendly way.

NOTES

1. "Digital Collections," *Meeting of Frontiers* <http://frontiers.loc.gov/intldl/mtfhtml/mfdigcol/mfdigcol.html> (accessed September 30, 2004) and "Partners," *Meeting of Frontiers* <http://frontiers.loc.gov/intldl/mtfhtml/mfprtnrs/mfprtnrs.html> (accessed September 30, 2004).

2. *Meeting of Frontiers* <http://frontiers.loc.gov> (accessed September 30, 2004).

3. "About the Site," *Meeting of Frontiers* <http://frontiers.loc.gov/intldl/mtfhtml/mfabout/mfabout.html> (accessed September 30, 2004). It states, among other things, that the "design of the site combines elements of two approaches used by the Library of Congress in presenting educational material in electronic form: the collections-based approach of the National Digital Library's *American Memory* [<http://memory.loc.gov>] program, and the method of integrating items from many collections to tell a single story that is used in *Exhibitions: An Online Gallery* [<http://www.loc.gov/exhibits/>]."

4. "America, Russia and the Meeting of Frontiers," *Meeting of Frontiers* <http://frontiers.loc.gov/intldl/mtfhtml/mfovrvw.html> (accessed September 30, 2004).

5. An example would be "Religious Flight and Migration: Old Believers," *Meeting of Frontiers* <http://frontiers.loc.gov/intldl/mtfhtml/mfcolony/col_OldBel.html> (accessed September 30, 2004).

6. Examples would be "Old Believers in the Altai," *Meeting of Frontiers* <http://frontiers.loc.gov/intldl/mtfhtml/mfcolony/gal_altai.html> (accessed September 30, 2004); illustrative map–"Map of Migration Routes, 1804-60," *Meeting of Frontiers* <http://frontiers.loc.gov/intldl/mtfhtml/mfcolony/mpmigration.html> (accessed September 30, 2004); timeline–"Timeline for the Russian Discovery of Siberia," *Meeting of Frontiers* <http://frontiers.loc.gov/intldl/mtfhtml/mfdiscvry/igddiscsibtl.html> (accessed September 30, 2004); and "for more items" lists–"California Missions," *Meeting of Frontiers* <http://frontiers.loc.gov/intldl/mtfhtml/mfcolony/fmiccal.html> (accessed September 30, 2004).

Making the Cyrillic OPAC a Reality

Jane W. Jacobs
Malabika Das

SUMMARY. The steps leading to the development of a Cyrillic OPAC at Queens Borough Public Library are presented by the authors. Issues covered include Cyrillic character display, font requirements, searching strategies, web browser interface development, authority and subject control, promotion, and publicity. The importance of librarian and customer involvement and training are discussed. *[Article copies available for a fee from The Haworth Document Delivery Service: 1-800-HAWORTH. E-mail address: <docdelivery@haworthpress.com> Website: <http://www.HaworthPress.com> © 2005 by The Haworth Press, Inc. All rights reserved.]*

Jane W. Jacobs, MLS, is Assistant Coordinator, Catalog Division, Queens Borough Public Library (E-mail: Jane.W.Jacobs@queenslibrary.org).

Malabika Das, MLIS, is Supervisor of Online Services, Information Technology and Systems, Queens Borough Public Library (E-mail: Malabika.Das@queenslibrary.org).

Address correspondence to: Queens Borough Public Library, 89-11 Merrick Boulevard, Jamaica, NY 11432 USA.

Special thanks to Slavic experts Elizabeth Ankersen, Galina Pershman, Olga Davydova, Galina Meyerovich, Olha Buchel, and members of *SLAVLIBS*; technical experts Fred Fishel and Sharon Small; Cyril programmer Ed Summers; project champions Stuart Rosenthal, Carol Sheffer, and members of the Queens Library, Catalog Division and Information Technology & Systems, who make it all work.

[Haworth co-indexing entry note]: "Making the Cyrillic OPAC a Reality." Jacobs, Jane W., and Malabika Das. Co-published simultaneously in *Slavic & East European Information Resources* (The Haworth Information Press, an imprint of The Haworth Press, Inc.) Vol. 6, No. 2/3, 2005, pp. 135-149; and: *Virtual Slavica: Digital Libraries, Digital Archives* (ed: Michael Neubert) The Haworth Information Press, an imprint of The Haworth Press, Inc., 2005, pp. 135-149. Single or multiple copies of this article are available for a fee from The Haworth Document Delivery Service [1-800-HAWORTH, 9:00 a.m. - 5:00 p.m. (EST). E-mail address: docdelivery@haworthpress.com].

Available online at http://www.haworthpress.com/web/SEEIR
© 2005 by The Haworth Press, Inc. All rights reserved.
doi:10.1300/J167v06n02_09

KEYWORDS. Cyrillic, Russian, library catalog, OPAC, encoding
.   scheme, vernacular display, character maps, native language fonts, web
browser interface development, authority records, subject control,
MARC, keyboard input methods, Unicode, translation, transliteration,
Queens Borough Public Library, New York, Sirsi

Cyrillic access points alone do not a Cyrillic catalog make. This is obvious to Slavic catalogers, but nonetheless worth considering in some detail. Displaying and retrieving Cyrillic records alone is daunting and providing a true interface and publicizing it can quickly become overwhelming. Online Public Access Catalogs (OPACs) are on international display in ever-increasing numbers and as Integrated Online Library System (IOLS) vendors move to Unicode, overcoming challenges to displaying native language scripts is crucial to providing access to library customers. The authors will highlight important issues in the creation of the Queens Borough Public Library's (Queens Library) Russian language interface and original script catalog.

The authors' direct experience is informed by (and to some extent limited to) the Queens Library's OPAC, *InfoLinQ* <http://web2.queenslibrary.org/>. *InfoLinQ* uses Sirsi Corporation's Web2 OPAC search engine in conjunction with the backend DRA Classic system (also a Sirsi product). DRA Classic uses MARC 21 Specifications <http://www.loc.gov/marc/specifications/spechome.html>, specifically the MARC-8 character sets. The library uses the Dewey Decimal Classification and Library of Congress Subject Headings. Original catalog records are obtained from OCLC, where Cyrillic is not yet implemented.

To say one has a Cyrillic catalog, in and of itself, suggests a loftier goal that few, if any American libraries, have yet reached. A number of Slavic languages besides Russian, notably Ukrainian, Bulgarian, Serbian, Belarusian, and Macedonian, use the Cyrillic alphabet. Cyrillic has also been adopted for writing many non-Slavic languages, such as Bashkir, Chechen, Kazakh, and Uzbek. It is at least theoretically possible, once Cyrillic characters are available, to provide catalog records and an interface in any or all of these languages. Public service demands and priorities will drive that decision. At the Queens Library, while collections and bibliographic records exist in Ukrainian (approx. 1,900), Bulgarian (approx. 79), Serbian (approx. 800), and Belarusian (approx. 80), the clear priority has been providing access in the original script to over 16,000 Russian records in the OPAC.

In 2003, Queens Library's Russian records, which previously existed in transliteration, were translated into Cyrillic using the Cyril program.[1] Thus, the appearance of Cyrillic in the catalog was quick, but not instantaneous. The Cyril program created 880 tags corresponding to selected fields and populated them with "detransliterated" Cyrillic characters. Subsequently more than 1,200 Ukrainian records were similarly converted. In a true Cyrillic catalog Bulgarian, Serbian, and Belarusian would also appear in Cyrillic rather than only in transliteration. However, for practical reasons, the Queens Library interface to be created will essentially be Russian even though the same technical requirements could easily be applied to other Cyrillic languages.

VIEWING CYRILLIC CHARACTER DISPLAY

Proper display requires the correct set-up for any OPAC and web browser. Recent versions of the Windows operating system and Microsoft's Internet Explorer (IE) web browser offer multilingual support and provide the necessary fonts that permit display of Unicode-based character sets. In the Queens Library environment, desktop PCs are set up with the Windows XP operating system, and IE 6.0 is the web browser of choice with the Queens Library's home page <http://www.queenslibrary.org> set as the default home page. Default browser and character encoding settings in IE 6.0 are determined by either HTTP header commands based on the RFC 2616 (HTTP/1.1) standard[2] or by META elements and HTTP-EQUIV attributes. Since the HTTP Header commands are not directly visible to users, the focus here will be on the META HTTP-EQUIV tags which are equivalent to HTTP header commands. META HTTP-EQUIV tags are embedded in the header field of HTML. The character set or *charset* attribute within the META tag will identify the encoding standard to be used to display native script characters in the browser:

```
<META HTTP-EQUIV="Content-Type" content="text/html; charset=ISO-8859-1">
```

A list of official names for character sets may be found at the Internet Assigned Numbers Authority's website <http://www.iana.org/assignments/character-sets>. Web pages that do not use either a charset HTTP header or a charset attribute within the META tag will default to a general encoding setup (i.e., West European), and consequently, web pages with Cyrillic characters may not display correctly. To view IE 6.0

browser settings in action, use the View Menu to go to the Encoding sub-menu. The active encoding scheme in use will be identified with a small bullet next to it. The encoding sub-menu, found within More, also allows one to change to a different encoding scheme (see Figure 1).

Remote users (i.e., those not accessing the OPAC through the Queens Library's network) and non-Windows and non-IE users (i.e., MacOS, Unix or Linux, Netscape or Opera) will need to check their support manuals and/or their browser versions to see if and how international character sets and displays are supported.

FONT SETTINGS

Font settings are an important but troublesome aspect of display. They work in conjunction with, as well as independently from, the browser settings. Fonts can be installed on a user's system and will correctly display native language characters, regardless of the application

FIGURE 1

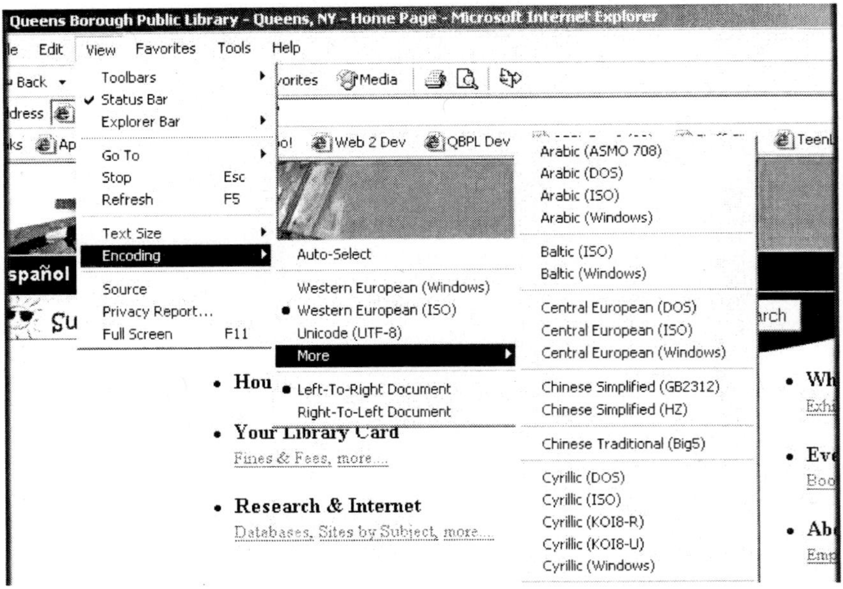

used (e.g., Microsoft Word, Microsoft Excel). Browser settings can only be set using HTTP headers or META HTTP-EQUIV tags. Publishers and printers customarily select fonts from familiar styles to which readers are accustomed and presumably prefer. English-speaking readers are accustomed to something similar to Times New Roman. However, Times New Roman does not provide for a full range of original scripts. The only one-size-fits-all fonts are Code 2000 and Microsoft's Arial Unicode MS. Both produce a legible but not particularly aesthetic display of Cyrillic letters (see Figure 2).

The real problem occurs with ligatures in transliteration rather than Cyrillic. Times New Roman has no ligatures and therefore cannot render either left or right ligature. Arial Unicode MS font incorrectly handles them as non-combining characters. Code 2000, which can be downloaded from *Unicode Support in Your Browser* <http://home.att.net/~jameskass/>, correctly combines the left or right ligature with the appropriate character and produces a correct display (see Figure 3).

The Code 2000 font has not customarily been bundled with Microsoft operating systems. Furthermore, although this font produces an acceptable printout, it is visually unappealing on the screen in IE 6.0. Therefore the most practical choice is to use Arial Unicode MS and hope devoutly for Microsoft to correct the ligatures' positioning.

FIGURE 2

Times New Roman: Железняк, Людмила

Arial Unicode MS: **Железняк, Людмила**

Code 2000:   Железняк, Людмила

FIGURE 3

Times New Roman: Zheleznilalk, Liluldmila

Arial Unicode MS: Zhelezni‾a‾k, Li‾u‾dmila

Code 2000:   Zheleznia͡k, Liu͡dmila

Once the OPAC and the workstation are properly configured, Cyrillic characters need to display at the record level. Users of Queens Library's OPAC will view the default Vernacular Display or they can use a toggle button to switch to the Non-Vernacular Display, which is the romanized record corresponding to any available 880 fields. The Web2 search engine uses a proprietary macro language to perform an IF-THEN test to determine the presence of vernacular characters. A true condition is determined by the presence of either a 066 field (in MARC-8 encoded records) or signaled by $6 in a regular display field such as field 100 or 245 (in Unicode encoded records). The toggle button will appear whenever the condition is true. If all fields that are selected for display are not provided with an 880 tag, a mixed display (combination of Roman and non-Roman) may result.

At the hit list level the situation is more complicated. In practice, a heading-level hit list will almost certainly reflect the search input. A search conducted with a romanized search argument will, in most American catalogs, retrieve a romanized hit list. This is logical, especially for names because, regardless of language, all records will contain roman letters and works in various languages will be collected under a single authorized (romanized) heading. (The implications for authority control of original scripts will be considered later.) For example, a search under "Sholokhov, Mikhail Aleksandrovich, 1905-" (transliterated) will return items in both the original Russian and translations into English, Persian, etc. Conversely a search for Шолохов, Михаил Александрович, 1905-" will return a hit list in Cyrillic that contains only Russian language materials. It will not inform Russian language readers of titles by Sholokhov in English or French, or in Belarusian, Serbian, or other languages.

ENTERING SEARCH ARGUMENTS

Of course any discussion of the search argument Шолохов, Михаил Александрович, 1905-" optimistically assumes an input methodology. For Windows users, several input methods are available, none entirely satisfactory. The best of the lot at present seems to be the onscreen keyboard. If a regional setting for Cyrillic is enabled from the Control Panel, the user can set the Language Bar to Russian. This results in keyboard keystrokes that are interpreted as Russian characters. Invoking the onscreen keyboard will display a keyboard template showing the

Russian character keymaps. Unfortunately this keymap is monolingual. A separate Ukrainian keyboard would have to be invoked in order to produce the Ukrainian umlaut *I*, *Ï* (UCS 0418) or ghe with upturn, *Г* (UCS 0491), since those characters are not used in Russian and hence are not included on the Russian keymap. A variation on this theme is the *Russian Keyboard: standard and phonetic* <http://ourworld.compuserve. com/homepages/PaulGor/kbd_e.htm>. This download works on the same principle as the Microsoft keyboard, but maps the Russian characters according to their corresponding (transliterated) English letters. Hence the Russian letter *К* (transliterated *K*) is located under the right middle finger and the Russian letter transliterated as *Ф* (transliterated *F*) under the left index finger. One drawback is that the Russian hard sign, or *tverdyi znak*, *Ъ* is absent. Overall this approach seems to be quite intuitive to Russian readers in the United States, but it does assume a familiarity with the English QWERTY keyboard.

Another method, reliable but clumsy, is the Character Map. Here the user invokes the Character Map from the Start Menu (Programs → Accessories → System Tools). Where Arial Unicode MS is installed it presents thousands of characters in Unicode sequence. The user selects characters to compose words or phrases that can then be copied and pasted into a search window. A variation on this concept entitled, *Babel Map* <http://uk.geocities.com/BabelStone1357/Software/BabelMap. html>, offers the same style of input with a more elegant front end.

All in all, none of these methods is especially obvious or convenient for the user. To facilitate Cyrillic input, the Queens Library has added a help page entitled: *How Do I Search Using Russian Vernacular (Cyrillic) Characters?* <http://web2.queenslibrary.org/web2/tramp2.exe/ goto/guest?setting_key=English&screen=help/cyrillic_search.html>. It is also available in Russian (*Kak iskat' russkoiazychnye materialy ispol'zuia simvoly kirillitsy?*) <http://web2.queenslibrary.org/web2/tramp2.exe/ goto/guest?setting_key=English&screen=help/cyrillic_search_ru_un. html>. This help page presents only the Microsoft keymap or onscreen keyboard method. It is reliably available in Queens Library branches and frequently available to remote users. Again, non-Windows and non-IE users will need to consult their system specific documentation to enter Cyrillic searches.

It should be noted that Sirsi Corporation has not added any equivalence to make Cyrillic searching case insensitive. Thus a search in for "чехов, антон павлович" will *not* find the titles available under "Чехов, Антон Павлович." The vendor has no plans to cure this deficiency in DRA Classic. We hope that later generations of software will include this innovation; it's worth testing when reviewing any system.

CREATING A RUSSIAN LANGUAGE OPAC INTERFACE

At the Queens Library the Russian language catalog interface is scheduled for release in June 2005. The development process will entail several steps, including organizing a technology team, a translation team, and a testing team (the translators and the testers may be the same individuals). Unicode-based development tools that work as WYSIWYG (What You See Is What You Get) HTML editors are required, and a project application such as Microsoft Project will help identify dependencies and milestones to see the project through to its expected completion date.

The process will begin with the technology team dividing the Web2 search engine file structure into segments and identifying which files should be translated first. Because the model will be English-based, all files from the English folder will be copied over to a newly created Russian file folder. Command line settings files, which show error messages, session time limit messages and field descriptions, will be separated from routine HTML files that are generally displayed to anyone who searches the OPAC. Printouts of the text in each individual file as well as screenshots (where applicable) will be created.

The technology team will then begin working with the translation team to review technical procedures that include a general overview of Web2 file structure and its proprietary macro language, using a Unicode-based editor to enter and display native language characters, tips, and best practices working in an application development environment, and previewing changes or edits in IE 6.0. As each file is translated, the technology team will work with the testing team to verify that the translation is displaying correctly and that it is the correct translation given the search circumstance.

The verification process is required because the Web2 search engine is based on conditional situations (e.g., If X is true THEN display Y) that may or may not show an instance of the newly translated phrase. Verification is also important because of Web2's proprietary macro language structure and an increased possibility of accidental macro deletions by translators.

```
<!–WEB2_INCLUDE FILE="IncStyleSheet.html"→
```

Because the above is structured as an HTML comment, WYSIWYG Unicode-based HTML editors do not see the comment displayed in the WYSIWYG view. It can only be seen in the HTML view. Translators, however, cannot work strictly in the HTML view, since numeric-based Unicode characters do not make intuitive sense–they are just numbers. It is only the WYSIWYG view that gives a true character representation.

Once the translation and testing processes are completed, the next steps will include creating additional graphics for web browser display, Help files (again modeled after the English) to help native Russian language speakers use the OPAC, and editing the primary setting file to create a new Russian Key that will lead catalog searches to the translated HTML files. With over fifty files to work with, time management will be critical to success.

AUTHORITY CONTROL IN RUSSIAN

Some significant limitations are inherent in the whole concept of 880 tagging. Authority control is at the top of the list. Simply creating a Cyrillic equivalent for the authorized form of a Russian name will often, but not always, produce a correct result. A good example is Boris Yeltsin (see Figure 4). The existence of case and gender in Russian, but not in English, can exacerbate the situation. Here a good example is Alexandra Tolstoy (see Figure 5). A cataloger with appropriate language skills, entering Russian original script directly, would have no problem producing an entry that a Russian customer would find useful, but the situation is more complicated with non-Russian authors. Consider the well-known and widely translated author Gabriel García Márquez (see Figure 6). There is little official guidance for transliterating French, Spanish, or even English into Cyrillic. The lack of a standard here makes complete reversibility of scripts impossible.

The obvious solution would be to add the appropriate heading (assuming it could be determined) in the 880 tag of the authority record. However, this 880 tag will often match a 400 field, NOT the 100 field. The corresponding 400 may not yet exist. Furthermore there is nothing to distinguish the correct approach for Russian versus any other non-Roman language. In the case of García Márquez, additional headings and corresponding transliterations would be necessary for Chinese, Arabic, and Korean.

FIGURE 4

100 1 Yeltsin, Boris Nikolayevich, $d 1931-(LC authorized form)

880 1 Ельцин, Борис Николаевич, $d 1931- (Correct Russian form)

400 1 El'tsin, Boris Nikolaevich, $d 1931- (Direct transliteration of
                                            correct Russian form)

FIGURE 5

100 1 Tolstoy, Alexandra, $d 1884-1979.   (LC authorized form)

880 1 Толстая, Александра, $d 1884-1979. (Correct Russian form)

400 1 Tolstaia, Aleksandra, $d 1884-1979. (Direct transliteration of
                                           correct Russian form)

Yet another complication arises where name headings contain actual text, such as is commonly included in 100 $c. A good example is Catherine II, Empress of Russia. Obviously detransliterating "Empress of Russia" makes little sense. To generate a useful entry one has to translate as well as transliterate (see Figure 7). The same problem crops up amid author/title headings. AACR2 provides for collective titles for Complete Works, Selections and works in a single form (e.g., Novels, Plays, Short Stories). It does not provide for translating them or detransliterating them. In the case of Turgenev's short stories, "Turgenev, Ivan Sergeevich, $d 1818-1883. $t Short stories." was converted to "Тургенев, Иван Сергеевич, $d 1818-1883. $t Повести и рассказы" (Turgenev, Ivan Sergeevich, $d 1818-1883. $t Povesti i rasskazy.). Although $t does not exactly contain an "alternate graphic" representation of the $t, it is clearly a sensible interpretation.

Although the Library of Congress is proceeding with the implementation of 880 tagging for authority records, some thorny problems like these examples remain unsolved. Resolving these issues through international cooperation and coordination of authority files is often discussed, but has proven difficult to implement. In 1993, the British Library and the Library of Congress agreed to the goal of establishing a single, shared name authority file to be created from the merger of their

FIGURE 6

100 1	García Márquez, Gabriel, $d 1928-	
400 1	Garsia Markes, Gabriel', $d 1928-	Russian
880 1	Гарсиа Маркес, Габриель, $d 1928-	
400 1	Garsiіa Markes, Gabriel', $d 1928-	Russian
880 1	Гарсия Маркес, Габриель, $d 1928-	
400 1	Garsia Markes, Gabriėl', $d 1928-	Russian
880 1	Гарсиа Маркес, Габриэль, $d 1928-	
400 1	Jiaxiya Makuisi, Jiabuli'er, $d 1928-	Chinese
880 1	加西亞‧馬奎斯, 加布里爾, $d 1928-	
400 1	Ghārsiyā Mārkīz, Jābrīl, $d 1928-	Arabic
880 1	جابريل غارسيا ماركيز, $d 1928-	
400 1	Garŭsia Marŭk'esŭ, Gabŭriel, $d 1928-	Korean
880 1	가르시아 마르케스, 가브리엘, $d 1928-	

two independent files. Yet despite much hard work the Anglo-American Authority File Project remains a work in progress.

At Hong Kong University of Science and Technology Library, a workable strategy has been developed for dealing with multiple scripts and different Romanizations providing for various approaches to the same name through different scripts.[3] Although they chose to construct their authority file in XML, a similar approach is almost certainly technically feasible in MARC. The problem would lie more in agreeing to a standard and persuading library system vendors to invest in a sound implementation.

Subject headings prove even more impossible to handle. Obviously an 880 alternate graphic representation cannot be applied to subject headings that are in English language and not transliteration. The translation involved is far more complex than the already perplexing exam-

FIGURE 7

100 1 Catherine, $b II, $c Empress of Russia, $d 1729-1796.

400 1 Ekaterina, $b II, $c Imperatritsa Vserossiĭskaia, $d 1729-1796.

880 1 Екатерина, $b II, $c Императрица Всероссийская, $d 1729-1796.

ples among name and name/title headings. The results would be dubious at best. With the chorus of English speakers who find Library of Congress Subject Headings (LCSH) variously illogical, archaic, arcane, or just plain incomprehensible, it is hard to imagine that translating them directly into Russian would improve the situation. It is highly probable that LCSH has some unintended American cultural bias that would make it further incomprehensible to Russian-speaking customers. In addition, translation is bound to add a further host of case, gender, word order, and other grammatical problems.

Theoretically one could employ a native Russian thesaurus such as *National Library of Russia Subject Headings Authority File* <http://www.nlr.ru:8101/eng/nlr/cat/sfile.htm>, but this would involve either a labor-intensive manual operation or a massive remapping of LCSH to Russian. These authority records are in RusMarc <http://www.rba.ru:8101/rusmarc/>, adding yet another level of complexity. (Note the use of field 250 for the authorized form, as opposed to the familiar USMARC 150 in Figure 8.) Even assuming that a deep-pocketed library (perhaps an oxymoron) was able to invest in Russian language subject headings, where (in MARC) would they go? Assuming a 6XX field with second indicator $7, the only available codes are:

rugeo

Natsional'nyi normativnyi fail geograficheskikh nazvanii Rossiiskoi Federatsii (National Normative File of Geographical Names of the Russian Federation) (Moskva: Rossiiskaia gosudarstvennaia biblioteka) [use only after Dec. 29, 2003].

rurkp

Predmetnye rubriki Rossiiskoi knizhnoi palaty (Subject Headings of the Russian Book Chamber) (Moskva: Rossiiskaia knizhnaia palata).

Neither of these works is readily available in print or online. Presumably a code could be added for a chosen thesaurus (see Figure 8). Could IOLS authority control modules handle it? Considering many systems are not yet handling *Guidelines on Subject Access to Individual Works of Fiction, Drama, etc.* (**gsafd**), or *Bilindex*, it seems unlikely.

Even apart from Name and Subject authority control, a record with Russian language access points is not truly a Russian language record. A host of fields, such as 5XX notes, 3XX data, etc., will nearly always be in the English language in the United States. Of course MARC records exist in other languages. MARC format now recognizes this by providing 040 $b for Language of Cataloging. This is defined as: "A MARC code for the language used in the textual portions of the record."[4] Interestingly, it is not repeatable. At least for the moment, records will remain inherently English with access points in Russian. A first step down the road to a truly multilingual catalog will be to revise MARC to recognize this possibility.

PROMOTION AND PUBLICITY

Is the world (or at least the library world) ready for searching original scripts? Both reference librarians and customers need training. Librarians not only need to be equipped with the searching skills for reference work, but also to be able to help customers use the tools and software to locate materials in OPACs. Queens Library's *InfoLinQ* can be searched, not only in Cyrillic, but with Chinese, Korean, or Arabic scripts. Queens Library offers workshops for its librarians to acquaint them with issues in different languages, available input tools, and searching

FIGURE 8

001: 1396212

250: ##$aАнтарктические экспедиции белорусские
[Belorussian Antarctic expeditions]

686: ##$aД890(887)022

651 0 Antarctica $x Discovery and exploration $x Belorussian.

650 7 $6 880-01 $a Antarkticheskie ėkspeditsii belorusskie. $2 nlrsaf

880 7 $6 650-01 $a Антарктические экспедиции белорусские. $2 nlrsaf

techniques. In such a large system (over sixty agencies) a librarian with the requisite language skill will not always be available to help. Hence all librarians need a minimal understanding of input methods as well as some printed or web-based instructions. It is worth noting that even if customers have some difficulty learning and using input methods, the inclusion of original scripts in the catalog is still valuable, because once they view vernacular characters in a hit list, they recognize the desired title much more quickly in the original script than in transliteration.

Of course, even before customer training is publicity. Customers need to know that Russian language materials are available and can be searched with original scripts. While it may seem easy, it is a message that can be surprisingly hard to get across. The customers who most need and want Russian-language materials are not always those with the best computer skills. As Russian speakers continue to arrive in Queens and new librarians are hired, the need for training continues.

Customer response to our Cyrillic OPAC has been difficult to gauge. Cyrillic Russian records in *InfoLinQ* have been available since the summer of 2003 and Ukrainian since the summer of 2004. DRA Classic/Web2 does not provide a way to track statistics on searches by script. However, it is possible to see how many hits are received on the help screens relating to Russian language searching, but this is far from foolproof. Some Russian language users may already be entirely familiar with input method editors and hence never need to visit the FAQ on entering Cyrillic search arguments. Anecdotally, reference librarians report some interest and questions.

CONCLUSION

In truth, a streamlined, easy-to-use Cyrillic OPAC is still a long way away. Although the Queens Library's *InfoLinQ* proves that a Cyrillic catalog is already technically feasible, there are still significant hurdles to leap. These include not only subject access and authority control, but also issues related to translation, transliteration, web browser display, input methods, and fonts. Ironically, perhaps the most serious challenges faced will not be technical as much as human factors: educating both librarians and customers. Without active involvement from both groups in the development process and regular usage, the effort made to do the necessary character conversions and create a Russian-language interface, the full potential of the catalog cannot be realized. In some ways the prospect of a Cyrillic OPAC exceeds customer expectations. However, this will certainly not be so for long.

NOTES

1. Jane Jacobs, Ed Summers, and Elizabeth Ankersen, "Cyril: Expanding the Horizons of MARC 21," *Library Hi Tech* 22, no. 1 (2004): 8.

2. The Internet Society, "Hypertext Transfer Protocol–HTTP/1.1," <http://www.w3.org/Protocols/rfc2616/rfc2616.html> (accessed August 26, 2004).

3. Kit-Tai Lam and Louisa Kwok, "XML Name Access Control Metadata Repository: An Experiment at HKUST Library," *HKUST Library Staff Papers & Reports*, <http://webarchive.ust.hk/webarch/20021129/info/reports/xmlnac.html> (accessed August 25, 2004).

4. *MARC 21 Concise Format for Bibliographic Data*, <http://www.loc.gov/marc/bibliographic/ecbdhome.html> (accessed August 26, 2004).

Adding Value to Slavic Electronic Texts: Approaches for Scholars and Librarians

Miranda Remnek

SUMMARY. Digital texts provide scholars with opportunities for rapid and meaningful analysis that were not available to earlier generations. This applies to scholars in Slavic studies as much as to scholars in other fields. But, for various reasons, many remain less than enamored of the possibilities. In simplifying ways of making e-texts useful, and in demonstrating their analytic value to the busy scholar, librarians can play a pivotal role. Hence, this article seeks to address the following topics: (1) Questions of value: scholarly imperatives and the maintenance of standards; encoding as a way of adding value to texts for analytical purposes; standardized encoding as a way of avoiding idiosyncratic analysis and ensure interoperability and reuse of data; (2) Development issues: attracting scholars to the graduated use of encoded texts; librarians as mediators: helping scholars exploit the benefits of analytical technologies; (3) Implementation issues: selecting appropriate texts for deep encoding; ensuring an appropriate infrastructure; facilitating customized approaches for different disciplines; (4) Programming issues: shaping datasets and interfaces for easy application and use: practical and theoretical issues. *[Article copies available for a fee from The Haworth Document Delivery Service: 1-800-HAWORTH. E-mail address: <docdelivery@haworthpress.com> Website: <http://www.HaworthPress.com> © 2005 by The Haworth Press, Inc. All rights reserved.]*

Miranda Remnek, PhD, MLS, MA, is Head, Slavic & East European Library, University of Illinois at Urbana-Champaign.

Address correspondence to: Miranda Remnek, 225A Library, 1408 West Gregory Drive, Urbana, IL 61801 USA (E-mail: mremnek@uiuc.edu).

[Haworth co-indexing entry note]: "Adding Value to Slavic Electronic Texts: Approaches for Scholars and Librarians." Remnek, Miranda. Co-published simultaneously in *Slavic & East European Information Resources* (The Haworth Information Press, an imprint of The Haworth Press, Inc.) Vol. 6, No. 2/3, 2005, pp. 151-167; and: *Virtual Slavica: Digital Libraries, Digital Archives* (ed: Michael Neubert) The Haworth Information Press, an imprint of The Haworth Press, Inc., 2005, pp. 151-167. Single or multiple copies of this article are available for a fee from The Haworth Document Delivery Service [1-800-HAWORTH, 9:00 a.m. - 5:00 p.m. (EST). E-mail address: docdelivery@haworthpress.com].

doi:10.1300/J167v06n02_10

KEYWORDS. Encoding, markup, text analysis, document analysis, TEI, XML, SGML, technology, research applications, Slavic

QUESTIONS OF VALUE

Scholarly Imperatives and the Maintenance of Standards

It need hardly be said, and yet bears repeating, that the notion of value has always resided at the center of scholarly research. The concept of peer review has thus guided validation of university faculties, and has also influenced the content of recognized journals and the approval of monographs for publication. This time-honored approach has raised issues for younger scholars–who spend time on the application of technology to research and feel disadvantaged when it comes to review by traditional validation mechanisms–but the need for quality control remains an essential part of the research process.

Indeed, as the era of isolated digital projects (and their presentation of digitized research texts) transforms itself into a new era of interwoven digital libraries, the question of validation, and a focus on value, becomes ever more important.[1] In addition to the ongoing need for evaluating levels of scholarly interpretation and the intrinsic value of the texts themselves, we must now consider the not inconsequential costs of preparation and maintenance when research materials are converted to, and stored in, digital format.

It will be countered that the organized preservation of research material and scholarship has always been a costly endeavor for libraries. But the addition of the digital overlay increases these costs measurably–both for the library that needs to accommodate new formats, and for the scholar who needs to learn new approaches. It follows that if a librarian or scholar is going to undertake the production or analysis of digitized research material, the time invested must be worth the expense; hence the texts created must be presented in ways that make them valuable for scholarly use.[2]

Encoding as a Way of Adding Value to Texts for Analytical Purposes

Digital collections exist in numerous formats. In part because of the expense involved with further processing, some project directors restrict their output to graphic images, often in the form of TIFF files. But as noted in regard to the early efforts of Slavic philologists, "While these images can represent much of the physical richness of original manuscripts, the ability to process the textual content of these electronic copies has been limited."[3] It therefore makes sense to produce digital versions of source material that are not only imaged, but also recognized using the process known as OCR (optical character recognition). But even OCR is not enough to ensure that the resulting, machine-readable text has been rendered sufficiently valuable for the purpose of scholarly analysis.

So what constitutes adding value to electronic texts? Basically, it involves identifying significant features represented by segments or words within a text, and increasing the value of the text by naming the segments so identified. This process of naming is accomplished by surrounding the segments with appropriate start tags and end tags (in angle brackets). Each set of tags represents informational value that is added to the text.

Here, for example, is a snippet from a short essay by Nikolai Karamzin, published in Russian in 1802 and entitled "The Book Trade and the Love of Reading in Russia." The text has been enriched with analytical tags that make it more valuable for scholarly analysis and information retrieval. The passage describes the activities of Nikolai Novikov, the eighteenth-century bookman: "After he had leased the University Printing House, he increased the <SEG ANA="pub-tech"> mechanical </SEG> means of book printing, had books translated, established stores in <SEG ANA="trade-prov"> other towns</SEG>, [and] in every possible way tried to entice the public to read . . ."[4] In other words, a scholar seeking evidence on the development of print technologies and the provincial book trade in Russia would be led to this source as a result of the added information.

This process is known as encoding, or markup. A more precise definition of the process of adding value "is to provide information which will assist a computer program to perform functions on that text."[5] If computers cannot independently incorporate the level of intelligent analysis needed, that intelligence must be embedded in the text.

Standardized Encoding: Avoiding Idiosyncratic Analysis, and Ensuring Interoperability and Reuse of Data

There are many forms of embedded markup. At the simplest level, encoding in HTML (Hypertext Markup Language) represents added value: it ensures that the document is readable in a browser. But HTML's approach to encoding is mostly presentational.[6] True, one can use HTML in a way that is based on naming the parts of a text (document analysis), rather than using purely presentational tags. This involves using the "class" attribute. Yet from that approach, it is not a big step to use XML encoding instead.

XML (Extensible Markup Language) is designed to support web publishing based on analysing the documents you want to represent and creating tags that are appropriate for *what you want to do with* them, rather than *how you want to present* them. In most cases, "wanting to do something" means "wanting to search and retrieve a document's contents." True, the Find feature in word processors or web pages will allow simple searches on a single text without additional markup. But when the researcher is performing non-keyword searches (especially on large quantities of text), markup becomes more crucial.

Some of these features characterized XML's forerunner, SGML (Standard Generalized Markup Language), which became an international standard in 1986. XML is a subset of SGML, intended to make it more usable for distributing materials on the web:

> XML differs from SGML primarily in simplifying the some-times-intimidating formalism of SGML in order to ensure that an XML parser [validation mechanism] is simple enough to embed in even lightweight software, including Web browsers. It differs from HTML primarily in allowing the user to specify new tags, marking types of elements not foreseen in the HTML specification, and making it possible for common off-the-shelf browsers and other software to handle such user-defined element types usefully.[7]

In performing document analysis for the purpose of retrieval rather than presentation, it is not always necessary to develop a tag set from scratch. Some already exist for certain purposes. For scholarly purposes an enormous contribution has been made in the form of guidelines developed by the TEI, or Text Encoding Initiative. The TEI was founded in 1987, the year after SGML became an international standard. The purpose of the TEI is to function as:

> an international and interdisciplinary standard that helps libraries, museums, publishers, and individual scholars represent all kinds of literary and linguistic texts for online research and teaching, us-

ing an encoding scheme that is maximally expressive and minimally obsolescent . . . [8]

Clearly, the TEI was developed at a time when SGML was the
markup language *de rigueur* when it came to analytical encoding. For
that reason, the comprehensive version of the TEI guidelines was somewhat complex, leading to the development of a condensed tag-set with
fewer elements known as TEI-Lite. The tags available for use within
this standard have become part of the TEI-Lite DTD (Document Type
Definition). This DTD is in use by most major e-text projects in the
U.S., and is available for downloading from the TEI website. The TEI is
now a membership organization, and access to workgroup materials is
restricted to members. But the TEI website provides links to many files
of value to the beginning encoder; among these are not only the TEI and
TEI-Lite DTDs, but also other files, including an introduction to TEI-
Lite in Russian (see links at <http://www.tei-c.org/Tutorials/index.
html>).

The TEI can be used for encoding many different types of research
texts irrespective of their discipline: literature, linguistics, history, philosophy, political science, etc. The TEI is somewhat weaker in the area
of bibliographic description, but efforts are currently underway to improve its flexibility in this area, too.

A basic characteristic of these forms is that they represent recognized
standards. But why is it so important for Slavic scholars to employ these
mechanisms? Two Bulgarian scholars provided in 1995 a very telling
overview of the history of computer applications to Slavic manuscripts,
and made clear the value of using established standards:

> There exists no complete coordination between Slavists and
> specialists in . . . Latin, Greek, and Hebrew paleography and
> codicology. This lack of coordination has led scholars to overlook
> the necessity of developing systems for Slavic studies which must
> be compatible with already existing systems for these other fields.[9]

Having identified as its five principles the standardizing of file formats, multiple use, independence from local platforms, preservation in
e-format, and orientation to well-structured data divisions according to
the Slavic traditions of orthography, textology, and paleography, these
scholars concluded that SGML (now XML) and its applications provided by the TEI corresponded most adequately to their principles. Of
course, where Slavic materials are concerned, other encoding issues

will continue to arise. To some extent the advent of Unicode has softened the impact of the difficulties caused by differing character sets, but challenges remain.[10]

To summarize, the need to maximize the analytical value of well-formed, enriched, and transferable digital documents is as important as the need to maintain the quality of scholarship itself.

But also important is the need to continue to expand awareness of this potential among the scholarly community. For, as indicated by a digital librarian at the Czech National Library, "It is clear that decisions on the standards and quality of digitization should *not* be made only by technicians, who are too focused on the possibilities of technology [italics mine]." Researchers are rarely "able to act without consulting computer experts," he says, but "their thinking is rooted in different disciplines,"[11] and this leads to the wasteful creation of resources that, though valuable in an absolute sense, may lose their their value when the precise needs of researchers are not fully met.[12]

I. DEVELOPMENT ISSUES

Attracting Scholars to the Graduated Use of Encoded Texts

Before they show any interest in the *how* of text encoding, however, most uninitiated scholars–and the librarians who assist them–will want to know *why* they should be interested in a process that, for the uninitiated at least, seems time-consuming to master, tedious to implement, and lacking in any obvious research outcome. True, growing familiarity with the potential of electronic texts and the disciplines they affect–like scholarly editing–has contributed to undeniable advances in the distribution of information literacy. However, skepticism persists; for instance, "the discipline [of scholarly editing] still seems quite arcane to the large majority of academics . . . "[13]

Yet individual Slavic scholars have realized for some time that the viewpoint of more traditional scholars can be turned on its head. It is not the application of technology that slows the well-honed research process, but rather the time-consuming research process that is alleviated by technology:

> Slavists who work with medieval manuscripts often must deal with vast corpora of unpublished texts, which, because of their unwieldy size, are very difficult to collate and analyze. Data collec-

tion also generally involves considerable time and expense for travel to overseas archives, and often results in reduplication of efforts among scholars who are collating the same unpublished texts for different projects. All signs suggest that this situation is about to change dramatically, however, as computer technology is now available for processing early Slavic texts on microcomputer, and for sharing textual data with other Slavists worldwide over the Internet.[14]

Besides the obvious benefits of avoiding expensive travel and reduplication of effort, the widespread sharing of textual data for consultation and commentary is a third non-specific benefit of interoperability. One more generic advantage can be seen: "The most important feature of the electronic medium is its ability to present different views of the same information quickly and flexibly. Given the proper encoding, an electronic text can be stored in numerous versions . . . ; readers can view the text in any configuration that is appropriate to their needs."[15]

As noted earlier, achievement of "proper encoding" starts with careful document analysis. But the process of analysis is useful not only because it ensures appropriate encoding, but also because it helps to clarify the goals of a project–whether the goal is purely research-oriented, or whether it involves successful digital production.

What, then, are the advantages of document analysis that the neophyte researcher should understand when launching a project to produce XML-compliant TEI-encoded texts? Staff at one London-based Computing Center suggest the following:

1. Ability to create documents that can be presented in different forms. This is not easy (consider the rate of error in non-XML-based documents like newspapers). And it cannot be done well without structural markup[16]
2. Ability to specify what the structure of a document should be, and automatically identify documents that don't comply (this is vital when a large amount of information is concerned)
3. Ability to use knowledge of structure in searching the documents
4. Ability to decrease reliance on current display technology, because you are not hardcoding current HTML into your documents[17]

Further discussion of these points is precluded by space limitations. For now, suffice it to say that document analysis almost always requires some knowledge of the subject area. This is why it is crucial that scholars be involved.

In attempting, therefore, to attract more scholars to the graduated use of digital technology, it is useful to begin by pointing out generic advantages like those mentioned earlier, and follow these with more sophisticated benefits that are specific to different disciplines. These might include TEI-structural encoding for comparing different editions of manuscripts, TEI interpretive encoding for literary texts or historical documents, and also qualitative data analysis tools or statistical packages. Some of these will be discussed more fully in the context of implementation.

However, it is also important to point out that scholars need to be educated in the existence and application of best practices. For one thing, those researchers who are drawn into the digital arena are just as likely to move on to create their own digital publications (referred to as born-digital material), rather than limit their involvement to the analysis of digital surrogates–and this raises even more questions for interoperability and archiving. Indeed, as noted in a recent study, "If scholars are to produce originally digital publications that are compatible with library needs and that allow libraries to collect at reasonable costs, then best practices for authoring have to be understood, established, and supported in some kind of networked, institutionalized workspace."[18] It is here that librarians enter the picture.

Librarians as Mediators: Helping Scholars Exploit the Benefits of Analytical Technologies

Despite the important contribution of the scholar to the formation of valuable digital collections, the role of the librarian is crucial in terms of both creation and maintenance. Librarians have long seen the necessity for standardized systems of classification and metadata creation, and current exigencies require that library professionals develop and maintain an awareness of today's requirements. Librarians can point the scholar to text creation resources, just as they have always helped to identify research tools.

A major resource endorsed by the Digital Library Federation (DLF) <http://www.diglib.org/> is *TEI Text Encoding in Libraries: Guidelines for Best Encoding Practices.* Listed on the DLF site under Standards and Practices, the original guidelines were first developed in

1999, and are currently undergoing a major revision. They recognized that:

> There are many different library text digitization projects, for different purposes. . . . [So] the Task Force has attempted to make these recommendations as inclusive as possible by developing a series of encoding levels. These levels are meant to allow for a range of practice, from wholly automated text creation and encoding, to encoding that requires expert content knowledge, analysis, and editing.[19]

II. IMPLEMENTATION ISSUES

Selecting Appropriate Texts for Deep Encoding

An important issue to be addressed before approaches to encoding are considered is the selection of appropriate texts. In keeping with the emphasis on value, any judicious project to enrich an e-text corpus involves prior selection of valuable material. That is, any project that allots more than the minimal time required to mark up a given collection should be certain that it is dealing with material that is worth the extra step. But the need here will depend on whether the impetus comes from the scholar, or the librarian.

The scholar who seeks to take advantage of computer technology will already, in most cases, have initiated a research project, and will have identified the material to be analysed. The need here will be to identify the existence of digital copies, or appropriate analysis software. In the first instance, a developing project sponsored by the Digital Projects Working Group of AAASS will be of assistance: the *Inventory of Slavic, East European, and Eurasian Digital Projects* <http://www. library.uiuc.edu/spx/inventory/>. Materials in the second category are harder to identify; one source is the Text Analysis Software page of the University of Virginia's Electronic Text Center <http://etext.lib. virginia.edu/textual.html>.

The librarian who selects materials for digitization and potential scholarly analysis will be more inclined to consider less personal issues, such as collection strengths at a given institution, or preservation needs. For guidance in selecting appropriate material for digitization (and indeed for most other aspects of the digital process), a fundamental source is the so-called *NISO Framework of Guidance for Building Good Digital Collections* <http://www.niso.org/framework/forumframework.html>.

Ensuring an Appropriate Infrastructure

Once the corpus to be handled is selected (and texts have been digitized and recognized using imaging/OCR software), it is necessary to verify the local availability of other needed elements of the digital infrastructure, including encoding and delivery software.

As regards encoding software, or XML editors, there are several possible options. They include commercial options like <oXygen/> 4.2 (July 15, 2004) <http://www.oxygenxml.com/>, epcEdit <http://www.epcedit.com/>, XmetaL <http://www.xmetal.com/>, and XMLSpy <http://www.altova.com/products_ide.html>. Open source options include jEdit <http://www.jedit.org/> and Emacs <http://www.tei-c.org/Software/tei-emacs/>. There are considerable differences among these products. Among the commercial varieties, Xmetal was the recognized XML-compliant successor to Author-Editor, widely used for SGML-based encoding. But it is now generally thought that a more accessible option for new practitioners in this field is <oXygen/>, a relatively simple product that is frequently updated (two new releases since spring 2004). As regards open-source variants, Emacs is a product that has been in use by TEI types for some time, but jEdit is generally reckoned to be a better choice for newcomers to the art of text encoding. For more information on several of these products, consult the TEI Consortium's software page.[20]

As regards delivery systems, a frequent choice is DLXS XPAT, a former commercial product that has gone through several incarnations and is now leased by the University of Michigan.[21] It should be noted that an XPAT license is not inexpensive. But a mini version, entitled XPAT Lite, *is* freely available for downloading, with a link at <http://www.dlxs.org/products/index.html>. However, the data size is limited to ten megabytes, and there is no Unicode support. Other options exist, including a British product called Anastasia (short for Analytical System Tools and SGML/XML Integration Applications, but appropriately named from the perspective of Slavists. . .).[22] As of June 24, 2004, this product has also become freely available, and the developers claim that "you can learn *online* how to publish a simple TEI document with Anastasia."[23] Still other possibilities are discussed in section IV of this essay.

Identifying and Facilitating Customized Approaches for Different Disciplines

A third issue affecting the implementation of a given digital analysis project concerns the disciplinary needs of the project in question. As noted by Milena Dobreva (who has been involved in the application of computers to the study of Bulgarian manuscripts), one of three possible approaches when one has to model how computers can be applied to a certain field is "to try to describe the specific task and data used in the field, and find which of the available computer tools can meet the needs of the field in the best way."[24]

However, one of the most vexing questions with regard to the development of adequate software for the needs of a given scholarly project stems from the disconnect between software developers and the host of scholarly practitioners whose methodologies differ immensely from discipline to discipline. These differences are no secret, but continue to assert their force. Its impact is lamented by Ruzena Bajcsy, a prominent electrical engineer and computer scientist of Slovak descent who now heads the Berkeley-based Center for Information Technology Research in the Interest of Society <http://www.citris-uc.org/>:

> The biggest hurdle for CITRIS is how to facilitate a group of independent investigators coming from very different cultures to work together in a meaningful way. Engineering and the physical sciences, as opposed to the social sciences and humanities, are profoundly different cultures in training, methodologies, the technology they use, and the questions they ask.

The problem, Bajcsy says, is that "Traditionally, academics tend to work alone. But . . . large-scale problems can't be solved by single professions . . . You need multiple skill-sets."[25] The need for multiple skills is undeniable, and underscores the need for scholars, librarians, and programmers to work together.

Also important, however, are extensible standardized schemes–like XML and the TEI–that allow text encoders in different disciplines to employ similar approaches to text analysis. Consider the passage from Karamzin cited earlier–concerning the development of printing and publishing in Russia in the 1700s and early 1800s. The underlying TEI-compliant encoding structure–as provided in Chapter 16 (Interpretation and Analysis) of the TEI-Lite element set <http://www.tei-c. org/Lite/U5-anal.html> is illustrated here:

```
<text>
<body>. . . .</body>
<back>
<div1 type="Interpretations">
<interpGrp type="Publishing">
<interp value="Commercial" ID="pub-commer">
<interp value="Patronage" ID="pub-patron">
<interp value="Technology" ID="pub-tech">
</interpGrp>
</div1>
</back>
</text>26
```

The encoding is standardized to the extent that it can be applied to texts in a variety of disciplines (literature, history, philosophy, etc.). The categories are chosen for the project in hand, but the structure at least is interdisciplinary, and interoperable.

III. PROGRAMMING ISSUES

Shaping Datasets and Interfaces for Easy Application and Use: Practical issues

Besides the implementation issues discussed above, scholars and librarians who seek to develop digital collections for analysis will need to be familiar with additional programming possibilities that will assist in the production of customized approaches.

At this juncture, the move towards open source software is ever more compelling, because it avoids the need for expensive proprietary software, and fosters interoperability.[27] Projects that do not have access to powerful and expensive delivery sytems like DLXS XPAT can achieve a surprising array of search options on the web by using open-source XSLT (Extensible Style Language Transformation) to deliver different representations of underlying XML-encoded files.[28] Mastering XSLT can be daunting to the beginner but graduated manuals exist.[29]

Another popular open source approach available for the database delivery of encoded texts (and other material) involves a combination of PHP scripting language and MySQL database software, where PHP is used to produce a customizable interface to the underlying MySQL database.[30]

Shaping Datasets and Interfaces for Easy Application and Use: Theoretical issues

Nevertheless, the question of just how to provide the best visualization and analysis features for the inquisitive scholar is not an easy task–despite the availability of programming software that can be used with relative ease to achieve customized interfaces, once skilled help is available.

Indeed, the question of how to represent its materials to Western researchers, as opposed to Russian scholars, was an issue raised in recent months by a major Russian digital repository known as FEB, or *Fundamental'naia elektronnaia biblioteka: Russkaia literatura i fol'klor* <http://www.feb-web.ru/>. This stunning collection of more than 50,000 encoded texts embedded in a structured system of digital scholarly editions was seeking to display its materials in the best possible way to a wider audience, but recognized that researchers in different communities have different approaches, and may require different features to satisfy their needs.

This realization is an interesting twist on the notion that different disciplines have different methodologies, and calls to mind a recent formulation reached by an IMLS Workshop on Opportunities for Research on the Creation, Management, Preservation and Use of Digital Content (Sept. 2003).[31] The workshop outlined three "specific research areas where it felt that IMLS should programmatically encourage proposals for applied research."[32] The first of these was "The Integration of Physical and Digital Experiences." Among the issues raised: "We do not know how the use of digital library collections affects the individual as library user. . . . Do they encourage or mitigate against the use of print and other artifactual resources? It is important to know how web-accessible collections affect the expectations of users." These ideas can be taken to apply directly to the question of how well digital library collections allow researchers to replicate the methodologies used with print materials.

With this in mind, important questions for the scholar and librarian as they seek to add value to encoded texts are:

> What do humanists and social scientists need from e-text sites? How do they differ? How should sites be constructed so as to serve differing research methodologies? How can sites promote the changes in humanities research methods (from a single researcher to a collaborative model) that some IT leaders see as essential to

maximize the benefits of technology? How can we involve more scholars in the building of ontologies? How can we promote expanded online analysis of encoded materials and interactive scholarly commentary (to replicate scholarly interaction in the physical environment)? How can we translate our research results into new web design and delivery software, so as to address more fully in software development the human needs of researchers (recommended by visionaries like Ben Shneiderman), and engender textbases that are maximally attractive and useful to scholarly communities?

CONCLUSION

Many exciting research questions remain, but it should be apparent that text encoding represents an important area in which scholars and librarians can come together to develop new approaches that will maximize the use of technology to save research time, and, more important, produce imaginative results that would not have been possible without the ability to harness the computational power of the computer.

NOTES

1. The focus on value can take several forms, involving not only the intrinsic value of the material being digitized, but also the value of the digital process for providing better access to the material. See *The Evidence in Hand: Report of the Task Force on the Artifact in Library Collections*, 41.

2. According to some Russian colleagues, the need for careful practices in this area is not only an issue for the local researcher or librarian; it is also a matter of national importance. See K. I. Vigurskii and I. A. Pil'shchikov, "Filologiia i sovremennye informatsionnye tekhnologii: k postanovke problemy," (Philology and Contemporary Information Technologies: Toward a Formulation of the Problem).

3. David Birnbaum, "Standardizing Characters, Glyphs, and SGML Entities for Encoding Early Cyrillic Writing," *Computer Standards and Interfaces* 18 (1996): 201.

4. See the University of Illinois's electronic archive, *Early 19th-Century Russian Readership & Culture*, <http://www.library.uiuc.edu/spx/rusread/> (accessed December 30, 2004). However, for copyright reasons this particular text is password-restricted, and does not display without authentication.

5. Susan Hockey, *Electronic Texts in the Humanities*, 24.

6. *XML Reference Guide: 1: Document Analysis* (London: Centre for Computing in the Humanities, King's College, <http://www.kcl.ac.uk/humanities/cch/refs/xml/xml-da.html> [accessed December 30, 2004]).

7. C. M. Sperberg-McQueen, "What is XML and Why Should Humanists Care?"

8. From the TEI website <http://www.tei-c.org> (accessed December 30, 2004).

9. Andrej Bojadzhiev and Anisava Miltenova, "The Necessity for Processing the Information in Slavic Medieval Manuscripts Using SGML and TEI."

10. The seminal source is Birnbaum, "Standardizing Characters, Glyphs, and SGML Entities."

11. Stanislav Psohlavec, "Digitization of Manuscripts in the National Library of the Czech Republic," 21-22.

12. Other recent sources on the importance of *value* in digital applications are: John Unsworth,"The Value of Digitization for Libraries and Humanities Scholarship"; and Angelika Menne-Harritz and Nils Brübach, "The Intrinsic Value of Archive and Library Material."

13. Julia Flanders, "The Body Encoded: Questions of Gender and the Electronic Text," 128.

14. Cynthia Vakareliyska, "Report on the First International Conference on Computer Processing of Medieval Slavic Manuscripts, 24-29 July, 1995, Blagoevgrad, Bulgaria."

15. Flanders, "The Body Encoded," 135.

16. The notion of encoding a document in ways that are other than, or more than, merely presentational is often, as here, called *structural markup* (characterization of parts of a document). Unfortunately, this notion is also sometimes called *semantic markup*–which can be confusing, because others use the phrase *semantic markup* in a more literal sense to convey the notion of content/thematic analysis (and in this sense, the phrase represents markup that differs substantially from so-called *structural markup*).

17. *XML Reference Guide.*

18. *The Evidence in Hand,* 69.

19. See "III: Recommendations," also entitled "Background," in *TEI Text Encoding in Libraries: Guidelines for Best Encoding Practices, Version 1.0 (July 30, 1999)*, <http://www.diglib.org/standards/tei.htm> (accessed December 30, 2004).

20. Available at <http://www.tei-c.org/Software/index.html> (accessed December 30, 2004).

21. See <http://www.dlxs.org/products/xpat.html> (accessed December 30, 2004).

22. See <http://server30087.uk2net.com/anastasia/> (accessed December 30, 2004).

23. See <http://anastasia.sourceforge.net/> (accessed December 30, 2004).

24. Milena P. Dobreva, *Applications of Computer Tools in Studying Medieval Slavonic Manuscripts* (Sofia, Bulgaria: Boyko Kacharmazov, 1995), 4.

25. "In Conversation: Ruzena Bajcsy" <http://www.citris-uc.org/people/leadership/director/bajcsy_interview.html> (accessed December 31, 2004).

26. For more information, see the Text Encoding Overview of the *Early Nineteenth-Century Russian Readership and Culture* project at <http://www.library.uiuc.edu/spx/rusread/rencode.html>.

27. A major source for keeping abreast of open source developments is *SourceForge.net* <https://sourceforge.net/> (accessed December 31, 2004).

28. For a glimpse at some wonderful examples of XSLT transformations based on texts available through UIUC's Early Nineteenth-Century Russian Readership & Culture project (see p. 2), see the presentation by Tom Habing (Research programmer at UIUC's Grainger Engineering Library), "'Quick and Dirty' Rendering With XLST and CSS and a Little JavaScript," to the Fourteenth Annual Slavic Librarians' Workshop/Digital Text Workshop held at UIUC in July, 2004, <http://g118.grainger.uiuc.

edu/slavic/> (accessed December 31, 2004). For more scholarly applications in the Slavic field using XSLT, see another presentation at the same workshop by David Birnbaum (Dept of Slavic Language & Literatures, University of Pittsburgh) entitled "On Beyond XML" <http://www.library.uiuc.edu/spx/slw-dtw/presentations/djb_onbeyondxml/index0.html> (accessed December 31, 2004). See especially his three XSLT examples further into the presentation: "Visualizing the Igor Tale," "Visualizing Russian Incantations," and "Visualizing the Structure of Mixed-Content Miscellanies."

29. A good place to start is Doug Tidwell, *XSLT* (Cambridge, Mass.: O'Reilly, 2001). Its cover title is *Mastering XLST Transformations.*

30. Several manuals are available. See, for example, Luke Welling and Laura Thomson, *PHP and MySQL Web Development*, 2d ed. (Indianapolis, Ind.: Sams, 2003).

31. Its "Report on the Workshop on Opportunities for Research on the Creation, Management, Preservation, and Use of Digital Content," is available at <http://www.imls.gov/pubs/pdf/digitalopp.pdf> (accessed December 31, 2004).

32. "Report on the Workshop on Opportunities," 3.

BIBLIOGRAPHY

Birnbaum, David. "Standardizing Characters, Glyphs, and SGML Entities for Encoding Early Cyrillic Writing." *Computer Standards and Interfaces* 18 (1996): 201-252.

Bojadzhiev, Andrej and Anisava Miltenova. "The Necessity for Processing the Information in Slavic Medieval Manuscripts Using SGML and TEI." Report on the First International Conference on Computer Processing of Medieval Slavic Manuscripts, 24-29 July, 1995, Blagoevgrad, Bulgaria. Available online at <http://www.ceu.hu/medstud/ralph/report.htm#andrej> (accessed December 30, 2004).

Dobreva, Milena P. *Applications of Computer Tools in Studying Medieval Slavonic Manuscripts.* Sofia, Bulgaria: Boyko Kacharmazov, 1995.

The Evidence in Hand: Report of the Task Force on the Artifact in Library Collections. Washington, DC: Council on Library and Information Resources, Nov. 2001. Also available online at <http://www.clir.org/pubs/reports/pub103/pub103.pdf> and at <http://www.clir.org/pubs/reports/pub103/contents.html> (accessed December 30, 2004).

Flanders, Julia. "The Body Encoded: Questions of Gender and the Electronic Text," in *Electronic Text: Investigations in Method and Theory*, ed. Kathryn Sutherland, 127-143. Oxford: Clarendon Press, 1997.

Flanders, Julia. "Learning, Reading, and the Problem of Scale: Using *Women Writers Online.*" *Pedagogy: Critical Approaches to Teaching Literature, Language, Composition and Culture* 2, no.1 (2002), 49-59.

"A Gentle Introduction to XML." In *TEI P4: Guidelines for Electronic Text Encoding and Interchange.* XML-compatible edition, May 2002. Available online at <http://www.tei-c.org/P4X/SG.html> (accessed December 31, 2004).

Hockey, Susan. *Electronic Texts in the Humanities.* Oxford: Oxford University Press, 2000.

Menne-Harritz, Angelika and Nils Brubach. *The Intrinsic Value of Archive and Library Material*. Marburg: Archivschule Marburg, 1997. Available online at <http://www.uni-marburg.de/archivschule/intrinsengl.html> (accessed December 30, 2004). Also available in German as *Der intrinsische Wert von Bibliotheks- und Archivgut: Kriterienkatalog zur bildlichen und textlichen Konversion bei der Bestandserhaltung: Ergebnisse eines DFG-Projekts*. Veröffentlichungen der Archivschule Marburg, 26. Marburg, Archivschule Marburg, 1997.

Miltenova, Anisava, and David Birnbaum, eds. *Medieval Slavic Manuscripts and SGML: Problems and Perspectives = Srednovekovni slavianski rukopisi i SGML*. Sofia: Marin Drinov, 2000.

Psohlavec, Stanislav. "Digitization of Manuscripts in the National Library of the Czech Republic." *Microform & Imaging Review* 27, no. 1 (Winter 1998): 21-26.

Robinson, Peter. *The Transcription of Primary Textual Sources Using SGML*. Office for Humanities Communication Publications, 6. Oxford, 1994.

Seaman, David. "The User Community as Responsibility and Resource: Building a Sustainable Digital Library." *D-Lib Magazine* 3, no. 7 (July-August 1997), <http://www.dlib.org/dlib/july97/07seaman.html> (accessed December 31, 2004).

Sitts, Maxine K., ed. *Handbook for Digital Projects: A Management Tool for Preservation and Access*. Andover, MA: Northeast Document Conservation Center, 2000. Available online at <http://www.nedcc.org/digital/dighome.htm> (accessed December 31, 2004).

Sperberg-McQueen, C. M. "What is XML and Why Should Humanists Care?" Abstract for a talk given at Conference on Digital Resources for the Humanities, Oxford, Sept. 1997. Available online at <http://www.w3.org/People/cmsmcq/1997/drh97.html> (accessed December 30, 2004).

Unsworth, John. "The Value of Digitization for Libraries and Humanities Scholarship." Presentation at an Innodata Isogen Symposium, Newberry Library, May 17, 2004. Available online at <http://www3.isrl.uiuc.edu/~unsworth/newberry.04.html> (accessed December 30, 2004).

Vakareliyska, Cynthia. "Report on the First International Conference on Computer Processing of Medieval Slavic Manuscripts, 24-29 July, 1995, Blagoevgrad, Bulgaria." Available online at <http://www.ceu.hu/medstud/ralph/report.htm#cynthia> (accessed December 30, 2004).

Vigurskii, K. I., and I. A. Pil'shchikov. "Filologiia i sovremennye informatsionnye tekhnologii: k postanovke problemy" (Philology and Contemporary Information Technologies: Toward a Formulation of the Problem). *Izvestiia Akademii nauk, Seriia literatury i iazyka* 62, no. 2 (2003): 9-16. Also available online at <http://feb-web.ru/feb/feb/media/philo-info.htm> (accessed December 30, 2004).

Vigurskii, K. I., and I. A. Pil'shchikov. "Informatika i filologiia: problemy i perspektivy vzaimodeistviia" (Informatics and Philology: Problems and Perspectives on Their Interaction." *Elektronnye biblioteki* 6, no. 3 (2003), <http://www.elbib.ru/index.phtml?page=elbib/rus/journal/2003/part3/VP> (accessed December 31, 2004).

XML Reference Guide. London: Centre for Computing in the Humanities, King's College. Available online at <http://www.kcl.ac.uk/humanities/cch/refs/xml/xml.html> (accessed December 30, 2004).

No Free Lunch:
Grant Adventures in the Digital Frontier

Bradley L. Schaffner

SUMMARY. Grant funding is not simply "free money." Even the best planned grant-funded projects can run into unanticipated problems and roadblocks, particularly if the endeavor is to work with content that is not controlled by the award institution. The goal of this article is to provide an overview of one such instance where a Slavic project ran into unforeseen problems. It will provide a summary of the undertaking and discuss the difficulties involved in completing this type of digital Slavic project in order to illustrate the challenges that future awardees may face when working on grant-funded projects. *[Article copies available for a fee from The Haworth Document Delivery Service: 1-800-HAWORTH. E-mail address: <docdelivery@haworthpress.com> Website: <http://www.HaworthPress.com> © 2005 by The Haworth Press, Inc. All rights reserved.]*

KEYWORDS. Russian archives, grant funding, Russia, United States, database, digital projects, Germans from Russia, U.S. Department of Education, University of Kansas, East View Information Services

Bradley L. Schaffner, MLS, MA, is Head, Slavic Division, Widener Library of the Harvard College Library, Harvard University, Cambridge, MA 02138 USA (E-mail: bschaffn@fas.harvard.edu).

Special thanks to Maria Carlson, Department of Slavic Languages and Literatures, University of Kansas, and Brian Baird, Heckman Bindery for their excellent advice and assistance on this article.

[Haworth co-indexing entry note]: "No Free Lunch: Grant Adventures in the Digital Frontier." Schaffner, Bradley, L. Co-published simultaneously in *Slavic & East European Information Resources* (The Haworth Information Press, an imprint of The Haworth Press, Inc.) Vol. 6, No. 2/3, 2005, pp. 169-182; and: *Virtual Slavica: Digital Libraries, Digital Archives* (ed: Michael Neubert) The Haworth Information Press, an imprint of The Haworth Press, Inc., 2005, pp. 169-182. Single or multiple copies of this article are available for a fee from The Haworth Document Delivery Service [1-800-HAWORTH, 9:00 a.m. - 5:00 p.m. (EST). E-mail address: docdelivery@haworthpress.com].

Available online at http://www.haworthpress.com/web/SEEIR
© 2005 by The Haworth Press, Inc. All rights reserved.
doi:10.1300/J167v06n02_11

Milton Friedman may have been thinking of grant funding when he said, "there is no free lunch." Indeed, most grants have restrictions on how the award can be used, but these limitations are generally well defined in the application instructions and are no surprise to anyone involved in the grant process. Unfortunately, experience also shows that there can be other, unexpected surprises associated with grant funding. Even the best planned grant-funded projects can run into unanticipated problems and roadblocks, particularly if the endeavor is to work with content that is not controlled by the award institution.

The University of Kansas (KU) Libraries' Slavic Department, in collaboration with the KU Center for Russian and East European Studies (CREES), recently received a U.S. Department of Education Title VI grant through the Technological Innovation and Cooperation for Foreign Information Access (TICFIA) program and found itself exactly in such an unexpected situation. Originally, the award was made to fund a project to digitize, preserve, and provide fully searchable machine-readable electronic access to a significant collection of archival documents in Russia. Although the archive administration holding the documents initially expressed interest in participating in this project, they changed their minds after the award, almost ending the project before it started. However, thanks to the understanding and help of Susanna Easton and her staff at the Department of Education's Office of Post Secondary Education, and the assistance and advice of Kirill Fesenko of East View Information Services, the principal investigators refocused the project on the creation of another archival resource, and the enterprise moved forward.[1] The aim of this article is to provide an overview of the project as it was conceived and discuss the difficulties involved in completing this type of digital Slavic project in order to illustrate the challenges that future awardees may face when working on similar grant-funded projects.

In 2001, the leadership of the American Historical Society of Germans From Russia (AHSGR) approached the KU Center for Russian and East European Studies with an intriguing proposal.[2] AHSGR expressed an interest in working in cooperation with CREES to establish a center for the study of Germans from Russia at KU. KU was a logical site for this institute, given that the state of Kansas is home to a large population of descendants of Germans from Russia, and the university has a robust Slavic Studies program. This initiative proposed to create a unique center for the study of the experience of Russian Germans in Russia.

Large groups of Germans emigrated at various times in the eighteenth and nineteenth centuries to the Trans-Volga region, to Odessa and the Black Sea area, to parts of Western Ukraine, and to other areas of Russia. An enormous body of materials on the demographics, social behavior, family life, history, culture, political activity, and other features of this population is housed in secondary Russian archives in those regions. This material is quickly disintegrating and being lost.[3] While the experience of the Russian Germans after they left Russia and came to the U.S. has been well documented, much less is known about the experience of the Russian Germans in Russia, and archival material is significantly more difficult to access.[4] This ethnically German population, living in the heartland of Russia, presents particularly interesting features for sociological, cross-cultural, anthropological, historical, and political study (the group was heavily persecuted under the Soviet regime).

Coincidentally, at about the same time that AHSGR approached CREES regarding their plan to establish a Germans from Russia research center, the Department of Education's Office of Post Secondary Education issued a call for proposals for the second round of their TICFIA grant program.[5] Although no formal agreement was made between AHSGR and KU (nor would an agreement ever be reached), CREES director Maria Carlson and KU Slavic Librarian Brad Schaffner agreed that the TICFIA grant program provided KU with an excellent opportunity to create an important digital resource related to the Germans from Russia. In addition, the project had the added benefit of providing important public outreach to a significant constituency of Germans from Russia in the Great Plains region and represented an important collaboration with the collections of the Kansas State Historical Society.

Based on suggestions by an AHSGR historian, Schaffner, with the help of Carlson and Brian Baird, the KU Libraries' Preservation Librarian,[6] developed a proposal to preserve and digitize the Tiraspol Consistory Records, held in the archives in Saratov Oblast' archive in Russia. Grant funds were requested to cover the cost of microfilming (to speed up the digitization process and for preservation) and digitizing the sixty-eight-volume, hand-written set of records. Each volume is about 200 pages in length, and contains birth (baptism), marriage, and death records. The collection provides valuable information about everyday life in imperial Russia. For example, the death records chronicle epidemics, crimes, and periods of social change and upheaval. In total, the collection provides a key primary resource for the study of village life in later imperial Russia.

The Roman Catholic Consistory for all of South Russia (many of the Germans were Catholic or Lutheran) was named for the small city of Tiraspol, in Ukraine. Since the 1840s, the Consistory had been located in Chernigov, Mogilev, and several other temporary locations. Since there was neither a Catholic Church nor suitable housing for the bishops in Tiraspol, it was decided to locate the Consistory in Saratov, where there was a Catholic seminary. Catholic churches in Russia made copies of their vital records (births, deaths, marriages, etc.) and annually forwarded these copies, or "Bishop's transcripts," to the Consistory in Saratov. Lutheran churches had to do the same. Regardless of where the church was in southern Russia, Ukraine, Volga, or the Caucasus, the transcripts went to Saratov.

Because the Tiraspol Consistory Records are chronological, handwritten entries, they are extremely difficult and cumbersome to use—in their current state they are of little value to scholars. The proposed TICFIA project was developed to address this problem by making the records fully searchable and easily readable. Because the books are hand-written, unless the researcher is a specialist in Russian and German pre-Revolutionary written script, it is often difficult or impossible to read the entries. For this same reason, it is impossible to use Optical Character Recognition (OCR) software to create the database with acceptable accuracy. Therefore, to improve accuracy of the finished electronic resource and to ensure that the project would be completed in a timely manner, the text was to be keyed manually. The goal of the project was to make the text fully searchable with the electronic version of each page linked to each high-quality TIFF image of the original document.

For archival purposes, the master negative microfilm would have been stored at the University of Kansas's off-site secure climate-controlled storage facility. The Saratov archive would also have a use copy of the microfilm. In addition, any library, student, researcher, or other interested party anywhere in the world would be able to order a copy of the Tiraspol Consistory Records for a nominal fee covering reproduction costs. However, primary and easiest access to the information would have been through a web interface that would allow scholars to search the text, view each page of the Tiraspol Consistory Records, and to read the text online.

NO FREE LUNCH

Although the Saratov Oblast' archive administration had originally expressed an interest in participating in this project (after a complex negotiation), when the grant was awarded, they changed their minds. They indicated that they would be happy to work on another project with KU, but not the Tiraspol Consistory Records project proposed for the grant. Over the next nine months, efforts were made to negotiate a resolution to this impasse.

At the onset of this stalemate, Schaffner asked Kirill Fesenko, of East View Information Services (East View was the vendor contracted to do the technical work on the project) to talk with the administration. Mr. Fesenko, and East View, have successfully negotiated hundreds of contracts with Russian archives, publishers, and other businesses, and Schaffner and Carlson felt that Mr. Fesenko was best equipped to lead the negotiations with the Saratov archive administration. Unfortunately, even with Fesenko's intercession, the administration would not change its stance on this issue.

Another approach to move the project forward was made by Ed Wagner of the AHSGR. He contacted a member of the German government, the Federal Government Commissioner for Matters related to Repatriates and National Minorities of the Federal Ministry of the Interior. This official expressed strong interest in seeing the KU TICFIA project completed and told Mr. Wagner that the German government, which has an interest in the records housed at the Saratov archive, would work with the archive administration in an effort to make this project a reality.[7] Unfortunately, even after the expression of interest by the German government, there continued to be no movement on the part of the archive administration to participate in the project.

As a result of all of these unsuccessful efforts, principal investigators Carlson and Schaffner were forced to conclude that KU would be unable to work with the administrators of the Saratov archive on the digitization of the Tiraspol Consistory Records. Schaffner's interpretation of the situation at the time was that the archive administration felt that the records had financial value, a belief reinforced when the grant was awarded for the digitization of the records. (This interpretation did indeed have some credence, as the reader will see at the conclusion of this article.) The intent of the grant, however, was to provide free access to important scholarly material, and KU was in no position to offer compensation to the archive for ongoing access to these records. When it first appeared that there might be problems working with the Saratov archive administration, Schaffner started exploring alternative projects of a similar size and scope of the original project.

NEVER SAY DIE: PROPOSAL FOR THE REVISION OF THE KU TICFIA GRANT

Because a successful conclusion to negotiations with Saratov quickly appeared doubtful, Schaffner, Carlson, and Fesenko devised an alternative project similar in size to the Tiraspol Consistory Records that could be completed using the current award. The new proposal was designed to appeal to a much broader audience of students and scholars. Grant funding would be used to create a searchable electronic database of regional and national guides to Russian Archives. In some respects, it was inspired by the project to microfilm regional archives guides proposed by Jared Ingersoll of Columbia University to the Slavic and East European Microfilm Project (SEEMP) of the Center for Research Libraries (CRL).[8] Whereas the goal of the Ingersoll project was to microfilm archival guides to preserve them and, as a result, also improve access, the KU project proposed to create an online database of guides to allow researchers to search numerous guides in a single, online search. The Ingersoll project will work with a much larger number of guides, whereas the KU project is working on a more focused group of guides selected by the Federal Archive Agency of Russia (Rosarkhiv).[9] This project will digitize approximately 105 central and regional archive guides for Russia.[10] The resulting database will provide the most comprehensive access to the holdings of the Russian archive system in one simple, user-friendly electronic format.[11] Creation of this database will allow students and scholars from anywhere in the world to identify the type and location of important archival holdings related to their research or areas of interest quickly and efficiently.

There is an obvious need for this project. Since the fall of the Soviet government, the Russian archive system, which houses most of the important documents for the study of contemporary and historical Russia, has been opened, to varying degrees, for research. Unfortunately, even as access to the archives themselves has opened up, prospective researchers continue to face a lack of easy access to information about holdings of specific archives, especially those in distant provinces of Russia. The researcher must locate individual guides to each archive in order to identify and use these archival resources. Many of the guides, however, are not readily available in any centralized location and the researcher must travel to the regional archive to consult the guide. This project addresses the problem of access through the creation of a single, easily searchable database of holdings for the Russian archive system.

In order to refocus the project, KU had to receive approval for this change from the Department of Education. Thankfully, these negotiations went smoothly, and the Department of Education staff quickly realized the value of the initiative and approved the proposed change to the KU TICFIA project.[12] Soon after the Department of Education approved the change, a contract was signed with Rosarkhiv for the project. Even before the contract was signed, Schaffner and Fesenko worked with representatives of Rosarkhiv, on the technical and content aspects of this project. Based on current progress, it is expected that the content will be digitized and at least a portion of the database available for use in early 2005.

WHAT WENT WRONG AND WHY THE PROJECT WILL SUCCEED

The principal investigators did a number of things right, which ensured that this grant would succeed; at the same time, they also made a number of missteps, which caused project delays and almost completely derailed the endeavor. The article will now examine both the innovations and problems of this grant project.

The grant will succeed because it was thoughtfully organized and planned out. From the onset, Schaffner wanted to design a grant that could be completed without any additional, grant-funded staff having to be hired for the project. There were two reasons for this approach: first and foremost, there are always challenges involved in hiring staff with special skills (in this case, Russian language and computer skills for working with databases). Recruiting qualified staff is made even more difficult when one is making temporary hires, because although this was designed as a three-year project, funding has to be renewed annually, with no guarantee of renewal. Therefore, because continual employment depends on grant renewals, the persons most likely to posses the skills needed for this project were also those most likely to be interested in long-term (rather than short-term) employment opportunities.

Additionally, the TICFIA grant required a one-third cost-share by the grantee (KU). The cost share could be financial, or it could be contributed cost. This meant that when the Department of Education awarded

$85,000 for the first year of this grant, KU had to provide at least $28,000 in cost-share. By using regular staff on the project, the percentage of their salary spent on the project contributed towards the cost-share. If additional temporary staff had been hired to run the grant rather than permanent staff, KU would then have had to make a financial contribution towards the project, something that was not institutionally feasible at the time of the application.

Second, and most important, it would be a waste of effort to try to complete this project from scratch. The author observed that many of the original TICFIA grantees spent a lot of time, effort, and money developing software and databases as part of the infrastructure for their projects, leaving less time and money to focus on the actual content of the project. This is unfortunate, given that the goal of the TICFIA program is to "access, collect, organize, preserve, and widely disseminate information on world regions and countries other than the United States that address our nation's teaching and research needs in international education and foreign languages."[13]

The design of the KU project centered on the idea of subcontracting as much of the technical work as possible to a vendor experienced in creating similar projects commercially. To this end, Schaffner had extensive talks with a number of vendors and publishers to discuss possible projects, their feasibility, and cost during the conceptual stage of the proposal. This grant will succeed in great part because of the intellectual engagement and professionalism of the staff at East View Information Services, the company with which KU subcontracted to do much of the technical work of the project.

A major advantage of working with an established vendor in the field of Slavic studies like East View is that East View already has in-country facilities and staff to work on a project, providing significant infrastructure cost savings. If KU staff were to attempt to complete this project in-house, the cost would have greatly increased due to additional technical, staff, and travel costs. By working with East View, these costs were substantially reduced. If the KU grant staff had attempted to complete this project in-house, they would have had to ship the appropriate equipment to Moscow, no small task given the red tape involved in bringing specialized camera and computer equipment into Russia, even for a short period of time. Along with paying to ship equipment to Russia, the grant would also have had to pay to send qualified staff to use the equipment or expend additional funds to train staff on site. Furthermore, other staff, fluent in Russian, would have to accompany this crew in order to communicate with the archive staff. Subcontracting with East

View to complete this part of the project meant that East View can exploit their qualified Russian-speaking in-country staff, which is already experienced in completing this type of work. In addition, East View has previously developed a number of large Cyrillic-language databases with great success, and as a result has experts on-site who would be available for the TICFIA project.

The principal investigators also anticipated that the negotiations with the Russian archives would be complex and time-consuming. Nevertheless, they did not expect that the original archives would drop out of the project altogether, particularly after the receipt of numerous e-mails in support of the Tiraspol Consistory Records project. Here KU also benefited from the expertise of East View's Kirill Fesenko, who led the talks to complete the project with the administration of the Saratov archive. When this discussion came to a dead end, Fesenko led the successful negotiation of the current project with the administration of Rosarkhiv. The staff at East View brought an enthusiasm and drive to this project that was not anticipated by the principal investigators. East View showed itself to be committed to completing this project in order to demonstrate that a commercial vendor can work successfully with a university on grant-funded projects to create and provide access to important research materials to the benefit of all.

The project will also succeed thanks to the flexibility and cooperation of the staff at the Department of Education's Office of Postsecondary Education. Susanna Easton and her colleagues understood the challenges posed by working in the FSU, and were willing to consider an alternative proposal for the grant. As a result of their flexibility, the scholarly community will soon have access to a resource superior to the project originally proposed.

Obviously, the story of this grant is not only one of success. The principal investigators made a number of errors in the formulation of this project that will be illustrated here for the benefit of future grant applicants. As mentioned at the beginning of this article, the original grant was an outgrowth of a potential project between KU and the AHSGR for the creation of a Germans from Russia study center. Due to a number of considerations, the principal investigators had less than six weeks to come up with an idea, develop a project, and submit a complex proposal (of approximately forty pages, including narratives and budget sheets) to the Department of Education. Prior to the official submission, the proposal first had to be reviewed and vetted by the KU Center for Research, no small task in itself.

Because time was short, Schaffner developed the grant project based on an idea suggested by colleagues at AHSGR. Although the KU Libraries do not actively collect genealogical resources, the Tiraspol Consistory Records are far more than genealogical records; they are a unique collection of documents that would be of use to Russian, German, and American scholars in a variety of disciplines. The records were also of extreme interest to the members of the AHSGR. Unfortunately, the full extent of this interest was not revealed until after the negotiations with the Saratov archive ended. It became clear that numerous descendants of Germans from Russia, many members of the AHSGR, had contacted the Saratov archive and local academics on a regular basis and had paid to receive genealogical information from the Tiraspol Consistory Records. Therefore, AHSGR had an interest in making these records freely available on the web to its members, while doing so was clearly not in the best interests of the Saratov archive. Had the principal investigators known that AHSGR members were paying to get information from the Tiraspol Consistory Records at the onset, they would not have moved forward on this project: it was clearly destined to fail. Why would the archive give up its cash cow? (However, one must ask why the Saratov archive administration originally agreed to work on this project with KU.)

Because Schaffner had never worked directly with the Tiraspol Consistory Records, he had to rely on third-party descriptions of the records as he developed the proposal. After the grant was awarded, Schaffner contacted the Saratov archive to request that they send several sample pages of the records so that East View could review the records to finalize their bid on the project. Saratov's silence regarding this request was the initial indication that the Saratov archive administration might have changed their minds regarding participation in this project.

The AHSGR was involved in this grant proposal because KU hoped to achieve three major things:

1. To develop a research center on the Germans from Russia. Several KU faculty do research in this area, and this population is of considerable historical, philological, and anthropological interest.
2. To promote outreach to regional populations, (which include a significant population of Germans from Russia), one of the major mandates of state institutions such as KU.

3. To enhance a strong collaborative relationship with the Kansas State Historical Society.

Members of the AHSGR were very enthusiastic about the TICFIA grant and offered considerable moral support when the award was announced. Unfortunately, most rank and file members did not understand how grants work. The award was made public approximately six months before the funding was made available for the project. During this time Schaffner received several dozen phone calls and e-mails from members of AHSGR inquiring where they could find the database. In addition, almost every caller, to a person, wanted to know about Schaffner's heritage–it was assumed that he too was a descendent of a German from Russia. Schaffner spoke with each person individually to explain that the project would not start for about six months and nothing would be publicly available for at least two years. He also explained that his family's background was Swiss; both of these pieces of news were received with disappointment.

On October 1, 2002, the first day of the federal fiscal year and the first day of the TICFIA grant, the calls started all over again. This time many of the callers knew that the project had received its first-year funding, and they wanted to know why the database was not yet available. While it was gratifying to find out that there was so much interest in this project, the time KU staff spent talking with people with a passing interest in the project could have been better used on completing other aspects of the grant.

When the Saratov archive administration decided to withdraw from the project, several highly placed members of the AHSGR considered going to Saratov to demand that the archive allow KU to have access to the Tiraspol Consistory Records. This was not diplomatically wise; moreover, no one was in a position to make such a demand. If this approach did not work, AHSGR wanted to explore the possibility of paying the administration for access to the records, although it was unclear what funds would be used to make this payment. Meanwhile, KU and East View were doing everything possible to negotiate with Saratov.

The Saratov archive administration was certainly within its rights to withdraw from the project, and they did. Taking the long view, the principal investigators concluded that offering cash payment to get the administration to participate in the grant would have been detrimental to other attempts to gain access to materials, because there would then be an expectation of monetary compensation for access to other archival records. The principal investigators would win the battle but lose the war.

CONCLUSION

One must take special care to consider every aspect of the possible challenges and problems that one faces when developing a grant involving materials held at another institution. It is an even greater challenge if the other institution is in a foreign country like Russia, where there is no strong tradition of open access to archives. As KU's experience shows, even having the initial consent of the foreign institution is no guarantee that the grantee will be given access to the material if funding is awarded for the project. If one is to go forward with this type of project, one must develop the project carefully, taking into account every point from the technical challenges, to staffing, to access. When working on Slavic digital projects, this author highly recommends that one consider working with an established contractor who has technical experience and in-country staff to complete the project. Such an approach can be extremely cost-effective, both from a technical and a logistical standpoint.

Many granting agencies now encourage partnerships between academia and other NGOs. If your grant initiative would benefit from such a partnership, be certain to factor in the time that you will spend on liaison work with your partner. Many organizations have not worked with scholarly granting agencies, and a principal investigator should factor in time spent explaining the process to the uninitiated partners.

Some readers may be wondering if it was worth the effort to create this project. After all, the author spent almost two years developing the initial proposal, negotiating the project, developing a new proposal and negotiating that project with the Department of Education and Rosarkhiv. (And this was a project designed to be extremely streamlined, so that the principal investigator could complete the work in addition to his regular full-time duties.) Only time will tell if it was really worth the effort. So, was it worth it? Absolutely. The author believes that the Access to Russian Archives database will greatly enhance Slavic scholars' ability to conduct archival research and is therefore worthy of grant funding and completion.

One last word of advice: whatever project you develop, always have a Plan B![14]

NOTES

1. Susanna Easton oversees the U.S. Department of Education's TICFIA Program. KU contracted with East View Information Services <http://www.eastview.com/> (accessed August 12, 2004) to work on the TICFIA grant. Kirill Fesenko is the East View staff member supervising the contract work.

2. Information on the AHSGR can be found at <http://www.ahsgr.org/> (accessed August 12, 2004).

3. Recent research has shown that 17.43 percent or more of all Russian and Soviet publications held in libraries are currently brittle. (Bradley L. Schaffner and Brian Baird, "Into the Dustbin of History? The Evaluation and Preservation of Slavic Materials," *College & Research Libraries* 60 (March 1999): 4.) Brittle materials will fall apart when used. Complicating matters is the fact that over 87 percent of all Russian and Soviet holdings are printed on acidic paper that will become brittle and deteriorate, becoming inaccessible to experts, students, and scholars in the field. (Schaffner and Baird, "Into the Dustbin of History?," 5.) Although the percentage of brittle materials may vary by institution, most research libraries face similar challenges with significant percentages of brittle collections. (Condition surveys at other libraries, such as Yale, the University of Illinois, and Syracuse University Library have indicated that the percentage of embrittled volumes can be as high as 35 percent of the entire collection. The geographic location of the library, as well as such storage conditions as climate control, play a major factor in the deterioration of printed materials. See: Thomas H. Teper and Stepanie S. Atkins, "Building Preservation: The University of Illinois at Urbana-Champaign's Stack Assessment," *College & Research Libraries* 64 (May 2003): 211-227; Gay Walker et al., "The Yale Survey: A Large-Scale Study of the Book Deterioration in the Yale University Library," *College & Research Libraries* 46 (March 1985): 111-132; Tina Chrzastowski et al., "Library Collection Deterioration: A Study at the University of Illinois at Urbana-Champaign," *College & Research Libraries* 50 (September 1989): 577-584; Randall Bond et al., "Preservation Study at the Syracuse University Library," *College & Research Libraries* 48 (March 1987): 132-147.)

4. For example, see The North Dakota State University Libraries' *Germans from Russia Heritage Collection* at <http://www.lib.ndsu.nodak.edu/grhc/index.html> (accessed August 13, 2004).

5. Information on this program can be found at <http://www.ed.gov/programs/iegpsticfia/index.html> (accessed August 10, 2004). Information on past and current projects can be found at <http://www.crl.edu/areastudies/ticfia> (accessed August 10, 2004).

6. Brian Baird is now Director of Preservation Services, Heckman Bindery, 1010 North Sycamore Street, P.O. Box 89, North Manchester, IN 46962, (800) 334-3628 ext. 111, brian_baird@heckmanbindery.com.

7. One thought was that the German government might provide financial support to the archive if the records were made available for the project.

8. For information on SEEMP see <http://www.crl.edu/areastudies/SEEMP/index.htm> (accessed August 16, 2004).

9. Information on Rosarkhiv can be found at <http://www.rusarchives.ru> (accessed August 20, 2004).

10. Detailed information on the project, including work in progress and completed can be found at <http://online.eastview.com/projects/RA/index.html> (accessed August 16, 2004).

11. Patricia Kennedy Grimsted, undoubtedly the premier Western expert on Russian and former Soviet archives, has a website devoted to Russian archives, ArcheoBiblioBase, which lists various archives, provides a brief overview of the institution's holdings, and its location. It also includes a great deal of other useful information regarding archives. ArcheoBiblioBase can be found at <http://www.iisg.nl/~abb/index.html> (accessed August 20, 2004). While the database does provide bibliographic information for archive finding aids, it does not list the actual holdings of the archives.

12. The negotiated change with the Department of Education went quickly and smoothly, thanks in part to the fact Schaffner and Carlson flew to Washington, DC to discuss the proposed grant changes in person with Susanna Easton and her staff. This face-to-face meeting helped move the negotiations forward.

13. From TICFIA's front page <http://www.ed.gov/programs/iegpsticfia/index.html> (accessed on August 20, 2004).

14. Anyone interested in discussing this project in more detail can contact the principal investigator, Maria Carlson, carlson@ku.ed, and/or the past co-principal investigator, Bradley Schaffner, bschaffn@fas.harvard.edu.

Digital Reference
in Slavic and East European Studies
with an Examination of Practice
at the University of Illinois
and the Library of Congress

Angela Cannon

SUMMARY. This article presents a survey of digital reference trends in the United States with an emphasis on services for Slavic and East European studies. It is based on the author's experience as a Slavic reference librarian at the University of Illinois (Slavic Reference Service) and the Library of Congress (European Division). Topics include the conflict between print and digital resources, coping with electronic serials, full-text databases and websites, digital communication tools such as e-mail, chat, and web forms, the proliferation of websites from

Angela Cannon, MA, MLS, is Reference Librarian, Library of Congress, European Division, Washington, DC 20540-4830 USA (E-mail: acannon@loc.gov).

The author would like to express her gratitude to the following individuals who either read this article and gave helpful suggestions or who took the time to provide me with information about the projects on which they are working: Helen Sullivan, Manager of the Slavic Reference Service at the University of Illinois; Alison Morin, Digital Reference Specialist of the Library of Congress QuestionPoint Team; Jane W. Jacobs, Assistant Coordinator, Catalog Division at the Queens Borough Public Library; Harry Leich, Russian Area Specialist, European Division, Library of Congress.

Opinions stated in this article are those of the author and not of the Library of Congress.

[Haworth co-indexing entry note]: "Digital Reference in Slavic and East European Studies with an Examination of Practice at the University of Illinois and the Library of Congress." Cannon, Angela. Co-published simultaneously in *Slavic & East European Information Resources* (The Haworth Information Press, an imprint of The Haworth Press, Inc.) Vol. 6, No. 2/3, 2005, pp. 183-217; and: *Virtual Slavica: Digital Libraries, Digital Archives* (ed: Michael Neubert) The Haworth Information Press, an imprint of The Haworth Press, Inc., 2005, pp. 183-217.

Available online at http://www.haworthpress.com/web/SEEIR
doi:10.1300/J167v06n02_12

Eastern Europe and the NIS, and opportunities for bibliographic instruction via the web. The article concludes with suggestions for keeping current and ideas for possible reference collaboration among Slavic and East European studies librarians.

KEYWORDS. Digital reference, electronic reference, virtual reference, Internet, online resources, Slavic, Eastern Europe, East Europe, Central Europe, Russia, NIS, University of Illinois, Slavic Reference Service, Library of Congress, European Division, European Reading Room, libraries, United States

INTRODUCTION

The introduction of digital technologies and the Internet has caused a revolution in the way libraries operate. Reference librarians have experienced this revolution just as much as catalogers, acquisitions staff, and librarians with other areas of responsibility. Libraries have invested an enormous amount of money in digital products and services, and to ensure that this money is not wasted, reference librarians have had to modify old, more traditional reference strategies to help users take advantage of these new tools. Besides learning new techniques, reference librarians are also getting involved in creating systems and content that enhance the user's research experience. The same is true for providers of more specialized reference services such as Slavic and East European (Slavic, for short) reference librarians in the United States. This essay is an overview of the trends in digital reference with particular emphasis on the Slavic field, highlighted by specific examples from my personal experiences as a Slavic reference librarian at two major U.S. research libraries, the University of Illinois at Urbana-Champaign (Slavic Reference Service in the Slavic and East European Library) and the Library of Congress (European Division). I will survey the impact the digital revolution has had on the provision of specialized reference services and explore the areas in which Slavic librarians have risen to meet the new challenges or, conversely, need to expand their participation, always keeping in mind a reference librarian's mantra, "whether our collections are large or small, whether our technologies are complex or simple, whether our patrons are worldwide or local, librarians care about *use*."[1]

In this essay digital reference is defined most broadly, encompassing all forms of electronic communication and data access such as e-mail, web forms, chat, the use of online databases and catalogs, the Internet, electronic courseware, and so on. The expression *virtual reference*, conversely, is restricted to reference communication via chat or some kind of real-time instant messaging software, although the two terms *digital* and *virtual reference* are often used interchangeably in the library literature. Since there is sufficient content to fill an entire book in this area, what follows is a modest selection of the many issues and resources concerning digital reference for Slavic and East European studies.

REVIEW OF THE LITERATURE

With the advent of e-mail and chat programs as part of mainstream reference practice in many libraries there has been an explosion of literature on digital reference in American library journals. For example, a search in *Library Literature* for the descriptor Reference Services–Automation yielded over 1,500 hits as of July 1, 2004. An online bibliography of articles related to digital reference is maintained by Bernie Sloan, Senior Library Information Systems Consultant at ILCSO; it contains over 600 citations as of its last update on November 18, 2003.[2] A national conference devoted to the topic[3] is now an annual event and there are even e-mail discussion groups just for digital reference participants.[4] Recognizing the importance of digital services to libraries worldwide, the Reference Work section of IFLA has recently created guidelines and standards for digital reference and the ALA Reference and User Services Association just did so as well.[5]

However, this research situation does not hold true for reference services provided by Slavic and East European librarians in the United States. In comparison, very little has been published about the practice of reference work for Slavic studies in general, and even less about its digital aspects. Although the literature for Slavic studies contains some descriptions of digital projects and is certainly flush with website reviews, these two topics represent only a fraction of what digital reference really encompasses. Reference topics tend to arise in Slavic library articles mainly devoted to other topics, such as cataloging or acquisitions. What follows is a brief survey of published works on some aspect of Slavic and digital reference.

Helen Sullivan, Manager of the Slavic Reference Service at the University of Illinois (SRS/UIUC), has written several articles that include information about the digital reference projects occurring at the SRS under her tenure. In her 2003 article, the discussion of various SRS reference practices illustrates the melding of electronic with traditional print resources in the Slavic reference environment. This article also provides an overview of other SRS digital reference projects, such as the development of an online guide to Slavic and East European reference sources and a chat service for Slavic studies questions.[6] Sullivan's 2002 article tackles the use of course management software for online dissemination of the SRS guide to Slavic bibliography as well as the nascent efforts to institute an international Slavic chat reference program.[7] Teresa Tickle also deals with the Slavic Reference Service, but at a time when e-mail requests and a website for the SRS were just beginning. She addresses the importance of using digital methods for outreach to a distant user community.[8] Michael Neubert focuses on answering various ready reference questions using such Russian websites as Internet telephone directories, online catalogs, and search engines.[9] Gordon Anderson investigates commonly-held subscription databases for their usefulness in Slavic research.[10] Marta Mestrovic Deyrup reports on U.S. Slavic librarians' involvement with information literacy programs.[11] Additionally, a number of subject-specific guides to electronic resources and websites have been published, such as Terri Tickle Miller on Internet resources for East European census data[12] and Peter Roudik surveying online sources for Russian laws.[13] In addition, Wojciech Zalewski's classic guide to Russian reference sources is now available on the web.[14]This brief survey shows that Slavic librarians in the United States are involved with digital reference even though the body of literature on the topic is modest. This is perhaps due to the scope of professional responsibilities of Slavic librarians: most of them are full-time catalogers or bibliographers with reference as only a small part of their duties. In addition, some hold positions that provide no incentives for research or publication, or that may even discourage work time spent on such activities. Thus many Slavic reference experiences, digital or otherwise, are not being recorded.

HOW REFERENCE HAS CHANGED
AND HOW IT HAS STAYED THE SAME

The traditional role of the reference librarian has been to guide readers in the use of the library and to direct them to reliable sources of information that might answer their questions. The digital revolution has not changed that basic premise; however, it has, depending on one's viewpoint, complicated or facilitated the reference librarian's ability to perform these tasks. Some believe the proliferation of online databases and websites has infinitely complicated the process, that there is so much information available it is impossible to keep up, impossible to hit a moving target, since the situation and the sites change on a daily basis. In addition, since one cannot see the sources, it is impossible to make a preliminary assessment of the scope of an electronic resource instantly in the way one can with a big fat reference book or a skinny little bibliography. One usually cannot skim the table of contents or indexes for a quick judgment of relevance. Databases and websites can have untold depths or be quite limited or haphazard in scope. The scope of the Internet also changes phenomenally every day.

Others feel that the often free access to online finding aids and catalogs and to bibliographic and full-text databases, greatly enhances their ability to help the patron satisfy his/her information needs. Being able to search another library's catalog instantaneously has shaved hours or even days off of a location query when the previous options were to telephone or write a letter to the other library. Even the millions of websites with unknown or questionable authority have the potential to provide valuable clues to finding the answer to a reference question. Concomitant with digital resources is a technological aspect to reference service that did not exist before. We need to understand the components of an online bibliographic record; decrypt the user interface of a database; help patrons make copies of desired material via floppy disk, CD-ROM, or scanning; and, for Slavic librarians and other foreign language specialists, help the patron with special encodings or keyboards.

The moving target issue is a legitimate cause for concern among reference librarians, for the problem of the stability of resources has entered the arena. Print resources do not change from day to day, rather they appear in new editions. Print resources also do not disappear–unless someone actively makes them disappear by stealing or misshelving. A reader does not need to take any kind of action to make a print resource readable. He/she can either read the printed alphabet or not. In the past the enormity of the publishing output was not as great an issue either, for libraries developed cataloging and classification schemes to cope with finding one item in a sea of many. With the Internet, however, not only are reputable publishers producing content, so are millions of individuals and groups whose output would not normally have been added to library collections. And to make matters worse, bibliographic or subject control with today's Internet resources is still in its infancy.

Initially, because of the specialized nature of the subject queries, the digital arena may not have seemed as important for Slavic and East European librarians as it was for general reference librarians, but times have changed. Now practically all of the countries in our region have online catalogs and significant web presences. New databases, Internet portals, e-libraries, and other valuable resources are emerging at a steady pace. And more and more Western digital products are either focusing on or including Slavic-related materials, for example East View Information Services's *Universal Databases*, and *JSTOR*, and *Project Muse*, to name just a few.

Now a constant for librarians of every sort is the ongoing theoretical debate about digital versus print. In my opinion, the digital revolution can be considered a tremendous boon to reference services, as long as one does not seek to replace or eliminate the contribution that printed resources bring to play. But in spite of the enormous changes technology has brought to the field, the digital world has not altered certain traditions of the previous print-only scene: the need for excellent searching skills, the requirement to stay current on important new sources, and the necessity to understand cataloging rules and indexing concepts in order to instruct a patron properly on how to use a particular tool. How much more complicated is it to show people how to e-mail articles to themselves than it is to help them with a cranky microfilm reader printer? Reference work is still reference work regardless of the environment, or, as Joseph Janes put it in his Library of Congress Luminary Lecture, "It isn't 'digital reference'; it's 'reference' . . . and that's what matters."[15]

Let three recent Slavic reference examples suffice to exemplify the value of print and digital resources as well as the necessary reliance on both in today's world. An SRS patron read a reference to Iambo the Elephant in Ivan Bunin's memoirs and wanted to know its significance. I checked various Russian subject encyclopedias such as circus and theater encyclopedias, historical encyclopedias, and even the major pre- and post-revolutionary general encyclopedias. There were no entries for Iambo, and likewise nothing about Iambo in the entries on elephants or circuses. There was also nothing about literary characters named Iambo in the Bunin criticism or reference books. Further, there was no information about a species of elephant called anything like "Iambo," admittedly a desperate avenue to explore. After checking the original source of citation, I tried a Russian search engine, Rambler, and voila! Iambo the Elephant appeared on several pages and even proffered a photograph. Although some of the pages with the information were of unknown authority and only partially explained Iambo's significance, they confirmed the veracity of Bunin's statement and encouraged me to search further, leading to the discovery, also on the Internet, of a scholar in the United States who has been researching the Iambo phenomenon. The patron who came to the SRS now had a substantive lead to conduct his/her own research on the topic. This question could not have been answered with print resources without the reference librarian crossing the line between reference work and research, and maybe not even then.

On the opposite side is the case of a printed source providing extremely quick access to bibliographic citations. A Library of Congress patron was looking for reader reactions to Nikolai Ostrovskii's communist classic *Kak zakalialas' stal'*. Within five minutes I had pulled the correct volume of the literary biobibliography set *Russkie sovetskie pisateli– rozaiki*, found the section for Ostrovskii, then the subsection of citations to works about this novel. In the list of over 130 citations there were many about readers' reactions. These results would have been impossible on the Internet unless the printed source has been digitized or some devoted Ostrovskii fan or scholar happened to have culled the citations and reproduced them on a website.

As many practicing reference librarians today can attest, a combination of print and digital resources is often the best mix. For instance, consider the following SRS request for information about the Palace Karabchevskii in pre-revolutionary St. Petersburg. The patron wanted to know where it was located and its connection to Belgians living in the city at the time. Simple enough, I thought foolishly. I determined the street address of the Belgian embassy and then started on the palace. I checked tourist and architectural guidebooks to St. Petersburg, the old city directory *Ves' Peterburg*, an encyclopedia of St. Petersburg, but no results. Then I started to investigate the Karabchevskii family using biographical dictionaries and necrologies. There wasn't an obvious link between this family and the city of St. Petersburg. So then I assumed the so-called palace was not a real palace, but rather a restaurant or hotel. Still nothing. Finally, by using the Russian Internet I found a reference to a rather famous lawyer in St. Petersburg named Karabchevskii and started to investigate him. From a website devoted to pre-revolutionary St. Petersburg addresses, I discovered that he lived in an elegant *osobniak* that was owned by his wife. Curiously, the address of her *osobniak* was next door to a temporary location for the Belgian embassy (which I had found in a printed volume). That's when I knew I must have the right Karabchevskii. This website referred to the *osobniak* under the name of Karabchevskii's father-in-law. That was the crucial piece of information I needed to investigate the building. In an architectural guide about the father-in-law's building I read that the lawyer Karabchevskii used to throw lavish parties at his wife's house and it became known anecdotally as the Palace Karabchevskii. This example clearly illustrates how both print and digital sources often intertwine today in a Slavic reference librarian's work. Finding the solution to this question required both kinds of sources, first the digital to give the identity of the man in question and to provide crucial clues to the name of the building, and second the print to provide the actual answer the patron was seeking.[16]

ONLINE CATALOGS, BIBLIOGRAPHIC AND FULL-TEXT DATABASES

It is indisputable that online catalogs and bibliographic databases are perhaps the most valuable contribution the digital world has made to reference work. Without leaving the country, or in many cases even leaving one's home, a researcher may search the collections of libraries around the world. Librarians and researchers are no longer constrained by the boundaries of their print collections. These wonderful tools enable verification of citations, locations for borrowing, determination of multi-volume holdings, and discovery of previously unknown resources for a topic of interest. In many cases the Internet and bibliographic databases serve as the jumping off points for beginning a question. Thus, when confronted with an unfamiliar name or place, a simple OCLC, OPAC, or Google search can help verify spellings, locations, or dates which then enable the reference librarian to focus better the direction of the search. I have used the *General'nyi alfavitnyi katalog knig na russkom iazyke (1725-1998)*[17] of the Russian National Library many times to check for first names, patronymics, and dates of life for an individual before I undertake further searching.

Most of the national libraries of the countries in our area now have at least an online catalog of recent items available via the Internet. Many university or scholarly institute libraries do as well. These catalogs may not have much retrospective depth at the present time, but the situation is changing rapidly. Some have added retrospective records to their OPACs, for example, the Russian National Library and the National Library of the Czech Republic. Others have provided scanned catalogs of paper card catalogs showing older holdings; for instance, both of the above-mentioned libraries and the Jagiellonian Library have done this.

The National and University Library in Ljubljana has a useful, scanned retrospective catalog covering 1774-1947, but unfortunately it has chosen a system that initiates a pop-up screen and a download of a plug-in that fails more often than not to load correctly; regardless, it is enormously useful for Slovenian research. Still others have followed different paths by scanning such major bibliographic tools as the *Katalog knjiga na jezicima jugoslovenskih naroda 1868-1972* (Catalog of Books in Languages of South Slavic Peoples) at the website of the National Library of Serbia, and the *Magyar Könyvészet 1712-1920* (Hungarian Bibliography) at the website of the National Széchényi Library, or by creating union catalogs of many libraries in a particular country, for instance the ones in the Czech Republic, Slovenia, Bosnia and Herzegovina, and Macedonia, to name a few.[18] Slovenia now hosts a unique catalog option called a database of researchers' bibliographies. The title is *Bibliografije raziskovalcev*, and it includes bibliographic citations for works by Slovenian researchers coded according to genre by the researchers themselves. Thus, when a bibliography is generated for an individual it may have sections for articles, books, conference papers, theses that the researcher has directed, reviews, interviews, etc. It is available through their COBISS system.[19]

These varied types of online catalogs not only aid Slavic reference librarians, but their patrons as well. We can show them how to use the catalogs in person or send URLs with basic searching tips if they are distance patrons. Searching tips and tutoring should include, of course, information about the necessity or non-necessity of using special keyboards for utilization of the catalogs. No blanket statement can be made about keyboards in East European library catalogs. Each must be tested to determine if the search results are different when diacritics or Cyrillic letters are used or not. Let two examples suffice to illustrate the problem. First, a search of the union catalog COBIB.MK of Macedonia shows that 92 hits result each time when searching a surname keyed in the following three ways: Pavic, Pavič, or Pavič written in Cyrillic. Searching various forms of Mancevski, Mančevski, or Mančevski written in Cyrillic also results in the same number of hits (97) for each spelling. Thus it appears that this catalog accommodates all forms; however a search of the variant forms of *Toshev* yields very different results: Toshev–8; Tosev–149; Tošev–147; Tošev written in Cyrillic–147. NKC, the online catalog of the National Library of the Czech Republic also yields varying results based on whether certain diacritics are keyed in or not. An author search for Dedic or Dědić yields 7 records, while a search for Dědič or Dedič results in 52 records. If a searcher does not know the correct diacritics for a name or term, he/she should at least be aware that multiple searches are necessary to locate all possible records. An added complication related to searching foreign databases is that there is no standard for transliteration of Cyrillic names into other alphabets. Thus, not only does the patron and the librarian need to remember the LC transliteration scheme for products in the United States, but they both must also be aware that German and French and Italian catalogs will use their own, non-LC, transliterations. Looking for Russian names or titles in a catalog from another Slavic country will also require adjusting to their unique transliterations. Anton Chekhov can serve as a common example of this situation–Russian: Chekhov (in Cyrillic); German: Tschechow; French: Tchékhov; Czech: Čechov; Serbo-Croatian: Čehov, etc. This situation also existed in the past when paper bibliographies were the standard tools, but somehow we expect more from digital tools: we expect name authority to connect us automatically to all versions of a name regardless of what we search in which catalogs. David Chroust's words of warning are well-taken, not just for OCLC and cataloging entries, but at all levels in online catalogs and databases everywhere, "Researchers would do well to anticipate variation rather than expect consistency . . ."[20] One search is never sufficient.

Just knowing that different keyboards may be an issue is a good start, but this knowledge must be taken a step further to their actual use: Slavic librarians need to know how to load and use the keyboards for themselves and be able to teach patrons. Loading special keyboards onto severely stripped-down public terminals is a constant struggle with the systems staff at both the University of Illinois and the Library of Congress, but worth the effort, so that one may instruct patrons and then let them fly solo with the various foreign tools. With regard to fonts and keyboards, an unusual program to reach out to specialized user groups is taking place at the Queens Borough Public Library. According to a press release dated November 10, 2003, this library, whose patron base is the "most ethnically diverse county in the United States," is making its foreign language titles searchable in their online catalog in the original scripts; thus Russian items may be viewed and searched in Cyrillic. This involves not only the processing of newly acquired items, but also applying a detransliteration program to retrospective materials. The library has provided its patrons both English and Russian instructions on how to access and use the Cyrillic keyboard that is made available on their website. They already are providing this service for Chinese, Korean, and Arabic, and are now experimenting with providing the same service with their other Cyrillic materials in Ukrainian, Belarusian, Bulgarian, and Serbian. If all goes according to plan, Greek and Urdu will be added sometime in 2005.[21]

The existence of searchable national bibliographies on the web is a positive trend worth some discussion. In the past, these highly valuable publications were collected heavily by major research libraries; thus the scholar at the smaller institution had difficulty taking advantage of their many benefits. This situation has changed dramatically in the past decade with many East European countries providing free access to their national bibliographies in some kind of online format. Besides the obvious need for bibliographic control, this trend may be related to a people's national identity. If indeed national bibliographies are "an important element in the preservation of a national culture,"[22] then we can expect even more developments of this type. Some countries are putting online versions of their national bibliographies on the web, such as the *Hrvatska bibliografija* (Croatian Bibliography) at the National and University Library or producing born-digital versions of their national bibliographies like the *Česká národní bibliografie* (Czech National Bibliography) at the site of the National Library of the Czech Republic. Both of these bibliographies take full advantage of the digital format by offering various types of searching, but the Hungarian national bibliography online has taken a different tack. It has produced an html version of each printed issue of the books section and provided links from the index to the individual records, but without a mechanism for searching.[23] For a searchable version of the Hungarian national bibliography, one must purchase a subscription to their CD-ROM. Regardless of format, the mere existence of these tools on a freely accessible platform is a remarkable occasion for scholars and librarians in our field.

The Russians, unfortunately, have decided to produce digital formats of their national bibliography in a for-purchase format. Thus, K. G. Saur is producing a searchable CD-ROM of the *Rossiiskaia natsional'naia bibliografiia* (Russian National Bibliography) and East View Information Services has recently started marketing an expensive database of the various Russian *letopisi*. East View has also included the sections of the Ukrainian national bibliography as part of its new Ukrainian Publications database. Having these extremely valuable tools in an electronic format makes the content more accessible for searching, but selling the information limits its reach to only a few wealthy research institutions.

On a more positive note, specialists at Indiana University have spear-headed a project to digitize back volumes of *Letopis' zhurnal'nykh statei* from 1956-1975 and provide an interface for searching.[24] This wonderful project has put a classic bibliographic tool into the hands of potential users anywhere in the world.

The next category of materials to be discussed is full-text databases and e-libraries. These sources allow the searcher to obtain the entire item online, for free, for a fee paid by the searcher, or via a library sub-scription. One example that I as a Slavic librarian can hardly imagine living without is the *Universal Databases* from East View. This package provides full-text access to hundreds of newspapers and journals from Russia and the CIS searchable in Cyrillic, transliteration, or English (for English language articles only). The interface is so easy to use that patrons get the hang of it immediately. Many of the regional newspapers contained in East View's databases are not available in this country in any other format, so not only is it providing searchable access to newspaper content, but searchable access to previously unavailable content as well. These full-text packages are valuable because they make it easier to find bits of relevant information inside articles and books, but they also voluminously expand smaller libraries' collections of Slavic and East European materials, that is if the smaller libraries can afford the price of a subscription. In addition to East View there are many aggregators providing the full text of scholarly journals in Western languages that have content pertinent to Slavic studies. *EBSCO Host* comes to mind with coverage of such titles as *Russian Review*, *Elementa*, *Scando-Slavica*, *Eastern European Quarterly*, *Russian Studies in Literature*, etc. All of the aggregators and their title coverage are too numerous to discuss in this survey, but they should be mentioned as valuable tools for digital reference in Slavic studies. Besides commercially produced full-text journals, there are e-libraries available for free on the Internet in almost all of the countries of the region. Many of these sites concentrate on digitizing the full text of classic works of literature. For example, the site *Fundamental'naia elektronnaia biblioteka "Russkaia literatura i fol'klor"* is loading the complete works of Lev Tolstoi based on the standard 100-volume set, along with such accompanying bibliographic aids for Tolstoi research as *Letopis' zhizni i tvorchestva Tolstogo*. This site is also in the process of adding the complete works of Lermontov, Tiutchev, and Pushkin, among others, and has digitized many years of the essential *Izvestiia Otdeleniia russkogo iazyka i slovesnosti Imperatorskoi Akademii nauk*. Another site with full-text access to Russian classics is *Mashinnyi fond russkogo iazyka* of the Russian Academy of Sciences, presenting the works of Chekhov, Bunin, Gogol, and Dostoevsky et al. This site came in handy for some of my recent reference questions concerning quotations from Chekhov's letters. Several quotes were found using the full-text version of Nauka's 1974 edition of Chekhov's letters. Having this work in a searchable format eliminated my need to use the index and skim many pages looking for the quotation, and the patron was able to view the full-text from his home in spite of the fact that his library did not hold this standard set of Chekhov's complete works.[25]

A wonderful trend that is extremely helpful to both reference librarians and researchers is the digitization of classic reference works. Everyone knows and has used the online subscription versions of the *Encyclopedia Britannica*, the *Oxford English Dictionary*, *Merriam Webster's Collegiate Dictionary*, and other familiar English reference tools, but there are now more and more digitized versions of traditional Slavic and East European reference books and dictionaries available for free on the Internet. The number of Russian titles is especially significant. The selection of tools currently available include the smaller edition of the pre-revolutionary Brokgauz encyclopedia, Dal's *Tolkovyi slovar' zhivogo velikorusskogo iazyka* (edition information not given on the site), *Literaturnaia entsiklopediia*, *Lermontovskaia entsiklopediia*, *Entsiklopediia "Slova o polku Igoreve,"* and *Russkii biograficheskii slovar'*.[26] Let these titles suffice as examples from other countries in Eastern Europe: *Nowa encyklopedia powszechna PWN*, *Słownik ortograficzny*, and *Ukrains'ka mova: entsyklopediia*.[27] The European Division (EurD) of the Library of Congress is getting in on the act as well by arranging for the digitization a number of older telephone directories from Eastern Europe and Rudolf Smits's *Half a Century of Soviet Serials, 1917-1968*. Although, strictly speaking, the country studies produced by the Federal Research Division of the Library of Congress are not really reference tools, they are mainstays in the reference collections of many of LC's reading rooms. Digitized versions of over 100 of them are on the FRD website.[28]

Electronic journals management systems have been developed to deal with the enormous number of online full-text publications. These tools essentially gather into one interface information about all of the online journals available at an institution and provide direct links to the databases, URLs, or aggregators that offer them, thus bringing the contents of the databases out into the open. Most of them show the extent of coverage per title and in which databases the titles can be accessed. The access is alphabetical by title with options (depending on the system) to search by ISSN, subject, vendor, or publisher. An article by Michael Brewer explains the use of a similar system, JAKE, but one that does not link the user to the online journal.[29] The Library of Congress uses three different systems that have much overlap–EZB: Electronic Journals Library, Serials Solutions, and TDNet–but each also includes unique titles.[30] Of the three, only EZB offers a subject category for various area studies such as "Slavonic." The other two have only very general subject groupings; thus patrons will have to explore the search options unless they are looking for a known item, which can be browsed in the alphabetical list. The basic searching function, however, is quite simple: one can search for a title word, the beginning of a title, or an ISSN, etc. In addition to the management systems, the Library of Congress also has its own interface to group together all of its electronic products such as databases, dictionaries, web search tools, and so on. This interface allows patrons to use the subject category European Studies to get a list of potentially relevant online tools. The University of Illinois has developed its own in-house electronic journals management interface based on TDNet data feeds. Besides managing full-text electronic serials, this interface also provides access to other types of digital products such as CD-ROMs that have been loaded onto a server, article indexes and abstracts, and online reference tools. Built into the interface is a range of subject categories, including some for area studies and Slavic and East European in particular.[31] The contents of East View's *Universal Databases* are accessible by title through two out of three of the Library of Congress's management systems, but this is not yet true for the University of Illinois's interface. These two libraries are not alone when it comes to home-built interfaces for electronic products management. Every library faces the same problem and many have come up with the same solution.

After discussing full-text databases and online journals, the bibliographic database seems less splashy, but these tools are enormously important for Slavic studies. Since their introduction in the early 1970s, bibliographic utilities like RLIN and OCLC have become mainstays of reference work in all specialties. They provide citations to works of many bibliographic types: books, journals, newspapers, visual media, sound recordings, archival collections, and the list goes on. Their importance cannot be overestimated, but bibliographic databases of other kinds also exist. There are article indexes, dissertation indexes, and indexes to contents of many kinds of materials based on subject. Many of the tools that are available via a Western subscription in this country and that have relevance for Slavic studies, including INION's *Russian Academy of Sciences Bibliographies* (RAS), already have been ably described in Gordon Anderson's article.[32] However, *ABSEES* and *EBSEES*, well known and well-used in the field, deserve mention as they are specifically geared to Slavic and East European studies.[33] Although *ABSEES* is a subscription product and its content overlaps to a great extent the content of other electronic indexes, it has the advantage of uniting many Slavic-related citations in one place, so a researcher and a reference librarian can use it as a good launching point. *EBSEES*, the equally valuable European counterpart of *ABSEES*, provides the same service and is available for free via the Internet. Besides *ABSEES*, *EBSEES*, and RAS, there are other interesting indexing tools in our field. Due to space constraints only two will be mentioned to highlight the situation. *SovLit: teksty, bibliografiia, issledovaniia*[34] is a combination journal index and full-text provider. It records the contents of several dozen Soviet literary journals and hundreds of *sborniki* (collections) from the 1920s and, in addition, is in the process of providing the full text of every item listed. This tool is not a traditional index in that there is no searching mechanism, but regardless, it stands to become an essential tool for Russian literary scholars and the reference librarians trying to help them. *BazTech: Polish Technical Journal Contents* is a more traditional indexing database with citations and abstracts to over 300 Polish journals in the fields of science and technology. The searching interface is simple, yet flexible enough to do complex searches. And it is freely available on the web.[35] With more and more of these kinds of tools being developed each year, Slavic reference librarians will have plenty of options to explore when trying to answer patrons' questions.

CD-ROMs are a sticky wicket, to be sure. What was once all the rage in the world of electronic data options is now a sort of neglected stepchild. Many Slavic librarians purchased such CD-ROMs as the national bibliographies for the Czech Republic, Slovenia, Slovakia, Russia, Hungary, or specialty CD-ROMs on Russian maps, Russian artists, or Polish language dictionaries, and now find themselves unable to serve them to their readers. Why? Because the hardware is no longer being supported or the public terminals in reading rooms have been disabled for security reasons, to the point that they cannot handle the CDs. There are probably a myriad of reasons why CD-ROMs have become a problem, but the bottom line is that today they involve extra work for the librarian and for the patron, in some sense defeating the purpose of making data more easily available in a searchable digital format. Before the University of Illinois purchased a Citrix server to make CDs accessible on the network via their Online Research Resources page, the SRS staff had to load the CD onto their personal machines and sit with the patron while he/she used the product. This was quite tedious if the patron was doing a detailed or comprehensive literature search on one of the national bibliography CDs. This situation still exists at the SRS for the CD-ROM products that have not been added to the server, either because the product was of such limited interest that it was not worth the server space and the bother, or because the publisher would not agree to allow it to be loaded. The advantage to the network server is that the products, which normally would require a patron to seek out assistance of the Slavic reference staff, are now readily available anywhere in the library. The disadvantage is that there may be no one around to assist with searching instructions or the inevitable font/keyboard issues that arise when using some of these products. The Library of Congress and likewise the European Division have dropped the ball when it comes to CD-ROMs. Many are acquired, cataloged, and sent to the Microform Reading Room. However, the staff there, though trained to load CDs onto a computer, lack foreign language skills or sufficient reference training to guide the patron on how to search the bibliographies. Some of the more popular titles (*Congressional Masterfile, SSCI, AHCI, Statistical Masterfile*) are loaded onto dedicated machines in the Main Reading Room's Computer Catalog Center, but other specialized CD-ROMs may not even be cataloged; rather they are held on the desks of reference staff to be shared with others at their discretion. The Slavic Reference Service also has a full drawer of uncataloged CD-ROMs that are hardly ever used and to which patrons have no access without a staff member volunteering information about their existence. Helping patrons with CD-ROMs in the EurD either means sending them to the Microform Reading Room or taking them to a librarian's desk and loading it onto a personal machine, thus repeating the same situation mentioned above, monitoring the patron's presence at a non-public machine. Since no solution is in sight, reference librarians either have resigned themselves to the uncomfortable situation or think long and hard before they recommend CD-ROMs for purchase, all the while muttering under their breath, "Why couldn't the publisher just have put this on the Internet?!"

GUIDES, WEBLIOGRAPHIES, BIBLIOGRAPHIC INSTRUCTION

The digital revolution has brought about a major change in people's expectations of libraries and librarians, that is, everyone should have a website. This attitude is perfectly in line with the way librarians in the United States try to foster independent activity in the library on the part of patrons. Reference librarians are happy to help instruct patrons on search strategies and use of the library's resources, but then expect the patron to venture forth independently, returning to the librarian for help when necessary. With library home pages that provide basic information and guides for more specific information, librarians are improving reference services by allowing the patron to find more information on his/her own before seeking assistance. Slavic librarians have participated in this trend by producing Slavic-oriented sites or collection guides, either to serve their libraries' patrons or to serve the Slavic community at large. For example, the Slavic and East European Library of the University of Illinois mounted the first version of its website in 1997. *REESWeb*, developed in 1993 and revamped in 2000, is the most notable example of an early endeavor for the entire community.[36] The European Reading Room created its own site in the mid 1990s. The website phenomenon not only allows Slavic librarians to engage in the positive act of preparing digital reference tools, but it also brings a troublesome trend to the fore: yet another new technology that librarians either have to master for themselves or rely on a second party to create for them. Nevertheless, many librarians have learned basic html encoding and how to use web design software. Some have acquired more technical skills in order to maintain control of their pages or simply to get their materials online when their institutions do not have the web design staff or the inclination to make Slavic content a priority.

Websites of Slavic librarians and/or Slavic collections in the United States contain a legion of information ranging from details on their scope to specific guides on how to conduct research in various disciplines. Some notable examples include the Slavic site at the library of the University of North Carolina at Chapel Hill, which includes descriptions about UNC's Slavic collections, a guide to resources for Soviet history, a list of irregular Russian periodicals received by the UNC library, a filmography of Russian videos held in the library, links to other useful resources, etc. The University of California, Berkeley has a more modest, but nicely designed site that offers the Slavic user, among other things, descriptions of the collections, lists of recent acquisitions, and links to other resources such as how to Cyrillicize a computer. More unusual for a Slavic librarian or collection's page is one that focuses on how to conduct a specific kind of research, such as Michigan State University's guide to finding translations, just one of the options for Slavic researchers at the site of MSU's Slavic Bibliographer.[37] One feature represented on most Slavic sites produced either by Slavic librarians or their corresponding Russian and East European centers or institutes is a list of links, annotated or not, to Internet resources from the various countries in our field. These lists are often called webliographies, meaning a bibliography of websites. The above-mentioned *REESWeb* is a dynamic example of this kind of site. Others are too numerous to mention here, but to illustrate some of the issues involved with such sites, the *Portals to the World* project at the Library of Congress and the *Internet Resources* site of the Slavic Reference Service will be discussed in more detail.[38]

The Library of Congress jumped into the portal arena when EurD Hungarian specialist Kenneth Nyirady loaded a briefly annotated list of useful Internet resources for Hungary onto the European Reading Room's website. His list inspired the project that came to be known as *Portals to the World*. The head of the Area Studies Directorate then mandated that a portal should be created for each country of the world. They were slowly compiled by the Library's specialists and enhanced by the work of the design team, who provided the template so all would have a similar look. An added contribution was the use of CORC to create pathfinders for bibliographic control.[39] In Illinois when the SRS decided to create a list of resources in 2000, it decided to take a slightly different tack from the others that already existed at that time. Instead of just unannotated links arranged by subject, the SRS wanted to locate and annotate not just regular sites, but portal sites, that is, sites that could provide an entry into a wealth of information on a particular topic, sites that in many cases could themselves be considered reference sources. Selection criteria were established, including such factors as longevity, authority (almost no personal sites were considered substantive or trustworthy enough for inclusion), amount of information provided, currency of site updates, statements of methodology by the sites' compilers, whether sophisticated programming on the site would inhibit access for people with older computers, etc. The resources were grouped by subject as well as by country, including a page for general resources that covered many or all of the countries in the region. The webliography, which was an attempt to help SRS patrons cope with the burgeoning number of web resources from Russia and

Eastern Europe, presented its own problems, however. In spite of the SRS staff's best efforts to pinpoint more stable resources, a number of them changed URLs or disappeared in the first year. Maintenance became a major issue, as the staff had moved on to other projects and no longer had the time to find new sites or record changes at the older ones. Much of this work was subsequently assigned to various graduate assistants. Maintenance is also an issue with the *Portals of the World*. Now that the pages for virtually all of the countries are completed, there is a need to update the ones that were done several years ago. One wonders whether those who made the original decisions to devote staff time and resources to such projects fully appreciated the scope of such a commitment for the libraries that created them.

What many of these sites have in common is an attempt to conduct some kind of bibliographic instruction from afar. Some are fairly simple with just lists of resources, print or digital, available at a particular institution, while others are quite complex, offering in depth coverage of a particular subject or detailed descriptions of sources with search strategies. In some cases the online guides are a replica or extension of what reference librarians used to prepare as paper handouts for patrons who came into the library. For these, the concept is not new, only the format or the inclusion of URLs is new. An example of a complex site with extensive coverage of one topic is *ArcheoBiblioBase*, maintained by Patricia Kennedy Grimsted and Rosarkhiv in Moscow.[40] This site describes guides to archives, provides information on how to use the archives, contact information, and often a brief history of particular archives. The next example is one that is totally devoted to bibliographic instruction including search strategies for Slavic researchers, the SRS's *Guide to Slavic Information Resources*, the brainchild of Helen Sullivan, Manager of the SRS.[41] It was created as a form of outreach for the SRS's patron base, which is comprised mostly of students and scholars not located on the campus of the University of Illinois and those who attend the Summer Research Laboratory in Urbana-Champaign. Patrons not only wanted the SRS to help them verify citations and locate materials for them, but also to give them advice on how to begin their research. The idea was to describe basic reference tools, electronic and print, for Slavic and East European studies. Arranged by type of resource, such as encyclopedias, dictionaries, national bibliographies, bibliographies of bibliographies, etc., and by country and topic, the guide provides full bibliographic citations, local call numbers and holdings, and annotations explaining the scope, authority, coverage, and special features of each resource. Many of the annotations are very detailed, as some sources are quite complex or multifaceted. The initial focus was on general resources and biography, but then the SRS made a concerted effort to cover the most essential bibliographic tools for every country in the region before branching off into subject specific guides. Thus, national bibliographies, periodical resources, library catalogs, and bibliographies of bibliographies have been completed for all the countries. The guide has grown so much that it now constitutes several hundred web pages, and every semester new sections are added. The most recent sections are Bulgarian Linguistics, Russian Archives, and Ukrainian Monographic Resources. A survey of the web statistics for the site show that all of the sections receive heavy use: from August 2003 through June 2004 the site registered an astounding 69,050 hits for users not on the University of Illinois campus. In fact, the statistics show that people are hitting on the pages that are under construction too, proving that there is a definite need for this kind of information. When the SRS staff are not working on requests, they are working on content for the guide to try to satisfy searchers' hunger for Slavic bibliographic information. The program also affords the SRS an excellent opportunity to collaborate with colleagues in Eastern Europe; thus reference librarians from Poland and Russia have been recruited to produce relevant sections. All of the Polish sections (Polish National Bibliography, Polish Biography, and the new, but not yet uploaded, Polish Gender Resources) were written by Barbara Bułat at the Jagiellonian Library, and the section on Russian Educational Resources was created by the reference staff of the Russian National Library. The Russian librarians are currently working on a guide to resources for Russian philosophy, while staff members of the SRS are finishing up Bulgarian history and Bulgarian literature. Next on the SRS agenda are sections for Russian governmental materials, Russian economics, and Russian statistics.

Rather than providing online bibliographic instruction, the EurD has focused on creating the country portals mentioned above and finding aids to the uncataloged Slavic and East European collections in the Library of Congress.[42] Since the Library is used heavily by genealogists, the collection of uncataloged foreign telephone directories has become a priority. Finding aids to over a half dozen European countries, mostly East European ones, are now completed. In the process of creating the aids, the staff has earmarked several older directories for digitization, with ones from Poland and Romania currently available and others from Russia, Bulgaria, and the Kingdom of Yugoslavia expected to be completed in 2005.[43] That these finding aids are being used can be attested by the reference questions coming in asking for a librarian to look up a particular surname in one of the directories. This demonstrates that an added bonus for the reference librarian who gets involved in the creation of webliographies, tutorials, finding aids, online exhibits, and other Internet content is that these sites often generate reference questions or spur greater use in the collections–which is why we are all here.

DIGITAL COMMUNICATION

The use of electronic technology to communicate with patrons has greatly facilitated the speed, cost, and accessibility of reference services for remote users.[44] Patrons no longer have to pay for postage stamps or for long distance phone calls to ask a question. By the use of various types of electronic communication, the lengthy process of exchanging letters is greatly reduced. Geography and distance in many cases are no longer serious barriers to service, for patrons can ask questions and receive guidance while sitting at home or in their offices. Privacy-minded or shy patrons also feel more comfortable asking for help with the anonymity of digital transactions. Since at both the SRS and the EurD the receipt of questions via some kind of digital format now has far outstripped numerically the receipt of questions received in person, by telephone, or mail, some discussion of these communication methods is in order.

The benefits and drawbacks of e-mail are many and have been discussed to a great extent in the published literature, so only a quick summary is given here. In addition to speedy, free delivery, e-mail also allows for delivery of large files such as word-processed documents, scanned images, or digitized works, which, if printed, could be physically hefty and/or incur significant mailing costs. Probably all Slavic and East European librarians are using e-mail to receive requests from patrons and colleagues, either by way of their personal e-mail accounts or through some generic e-mail reference account. Both the SRS/UIUC and the EurD at LC receive requests via general reference accounts and librarians' personal e-mail.

Web forms are also a very prominent method for directing digital communications between a librarian and a patron. The resulting information is transmitted to a file or often to an e-mail account accessible to the librarian. Web forms require that a person fill out information in a questionnaire that helps the librarian to better understand the question and/or identify the patron. Some common questions, besides patron name and contact information, include educational level of the patron, foreign languages the patron can read, whether the patron has access to interlibrary loan services, verification of institutional affiliation, and what sources the patron has tried in order to answer the question on his/her own. These questions are usually an attempt to compensate for the lack of the all-important reference interview in this asynchronous form of communication. Of course, both e-mail and web forms have a disadvantage for patrons: they can only assume that their messages have reached an actual librarian's desk, for they will have no human confirmation of this until a reply is sent, be it one hour, one day, or one week later. Again, both the SRS/UIUC and the EurD at LC make use of web forms to receive requests from patrons.[45]

QuestionPoint (QP), the collaborative digital reference venture of the Library of Congress and OCLC, combines many forms of digital communication into one package, as well as offering reference question tracking and management, a referral system, and a knowledge base. Launched in the spring of 2002, QP funneled over 170,000 requests through its system in 2003 with the Library of Congress receiving over 50,000 of the total. QP has a local component for managing an individual library's requests and a global component that allows for national and international question referrals. Libraries that choose to subscribe may decide which aspects of QP to utilize. Basically, any patron anywhere at any time of day can submit a reference question. If the patron's local library cannot answer it or is not open for business, the question may be answered by another library in the local library's cooperative QP group. Another option is for the library to submit the question to QP for routing to the Global Reference Network, using an algorithm to determine which library or libraries would be best able to answer the question, based on how the libraries represent themselves using RLG Conspectus levels and other factors. The local library may also opt not to participate in routing or cooperative groups and let the question wait until business hours begin the next day. Fortunately, QP seems simple enough for the patron. One asks and one receives an answer by using a web form. But the system is quite complex in the number of tasks it handles and versatile in its functionality. Once a question is submitted to an institution (in particular one as large as LC) the question may be routed to the appropriate reading room or to a particular librarian. Each reading room has its own account, as does each librarian. Librarians may claim questions to answer or they may be assigned. By logging into his/her account a librarian can view open and closed questions, answer questions that appear in the patron's e-mail, send attachments, refer questions, view transcripts of every transaction related to a particular question, edit questions, and file questions as closed. If the patron in turn responds, QP automatically routes the response to the librarian who was working on the question. Administrators can view all of the questions and answers that pass through QP, set up scripts to answer frequently received questions, and study reports based on the system's statistics functions. Besides web forms, QP offers a chat program with two versions, basic and enhanced, the difference for the librarian being that enhanced allows for co-browsing (more on this below) and has video and voice capabilities.[46] The EurD began using the QP web forms with the rest of the Library of Congress in spring 2002 and received over 1300 requests in 2003 and 668 in the first six months of 2004.[47] Because the QP Ask A Librarian button is prominently displayed on the website of the European Reading Room, most patrons use that option. Nevertheless, in 2003 almost 200 were referred by some other division in the Library, and an additional handful came from the Global Reference Network. Requests received via the generic EurD e-mail reference account (non-QP) have dropped off dramatically since the introduction of QP.

Although e-mail and web forms are now fully integrated into most reference services, they lack the immediacy of telephone or in person questioning. Thus, we have our first argument for virtual reference or chat, a digital area where most Slavic librarians in the United States are not on the cutting edge–or even in the game, for that matter. Chat reference is often referred to as real-time or synchronous reference since the patron is able to communicate directly with the reference librarian and engage in immediate and continuous interaction at his/her time of need. Chat not only serves the patron who craves immediacy, but also some who feel more comfortable communicating in a digital fashion rather than conversing face-to-face with a librarian. The benefits of the "conversation" accrue without the actual personal contact. An added benefit is that a transcript of the entire transaction including URLs of pages pushed or visited is e-mailed to the patron after the session for future reference. In my opinion, however, the true benefit of virtual reference is not the ability to send and receive text messages (not much different from the telephone except for the slower speed), but the function of co-browsing, that is, when both the librarian's and the patron's computers visit Internet sites together and see the same pages. It is this feature that elevates chat beyond a mere digital communication tool into a tool for bibliographic instruction as well. When looking for a particular piece of information that is likely to be found on the Internet, the librarian can lead the patron to the site and show him/her exactly where and how to find the information. The SRS has on occasion led a patron via co-browsing to another university's online catalog or to an East European search engine and performed the search with the patron able to view the results as they appear. The text dialogue box, constantly running alongside the browser window, allows the Slavic librarian to show the patron how to change the encoding of a particular site while the patron is viewing the page, try different search strategies, or provide other explanations. If you believe the adage that a picture is worth a thousand words, you will understand how powerful a tool co-browsing is and that it should be in every reference librarian's arsenal.[48]

Not all chat programs allow for co-browsing. Many just have text messaging, while others enable the librarian only to push selected pages, that is, the librarian sends selected URLs to the patron for viewing rather than the patron seeing everything the librarian sees. With these limitations, chat is little more than a new way to receive reference requests, a distance communication tool that allows for a reference interview. Many library staff initially are resistant to this new technology. They feel pressure to perform quickly and believe that chat requires a sophisticated knowledge of the Internet and strong familiarity with an enormous number of websites. This is not necessarily true, for the most important skill a librarian needs to have for a successful chat session (with or without co-browsing) is the ability to search. Knowledge of one's local institution is also quite important since the most common chat questions are related to a library's holdings, layout, or policies.[49] And in the end, the patron is happy to have made contact, to know that someone on the other end is working on the request, and is usually willing to have the librarian e-mail later with follow-up. Other worries about instituting new chat services involve increasing workload. The initial fear of being swamped with chat requests once a new service is offered (similar to the fears once instilled by new e-mail services) is proving to be a red herring. Most U.S. libraries that offer the service have shown statistically that chat patrons are not overwhelming in number.[50]

No form of technology is without its drawbacks. A significant problem for co-browsing is frame-busting, a situation that occurs with some security sites or complex searchable sites like search engines, databases, or online catalogs. Frame-busting usually causes the chat software to disconnect the patron, and the librarian may or may not be aware of what has happened. Sometimes the librarian's system will freeze as well. Unfortunately, this situation obtains for some of the most potentially useful Slavic sites such as the Russian National Library's scanned card catalog mentioned above. Thus, the librarian can only lead the patron to water, so to speak; the patron will have to indulge on his/her own. In addition, librarians cannot co-browse with a patron in most subscription databases including one of the most powerful, *WorldCat* (OCLC). Docutek, the chat software of the SRS, recently added a work-around to alleviate some of this problem. Called the PrintKey Pro, it enables the librarian to go to a site without the patron in tow, search it, find the needed record, and then take a screen shot of the page and e-mail it to the patron, all while still maintaining the chat session with the patron.

Digital communication tools for reference in general (e-mail, web forms, and chat) are faulted across the board for the slowness of the actual transaction or completion times. For example, the consensus seems to be that the average chat session lasts longer than a comparative phone or in-person reference conversation, possibly even twice as long.[51] If a reference interview needs to occur via e-mail, the back-and-forth is extremely slow. Thus on the one hand, digital communication accelerates the overall process compared to the postal service or traveling long distances to visit a library, but on the other hand, compared to the query posed in person, it prolongs the transaction. When making comparisons, however, one must keep in mind that even in the past many reference questions were submitted from a distance, not in person.

As of July 2004, the only Slavic chat reference service at a U.S. library is the one at the Slavic Reference Service of the University of Illinois, which was initiated in January 2000 using the chat function of WebCT, an online courseware package purchased by the University. Docutek's VRL Plus, the current SRS software of choice for chat, allows co-browsing and page pushing, but was ultimately selected over WebCT's chat because patrons did not need a login and password and because of its ability to display Cyrillic fonts. In 2001, it was the only such software with this feature. Patrons may access the service from 9:00 a.m. to 3:00 p.m. central time. All chats are conducted in English, but the SRS has introduced an international component into its service by acting as a broker of chat requests for patrons who would like to interact with reference librarians at the Jagiellonian Library or the Russian National Library. In an ironic twist to the usual benefits of chat, the patron must schedule an appointment because of the time differences and the foreign libraries' inability to provide constant staff time to monitor the service. Although chat is available as part of QuestionPoint, most of the reading rooms in the Library of Congress have opted not to use it, including the European Reading Room. The new enhanced version of QP's chat software has some technical difficulties with the co-browsing function, a problem that can dissuade a patron who has had an unfortunate experience from trying the service a second time. In addition, there is staff resistance to the whole concept of chat, partially because of desk scheduling problems, partially because of views similar to those mentioned earlier, but mostly because many feel that it is an inappropriate format to receive complex requests. The EurD has an additional complication in that most of its librarians are specialists in a particular geographic region or language. If a patron were to enter the chat intending to ask for help with Hungarian, but the chat was being staffed by the Scandinavian specialist, chances are it would be a fruitless endeavor. Helen Sullivan, Manager of the SRS, also faced a recalcitrant staff when trying to introduce chat, but patience and training paid off in the end with a workable program now in place. Of course, the small number of requests received also eased the concerns. Like many other chat services, the SRS is facing lower than expected statistics with only about three or four chat requests per month. This may be a result of the national trend mentioned above, but certainly the numbers are affected by a host of factors, for instance, the specialized nature of most Slavic and East European studies requests, the limited number of patrons in Slavic area studies versus those handled by general reference desks, and the difficulty in advertising such a specialized service. Regardless of how one feels about chat, it is probably here to stay, and Slavic reference librarians should get more involved lest they be left behind. After all, chat is a medium preferred by the younger generation of library users, some of whom will become the future scholars in Slavic studies.

REPRODUCTION AND DOCUMENT DELIVERY

Document delivery is an area that has profited greatly from digital technologies. Not only are requests transmitted and managed electronically via systems such as OCLC and RLIN, now the documents themselves are being duplicated and delivered electronically as well via scanning or faxing, ARIEL or e-mail. Slavic librarians are taking advantage of all of these methods. Both the SRS and the EurD[52] have standard flatbed scanners for the use of library staff only, but additionally, the SRS has just recently installed one in the public area for patrons' use. Librarians can scan an article or image and e-mail it to a patron instead of photocopying and mailing with the inherent savings of time and money using the digital methods. Walk-in patrons may obtain a scanned copy only if a staff member offers to do it for them. The SRS, however, has an additional option that patrons make heavy use of, a scanner and CD-burner attached to a microfilm/microfiche reader-printer. This machine enables users to scan an unlimited number of images from any microfilm or microfiche of reasonable quality at no charge and take those images with them when they leave. Patrons incur charges only if they opt to print an image on paper. Supplemental software was loaded early in 2004 to allow the images to be scanned into PDF format instead of just making TIFF or Bitmap files. An image editor is available on the attached computer to convert files to other formats and to tweak images by cropping, lightening, inserting text boxes for citations or explanations, adding arrows or highlighting, etc. Anyone who has attended the Summer Research Laboratory at the University of Illinois in the past several years knows that this machine is the most sought-after spot in the library, with sign-up sheets needed to allow everyone a turn. Besides scanning, other digital delivery options for library patrons include downloading to a disk or e-mailing articles or citations directly from a database. These options are likewise very popular with patrons and thus the reference librarian needs to know how to help them accomplish these tasks.

Concomitant with progress come problems, it seems. In the past, interlibrary loan librarians and photoduplication specialists were the ones who had to worry about providing copies of items and the related legal issues, but with the emergence of digital technologies, reference librarians also are involved. Subscription databases of citations or full-text materials present potential problems for the reference librarian who is focused on providing and helping to locate information for patrons. If a librarian is doing a literature search for a remote patron, the first instinct would be to search a database and send the resulting hit list to the patron for him/her to decide which citations might be important for the topic. By the same token, if searching a full-text database, sending the germane articles would be a desirable tactic. Such actions could violate license agreements between the library and the vendor; thus reference librarians now need to be aware of the content of the license agreements for the databases that they use. Some are very liberal, allowing such distribution of citations and full-text; others are extremely restrictive, limiting their use only to individuals in the library building. Another issue involves making digital copies. All Slavic reference librarians make occasional photocopies of articles for patrons and send it to them, bypassing the traditional and often slower or less foreign-language-focused interlibrary loan offices. Fortunately, with the new and ubiquitous scanners, the same terms of fair use are applicable, as they should be, since logically there is really no difference between making a photocopy of an article under fair use and making a digital copy under the same conditions. The latest digital reproduction method gaining a foothold in research libraries is the digital camera. Each library must establish its own guidelines regarding the acceptability of patron use of digital cameras, for they are growing in popularity if the patrons who frequent the European Reading Room can be considered a good barometer of area-wide trends.

KEEPING CURRENT

Frankly, the best way to keep current on developments in the world of Slavic digital reference is to work on requests and to treat each one as brand new. Do not make assumptions that only one specific source can help. If you try the digital sources before you turn to an old favorite, you may be surprised to discover something new. In the course of your investigations you may stumble across a wonderful tool that may or may not help with your question, but might come in handy with another. This was the case for me with the journal index and full-text source *SovLit* mentioned earlier. In my opinion, one of the benefits of being a reference librarian is the lifelong learning that accrues with new reference requests. As long as there is a willingness to accept new challenges and try new things, staying current will come naturally. Short of that, there are some strategies that can help. An obvious method for keeping current is to read the core journals in the field. For example, ACRL's Slavic and East European Section *Newsletter* has been publishing an annotated list of notable websites since 1995. *Slavic & East European Information Resources* has as a regular feature called "The Internet." Perusing more general serials can also be beneficial for professional development. For digital issues, try the online magazine *Dlib* <http://www.dlib.org/>, which covers all the latest trends, or *Internet Reference Services Quarterly*, which has articles devoted to various aspects of digital reference. One could also, once a year or so, examine the sites presented on various Slavic portals compiled by our colleagues, such as the ones at the Center for Russia, East Europe, and Central Asia at the University of Wisconsin. Monitoring the postings on *SLAVLIBS*, our listserv that serves as a professional forum for developments in the field as well as a quasi-referral system for Slavic and East European reference questions, is a must for the hot topics and daily information in the field. If that is not enough, try signing up for a more general library listserv, such as the two for digital references services mentioned earlier, or subscribe to one of the Slavic and East European lists for scholars, such as *SEELANGS* or *H-Russia*, to keep in touch with the issues that concern our main patron groups. A very traditional method for staying current is conference attendance, but this year consider going to one on digital reference in addition to the standard ALA and AAASS. The VRD conference may really open your eyes to what reference librarians on the front lines of very busy services are facing on a daily basis. Do not be afraid to offer new services, for the experiences you have may help with other projects down the line. For instance, the SRS arranged for special groups at its annual Summer Research Laboratory to use the threaded discussion group feature in an online courseware package. The idea was not a big success, but the patrons became more familiar with the courseware and the other materials that the SRS had loaded into the program, such as the online bibliographic guide to Slavic information resources.

Perhaps one of the most challenging issues is how librarians can keep current on new search tools and the latest technologies. Most reference librarians understand that one needs to use more than one search engine for better results. Certainly all Slavic reference librarians understand the necessity of using vernacular search engines, but do we really understand how different all of these engines are? As much as everyone loves Google and its foreign language versions or one of the myriad of others that has become a favorite, no engine searches the live web every time; rather they search their own databases, which are updated according to varying schedules. Each one also has a different database, probably with none covering more than twenty-five to thirty percent of the entire Internet. Using a meta-engine like Copernic is one way to test the effectiveness of your favorite engines and to do a more comprehensive search as well, because meta-engines search multiple search engines' databases at the same time. To find a list of the dozens of meta-engines, simply do a search on your favorite engine for *meta-engines*. Another hot tool these days is the blog or weblog, a kind of online journal or diary of postings on a particular topic, which may also include links to sites of interest. Librarians have created a number of library- and reading-centered weblogs. For instance, *LISNews* <http://www.lisnews.com/> has been around since 1999, and covers news and issues of interest to librarians. In fact, blogs are not just a way to keep current; they are now being discussed as possible reference tools allowing librarians to work collaboratively on questions by each posting ideas and sources on a blog that a patron can access.[53] Other suggestions for keeping technologically current, such as using website monitoring software and RSS feeds that deliver content of your choice directly to you so that you do not have to spend time hunting it down, are examined in detail in Steven Cohen's recent book *Keeping Current*.[54] His tips on learning about the latest technological tools, something every reference librarian should take the time to do, are well worth reading.

THE FUTURE

Who can say what the future will bring? By the time this article appears in print, digital Slavic reference may have evolved new trends, new tools, and new partnerships. The key is to keep service as our top priority and keep open minds with regard to developments in all aspects of reference work. In this age of expanded publishing and the digital revolution, cooperation with our peers is essential. The Slavic Reference Service is open to opportunities for reference cooperation with East European partners. It already has established relationships with the reference departments and librarians at the Jagiellonian Library in Cracow and the Russian National Library in St. Petersburg, for chat and for the development of modules to the online bibliographic guide mentioned above. Expansion of the SRS's cooperation to include other East European countries is being investigated. QuestionPoint offers a unique and as yet unexplored opportunity for cooperation via its Global Reference Network (GRN). The GRN allows libraries to refer questions and receive questions from partners around the world. Within QP each partner may form cooperative groups based on three forms of communication (chat, web forms, referrals) and any chosen subject criteria. For example, there is a group of U.S. medical libraries, a group for libraries in the state of Washington, a group concerned with anti-Semitism and bigotry, etc. Why couldn't there be a group devoted to Slavica? All of the reading rooms in the Library of Congress have their own accounts and may form groups on their own. Thus, the European Reading Room could join a global Slavica group without impacting the rest of the Library of Congress. Large university libraries that use QP could set up a Slavic and East European account to separate the main service from the specialized one. Profiles can limit the questions by language of communication just as patrons can specify the language in which they wish to communicate. The most significant barrier to this scenario is that a subscription to QP is probably too expensive for most of the libraries in our countries, approximately $2,000 per year for the basic subscription and $2,000 more if they opt for the enhanced version. However, there is an option to share a QP library profile and thus also share the cost. Thus, one country could purchase a profile that up to twenty libraries could share. To date, the only East European country that has purchased a subscription to QP is Slovenia (Reference Service in the System COBISS.SI), but others are sure to follow as their economic situations improve.

Slavic librarians need to continue to produce such digital reference tools as guides, tutorials, and finding aids. Involvement in digital projects that would make reference books or bibliographic databases available to our users is of particular importance, for if we do not promote the interests of Slavic and East European scholars, who will? Those volunteers who contribute abstracts to *ABSEES* and *EBSEES* are worthy examples for us all. New forms of digital communication that we have yet to try, such as chat or streaming video for bibliographic instruction, should be one of our priorities since the predominant users are today's undergraduates,[55] the Slavic and East European scholars of tomorrow. Other communications tools that we have not even envisioned for reference work may become standard in a few years; for instance, cell phone text messaging systems are now being mentioned as possible reference tools.[56] The very fact that so many new digital tools are currently available and being produced, either fee-based or for free, combined with the amount of money libraries are investing in them, is sufficient reason for reference librarians to expand their repertoire of digital communications tools as well. Whatever the future may bring, we need to be ready or at least willing.

NOTES

1. Deanna B. Marcum, "Library Collections for the 21st Century: Rethinking Our Strategies," Keynote Address to the 2004 Nylink Annual Meeting, text of speech circulated to Library of Congress staff via e-mail in May 2004).

2. Sloan's *Digital Reference Service Bibliography* can be found at <http://www.lis.uiuc.edu/~b-sloan/digiref.html > (accessed July 1, 2004).

3. The Virtual Reference Desk hosted its sixth annual Digital Reference Conference on November 8-9, 2004. See <http://www.vrd.org/conf-train.shtml> (accessed July 1, 2004) for details about this and previous conferences.

4. The discussion groups referred to include *Dig_Ref* at <http://vrd.org/Dig_Ref/dig_ref.shtml> (accessed July 1, 2004) and *Livereference* at <http://groups.yahoo.com/group/livereference/> (accessed July 1, 2004).

5. See *IFLANET* <http://www.ifla.org/VII/s36/pubs/drg03.htm> (accessed July 22, 2004) and the ALA website <http://www.ala.org/ala/rusa/rusaprotools/referenceguide/virtrefguidelines.htm> (accessed August 3, 2004) for more details.

6. Helen Sullivan, "Slavianskaia spravochnaia sluzhba: tendentsii razvitiia i novye vozmozhnosti," in *Informatsionno-bibliograficheskoe obsluzhivanie* 1: *Istoriia i sovremennoe sostoianie: sbornik statei* (Sankt-Peterburg: Rossiiskaia natsional'naia biblioteka, 2003), 183-191.

7. Helen Sullivan, "Slavic Bibliography Online: WebCT as a Resource for Online Instruction," *Slavic & East European Information Resources* 3, no. 1 (2002): 21-33.

8. Teresa E. Tickle, "Expanding Outreach to a Unique User Community: The Slavic Reference Service and the Internet," *The Reference Librarian* 67/68 (1999): 69-83.

9. Michael Neubert, "Using Russian Internet Resources for Ready Reference: Good Enough for Prime Time?" *Slavic & East European Information Resources* 1, no. 4 (2001): 69-77.

10. Gordon B. Anderson, "Save Yourself a Trip: A Guide to Exploiting Your Home Library's Bibliographic Databases for Slavic-Language Research Materials," *Slavic & East European Information Resources* 1, no. 1 (2000): 13-28.

11. Marta Mestrovic Deyrup, "Report on *SLAVLIBS* Survey on Information Literacy," *Slavic & East European Information Resources* 5, no. 1/2 (2004): 41-46.

12. Terri Tickle Miller, "The Census Online: Internet Census Resources for Eastern Europe and the Former Soviet Union," *Slavic & East European Information Resources* 3, no. 4 (2002): 51-63.

13. Peter Roudik, "Researching Russian Laws: A Guide to Major Online Information Resources," *Slavic & East European Information Resources* 2, no. 3/4 (2001): 99-105.

14. *Russian Reference Works* <http://www-sul.stanford.edu/depts/hasrg/slavic/3refint.html> (accessed July 25, 2004).

15. Joseph Janes, "Why Does Digital Reference Matter?" presented as a live webcast February 10, 2003 <http://www.loc.gov/rr/program/lectures/janes.html> (accessed July 18, 2004).

16. A testament to the rapidly changing nature of the Internet is that upon retracing my steps several years later to refresh my memory for this article, I discovered a recent site about Karabchevskii that links him right away to his father-in-law's *osobniak*, although it did not provide the explanation about the moniker of Palace Karabchevskii.

17. Available at <http://www.nlr.ru:8101/poisk/index.html#8> (accessed July 29, 2004).

18. The two bibliographies are available at <http://nainfo.nbs.bg.ac.yu/katalog/> and <http://www.arcanum.hu/oszk/> respectively (both accessed July 29, 2004).

19. Slovenia's database: <http://splet02.izum.si/cobiss/Bibliographies.jsp?init=t> (accessed July 30, 2004). Serbia had a similar researchers' database entitled *Bibliografije istraživača* at <http://vbs.nbs.bg.ac.yu/cobiss/>, but it no longer is available to Internet searchers.

20. David Zdeněk Chroust, "Slavic-Language Material in OCLC and the Search for Matching Records: Reconsidering an Overlooked Problem," *Slavic & East European Information Resources* 1, no.4 (2001): 41-67, p. 56. This article provides a good overview of some of the complications with transliteration systems.

21. The press release was provided by Jane W. Jacobs in a personal communication. For more information about this program see the instructions for patrons and

Russian language information at <http://web2.queenslibrary.org/web2/tramp2.exe/goto/ guest?setting_key=English&screen=help/cyrillic_search.html> and <http://www.queenslibrary. org/russian/index.asp> (accessed August 2, 2004). For details on the process of changing the records into Cyrillic see Jane W. Jacobs, Ed Summers, and Elizabeth Ankersen, "Cyril: Expanding the Horizons of MARC21," *Library Hi Tech* 22, no.1 (2004): 8-17.

22. Ross Bourne, "National Bibliographies and the Technological Gap," *International Cataloguing and Bibliographic Control* 24, no. 2 (April/June 1995): 26-29, p. 26.

23. *Hrvatska Bibliografija* (Niz A, B, C) is available at <http://www.nsk.hr/ bibliografije/index.html>; *Česká národní bibliografie* is available at <http://aip.nkp. cz/index.htm>; the *Hungarian National Bibliography, Bibliography of Books* is available at <http://www.oszk.hu/mnbkb/index-en.html> (all accessed August 2, 2004).

24. Available at <http://webapp1.dlib.indiana.edu/letopis/index.jsp?lang=en> (accessed August 2, 2004). For more information about this project see Murlin Croucher, "Digitizing and Making a Web Site for the Soviet *Letopis' zhurnal'nykh statei*, 1956-1975," *Slavic & East European Information Resources* 3, no. 2/3 (2002):179-183.

25. These two sites are available on the web at <http://feb-web.ru/> and <http:// www.irlras-cfrl.rema.ru/> (both accessed August 2, 2004). Editor's note: more about FEB-web can be found in the article by Joseph Peschio, Igor Pil'shchikov, and Konstantin Vigurskii in this volume.

26. Brokgauz available at <http://www.encyclopedia.ru/internet/bol.html>, Dal' available at <http://infolio.asf.ru/Sprav/Dal/index.htm>, all literary encyclopedias available at <http://feb-web.ru/feb/feb/voc.htm> (all accessed August 5, 2004). *Russkii biograficheskii slovar'* available at <http://www.hi-edu.ru/xPol/> (accessed August 20, 2004). While preparing this section of my essay, I came across the classic case of the instability of Internet resources. About half of the digitized reference tools I had used in the recent past were no longer accessible as of August 5, 2004. Some, which were previously free, are now available only by subscription at <http://www.rubricon. com/>. Others have simply disappeared.

27. Polish encyclopedia available at <http://encyklopedia.pwn.pl/0_3.html>, orthographic dictionary at <http://so.pwn.pl/>, selected entries from Ukrainian linguistic encyclopedia at <http://litopys.narod.ru/ukrmova/um.htm> (all accessed August 5, 2004).

28. Country studies available at <http://lcweb2.loc.gov/frd/cs/cshome.html> (accessed August 5, 2004). The two volumes of *Half a Century of Soviet Serials* can be found at: <http://lcweb2.loc.gov/service/gdc/scd0001/2004/20040720001ha/20040720001ha. pdf> and <http://lcweb2.loc.gov/service/gdc/scd0001/2004/20040601001so/20040601001so. pdf> (accessed December 25, 2004).

29. Michael Brewer, "Using JAKE: A Guide for the Slavic Specialist," *Slavic & East European Information Resources* 3, no. 4 (2002): 79-84.

30. The following link shows the electronic journals management systems that are available at public terminals in the Library of Congress: <http://www.loc.gov/rr/ ElectronicResources/ejournals.php> (accessed July 28, 2004). They have been designated as E-journal Search Tools. All of the titles in the Full-Text E-Journals Collections are represented in at least one of the three systems.

31. To view the UIUC Online Research Resources interface see <http://www.library. uiuc.edu/orr/> (accessed July 28, 2004).

32. Anderson, "Save Yourself a Trip."

33. For more information about the history and status of both *ABSEES* and *EBSEES* see Aaron Trehub, "Building a World Bibliography of Slavic and East European Stud-

ies: *ABSEES, EBSEES,* and Beyond," *Slavic & East European Information Resources* 3, no. 2/3 (2002): 103-119.

34. Available at <http://www.ruthenia.ru/sovlit/index.html> (accessed August 3, 2004).

35. Available at <http://baztech.icm.edu.pl/indexeng.html> (accessed August 3, 2004). For more information about this database see Lidia Derfert-Wolf, "BAZTECH: Polish Technical Journal Contents," *Slavic & East European Information Resources* 5, no. 1/2 (2004): 149-154.

36. *REESWeb* is available at <http://www.ucis.pitt.edu/reesweb/> (accessed August 6, 2004). For more information about the origins and changes in REESWEb see Mark Weixel, "Restringing the Threads of *REESWeb,*" *Slavic & East European Information Resources* 1, no. 1 (2000): 105-108.

37. UNC's site available at <http://www.lib.unc.edu/cdd/crs/international/slavic/>, Berkeley's site available at <http://www.lib.berkeley.edu/Collections/Slavic/>, MSU's site available at <http://www.lib.msu.edu/ticklet/> (all accessed August 4, 2004).

38. *Portals to the World* available at <http://www.loc.gov/rr/international/portals.html>; SRS *Internet Resources* available at <http://www.library.uiuc.edu/spx/resources/guide.htm> (both accessed August 4, 2004).

39. For more information about *Portals to the World,* see Kenneth Nyirady, "Country-Specific Information Portals at the Library of Congress," *Slavic & East European Information Resources* 3, no. 1 (2002): 69-71.

40. *ArcheoBiblioBase* is available at <http://www.iisg.nl/~abb/> (accessed August 4, 2004).

41. Available at <http://www.library.uiuc.edu/spx/class/titlepage.html> (accessed August 4, 2004). See Sullivan, "Slavic Bibliography Online" for more details about the development of the guide.

42. The librarians who work in the European Division of the Library of Congress are not involved in reference work full-time like the SRS staff. All have additional responsibilities such as collection development, outreach, special projects, etc.

43. Finding aids to telephone directories are available at <http://www.loc.gov/rr/european/tel.html> (accessed August 6, 2004).

44. Although digital communication is less expensive for patrons, some kinds of it, for instance chat, are more expensive for libraries. See note 48.

45. Web forms for SRS/UIUC may be viewed at <http://www.library.uiuc.edu/spx/srssubmitreq.htm> (accessed July 14, 2004) and for the EurD/LC at <http://www.loc.gov/rr/askalib/ask-european.html> (accessed July 14, 2004).

46. Another difference is that the basic chat is totally html based, while the enhanced chat requires that the patrons download software onto their machines and enable Java. In fact, the entire QP system is html-based except for the enhanced chat. For more information on QuestionPoint, see <http://www.questionpoint.org/> (accessed July 18, 2004).

47. A note of explanation is required: the statistics for the EurD include not only Slavic and East European reference questions, but also those pertaining to Western Europe except for Spain, Portugal, and the UK. Those three are covered by other reading rooms in the Library. Since statistics are not kept for subject or geographic region, only a rough approximation can be made of the number of questions received concerning Slavic and East European studies, that being about 75% of the total.

48. For an eye-opening and entertaining dissenting opinion of the value of digital reference, and of chat in particular, see Jonathan D. Lauer and Steve McKinzie, "Bad

Moon Rising: A Candid Examination of Digital Reference and What It Means to the Profession," *The Reference Librarian* 79/80 (2002/2003): 45-56. The authors believe the profession has gone "bonkers" over digital reference and refer to digital communication tools as "inferior gadgetry."

49. Jana Ronan and Carol Turner, Online summary of *Chat Reference*, SPEC Kit 273 (Association of Research Libraries, December 2002) <http://www.arl.org/spec/273sum.html> (accessed July 30, 2004).

50. Steve Coffman and Linda Arret, "To Chat or Not to Chat: Taking Another Look at Virtual Reference, Part 1," *Searcher: The Magazine for Database Professionals* 12, no. 7 (July/August 2004): 38-46, <http://www.infotoday.com/searcher/jul04/arret_coffman.shtml> (accessed July 2, 2004). This article reviews the history of the competition of commercial versus library virtual reference services and cites usage and cost statistics. It turns out that chat services are quite expensive to set up and maintain.

51. The concept of lag time is discussed in R. David Lankes, "The Digital Reference Fallacy," *The Reference Librarian* 79/80 (2002/2003): 35-44. Coffman and Arret in "To Chat or Not to Chat," mention the chat experiences of commercial call centers; Lauer and McKinzie, in "Bad Moon Rising," summarize evidence from other published studies that mention the slowness of digital reference.

52. The details about photoduplication and document delivery pertaining to the EurD do not include the methods and services provided by the Library of Congress Photoduplication Service or Collections Access, Loan & Management Division, rather they are meant to elucidate what the librarians in the EurD have at hand to serve patrons directly. Likewise, there is no discussion of the Interlibrary Loan department at the University of Illinois Libraries, only methods and tools for the SRS.

53. Jeffrey Pomerantz and Frederic Stutzman, "Lyceum: A Blogsphere for Library Reference" (Paper presented on panel "Weblog Applications in eLearning, Business and Libraries," Thirteenth International World Wide Web Conference, New York, NY, May 18, 2004), <http://www.ils.unc.edu/~jpom/conf/Lyceum.pdf> (accessed August 6, 2004).

54. Steven M. Cohen, *Keeping Current: Advanced Internet Strategies to Meet Librarian and Patron Needs* (Chicago: American Library Association, 2003).

55. Ronan and Turner, Online summary of *Chat Reference*, SPEC Kit 273.

56. Mentioned in a posting by a librarian in Syracuse, NY to *DIG_REF* listserv, July 27, 2004.

Index

Page numbers followed by f indicate figures; those followed by t indicate tables.

BOOK ORDER FORM!

Order a copy of this book with this form or online at:
http://www.haworthpress.com/store/product.asp?sku=5685

Virtual Slavica
Digital Libraries, Digital Archives

____ in softbound at $22.95 ISBN-13: 978-0-7890-2686-6 / ISBN-10: 0-7890-2686-4.
____ in hardbound at $49.95 ISBN-13: 978-0-7890-2685-9 / ISBN-10: 0-7890-2685-6.

COST OF BOOKS _____

POSTAGE & HANDLING _____
US: $4.00 for first book & $1.50
for each additional book
Outside US: $5.00 for first book
& $2.00 for each additional book.

SUBTOTAL _____

In Canada: add 7% GST. _____

STATE TAX _____
CA, IL, IN, MN, NJ, NY, OH, PA & SD residents
please add appropriate local sales tax.

FINAL TOTAL _____
If paying in Canadian funds, convert
using the current exchange rate,
UNESCO coupons welcome.

❑**BILL ME LATER:**
Bill-me option is good on US/Canada/
Mexico orders only; not good to jobbers,
wholesalers, or subscription agencies.

❑**Signature** _____

❑ **Payment Enclosed: $** _____

❑ **PLEASE CHARGE TO MY CREDIT CARD:**
❑Visa ❑MasterCard ❑AmEx ❑Discover
❑Diner's Club ❑Eurocard ❑JCB

Account # _____

Exp Date _____

Signature _____
(Prices in US dollars and subject to change without notice.)

PLEASE PRINT ALL INFORMATION OR ATTACH YOUR BUSINESS CARD

Name

Address

City   State/Province   Zip/Postal Code

Country

Tel   Fax

E-Mail

May we use your e-mail address for confirmations and other types of information? ❑Yes ❑No We appreciate receiving
your e-mail address. Haworth would like to e-mail special discount offers to you, as a preferred customer.
We will never share, rent, or exchange your e-mail address. We regard such actions as an invasion of your privacy.

Order from your **local bookstore** or directly from
The Haworth Press, Inc. 10 Alice Street, Binghamton, New York 13904-1580 • USA
Call our toll-free number (1-800-429-6784) / Outside US/Canada: (607) 722-5857
Fax: 1-800-895-0582 / Outside US/Canada: (607) 771-0012
E-mail your order to us: orders@haworthpress.com

For orders outside US and Canada, you may wish to order through your local
sales representative, distributor, or bookseller.
For information, see http://haworthpress.com/distributors

(Discounts are available for individual orders in US and Canada only, not booksellers/distributors.)

Please photocopy this form for your personal use.
www.HaworthPress.com   BOF05

11/20/2018